KEEP
MARCHING

How Every Woman Can Take Action and Change Our World

KRISTIN ROWE-FINKBEINER

WITHDRAWN

 hachette
BOOKS

NEW YORK BOSTON

Hachette Books
Hachette Book Group
1290 Avenue of the Americas, New York, NY 10104
hachettebooks.com
twitter.com/hachettebooks

First Edition: May 2018

Hachette Books is a division of Hachette Book Group, Inc. The Hachette Books name and logo are trademarks of Hachette Book Group, Inc.

The publisher is not responsible for websites (or their content) that are not owned by the publisher.

The Hachette Speakers Bureau provides a wide range of authors for speaking events. To find out more, go to www.hachettespeakersbureau.com or call (866) 376-6591.

Names: Rowe-Finkbeiner, Kristin, author.
Title: Keep marching : how every woman can take action and change our world / Kristin Rowe-Finkbeiner.
Description: New York : Hachette Books, 2018. | Includes bibliographical references and index.
Identifiers: LCCN 2017054730| ISBN 9780316515566 (trade pbk.) | ISBN 9781549167904 (audio download) | ISBN 9780316515559 (ebook)
Subjects: LCSH: Women—Political activity. | Feminism. | Social action. | Social movements.
Classification: LCC HQ1236 .R59995 2018 | DDC 305.42—dc23
LC record available at https://lccn.loc.gov/2017054730

ISBNs: 978-0-31651-556-6 (trade paperback original), 978-0-31651-555-9 (ebook)

Printed in the United States of America

LSC-C

10 9 8 7 6 5 4 3 2 1

To everyone who has ever marched for women's rights,
who is marching now, and who will in the future.

Contents

Introduction

"Always remember, you have within you the strength, the patience, and the passion to reach for the stars to change the world."

—HARRIET TUBMAN

Millions of women became part of a wave of powerful, inspiring voices—reverberating through Washington, DC, and across the country and globe at over six hundred sister marches—on January 21, 2017. Longtime activists Tamika Mallory, Carmen Perez, Linda Sarsour, and Bob Bland co-chaired the Women's March[1] of 2017, encouraging and helping women across the nation and around the world mobilize like never before.

It was the largest outpouring of people on a single day in the history of our nation.[2]

That was just the beginning. The Women's March marked a turning point in our nation in much the same way that past marches and movements for equity, equality, and justice have done. Each of these turning points ultimately not only left their marks in our history books but also helped shape the culture we live in, produced legislative action that advanced many of the freedoms that we've come to enjoy, and provided a foundation for the ground we stand on today.

What got people out their doors and onto the streets for the Women's March was what happened on Election Day in 2016.

That day, the issues that many women care deeply about were either ignored or flat-out undermined by a shocking amount of support for—or at least tolerance of—sexist, racist, and xenophobic policies and behavior. That support included 53 percent of white women who voted for Donald Trump, a man with a well-documented history of racism, misogyny, and xenophobia.[3]

In other words, in the face of hate, many white women didn't stand up for themselves—or for every woman in the nation. That being said, many women did stand up against the onslaught of hate. A full 94 percent of Black women voted against Trump, as did nearly 70 percent of Latina women.

Since the 2016 election, it's clear that a lot more women are waking up to the fact that we can't take our rights for granted and that we can't afford to be a nation divided.

It's time to stand together, to keep marching together, to rise for and with one another.

Keep Marching

In *Keep Marching*, my hope is to help you become more knowledgeable about the struggles and fights women in our nation face today—as well as how you can play a role in solving these challenges. The list of top priorities for the women of our nation is broad and diverse, just like we are as a country. So, in addition to covering issues like the wage gap and access to health care, I've also included chapters on ending mass incarceration and supporting fair treatment of immigrant families. We have a lot of work to do. But we also have a lot of power to do that work.

Remember, when we stand together, we are 164,148,777 strong. That's power. We contribute a massive amount to our nation, to our economy, to our communities, to our families, to the future—in both unpaid and paid ways. According to the U.S. Census data as of 2015: 62 percent of us women are white non-Hispanic, 17 percent Hispanic, 13 percent Black, 5 percent Asian, 2 percent two or more races, 1 percent American Indian/Alaska Native, and 0.2 percent Native Hawaiian/Other Pacific Islander.[4]

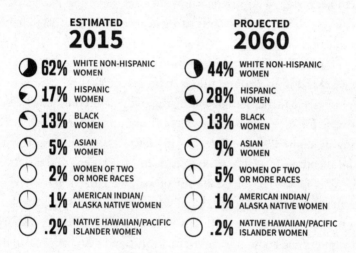

ESTIMATED 2015

- 62% WHITE NON-HISPANIC WOMEN
- 17% HISPANIC WOMEN
- 13% BLACK WOMEN
- 5% ASIAN WOMEN
- 2% WOMEN OF TWO OR MORE RACES
- 1% AMERICAN INDIAN/ ALASKA NATIVE WOMEN
- .2% NATIVE HAWAIIAN/PACIFIC ISLANDER WOMEN

PROJECTED 2060

- 44% WHITE NON-HISPANIC WOMEN
- 28% HISPANIC WOMEN
- 13% BLACK WOMEN
- 9% ASIAN WOMEN
- 5% WOMEN OF TWO OR MORE RACES
- 1% AMERICAN INDIAN/ ALASKA NATIVE WOMEN
- .2% NATIVE HAWAIIAN/PACIFIC ISLANDER WOMEN

Women are a fierce and rising force in our nation—and in our economy. We became half of the full-time labor force in our nation for the first time in the last decade.[5] We make the vast majority of consumer purchasing decisions in our consumer-fueled economy.[6] We push $11 trillion of value into our world economies through our unpaid work.[7] We own 11.3 million American businesses, which employ over 9 million people and generate over $1.6 trillion in revenue. We earn the majority of college and graduate degrees.[8] Single women are more than twice as likely to buy a home as single men (17 vs. 7 percent).[9]

Women play a role in every aspect of our country's businesses; families; nonprofits; schools; churches; communities; city, county, state and federal governments; and American life. Women are rising as breadwinners, voters, and leaders, all while juggling an unprecedented number of roles at the same time.

The responsibility of building a movement together may be great, but the gains we can make together will be nothing short of revolutionary. *Keep Marching* is for every woman who is stepping into her power, who wonders how the heck we're going to fix our nation's problems, who wants to dig deeper, or who wants to help create positive change.

This book is for all of us who show up for marches, in movements, and in our communities; who give back; and who want answers and tactics for navigating the struggles in our daily lives. It's also for all of us who have worked our butts off for democracy, ringing doorbells on cul-de-sacs in New Jersey, attending town hall meetings in Idaho, making calls in Mississippi. And it's also for all of us who haven't done any of that, who maybe have never been even remotely political, but who now find ourselves awake at night, staring at the ceiling, worrying about the safety of our daughters and about our children's future, and who have realized that we must be our own heroes on their behalf.

And this book is being written in no small part in thanks to every woman leader, especially women of color, who has rightfully told me, "Go get your people." This is me, getting my people. This is my call to every imperfect, glorious woman in America to keep marching.

Together we can change the fact that many of the policies that most directly impact our daily lives and economy are all too often swept under the rug and ignored. Together, we can inspire more women to participate in our democracy so that the laws of our land truly reflect the contributions and needs of all those who live here.

As the co-founder and executive director of MomsRising, a nonprofit organization with over a million diverse and powerful women in every state of our country, I've seen the power of women and moms taking action. With that in mind, I've written *Keep Marching* as a road map. This is a blueprint for how we build and wield power as women. This is an atlas showing how to advocate for policies that improve not only our own lives but also the lives of future generations. This is a diagram of how we can win.

That being said, I hope you write in the margins of this book, tear the pages out that you don't agree with, write in your own new ideas, be in conversation with the concepts, add to what I've written, and work together in order to build a country that truly does work for us.

Keep Marching highlights and celebrates the contributions that women make every day to our country, as well as the barriers we unfortunately continue to face generation after generation. By providing the facts of what's happening to women and families nationwide, as well as providing solutions, this book is focused on informing and giving you the power to implement change—in your own life, in the lives of women you know, and in the lives of women you don't. Combining statistics, stories, and actionable advice, this book is intended to be a practical handbook for those of us—and our allies—who want to do something to help advance women's rights and fix our nation, but who don't know what or how.

In this book, you'll find not only illuminating facts but also practical advice. The topics in this book reflect the priorities of the over a million women I've encountered through MomsRising, as well as the Unity Principles at the 2017 Women's March. Many of the action plans that appear at the end of each chapter are based on a document that we at MomsRising created.[10] This document includes tactics that we have used over the past decade to enact and encourage change. These tactics are accessible to anyone and can be tremendously effective. Know one thing: You are needed.

This Is *Our* Time to Rise

In order to truly change the status quo, we must not advocate for just one policy to change—but many. Not just one female leader—but thousands. It's up to us to stand up for our sisters, our communities, and our nation.

If you ever feel overwhelmed by the hurdles ahead of us, remember this inspiring chant from the Women's March:

When women are under attack, what do you do?
    Stand up, fight back!
When Black lives are under attack, what do you do?
    Stand up, fight back!
When Muslims are under attack, what do you do?
    Stand up, fight back!
When immigrants are under attack, what do you do?
    Stand up, fight back!
When trans people are under attack, what do you do?
    Stand up, fight back!
When any of us are under attack, what do you do?
    Stand up, fight back!

It's *our* time to make history/herstory/ourstory. I invite every woman in America to keep marching forward. I may not be able to predict the future but I do know one thing for sure. As women, we will not be bullied. As women, we will not be silenced.

As women, we *will* rise.

1

Waking Up

"We are the leaders we've been waiting for."
—Grace Lee Boggs

Driving to pick up my daughter from school, I started noticing bursts of colors in the yards as I passed. Light blue, lime green, hot pink, deep purple, sunny yellow, bright orange, sapphire blue. Yard signs adorned lawns even though the election season was over and done. I got curious. The print on the signs was too small to read as I zipped by, so I pulled my car over in front of one house to read the words:

In this house we believe Black Lives Matter, no human is illegal, love is love, women's rights are human rights, science is real, water is life, and injustice anywhere is a threat to justice everywhere.

In this book, that's the belief, too. Now some people will say: "Hey, Kristin—This book is about women's rights! Why such a broad spread of topics?" To this I say: As women, we're all mosaics of many different experiences, perspectives, and backgrounds.

1

As such, the top priorities of a modern women's movement must reflect all that is our lives, our contributions, our needs, the barriers we face, and the paths we need to take to break those barriers down.

None of us are single-issue people.

Not all of us are ever going to agree on every issue, policy, action, or stand.

That's okay.

What's most important is to keep believing in and inspiring each other, knowing that together women can—and must—be a nation-changing force.

When each of us does better, we all do better. When the most discriminated-against women among us rise, we all rise. If one group of women is left behind, we all suffer. Our freedoms are intertwined.

And thus, our struggles are intertwined, too.

INTERSECTIONALITY

Intersectionality reinforces the idea that our individual freedoms and struggles are intertwined, yet different. Award-winning author Dr. Kimberlé Crenshaw created the important concept many years ago. Essentially, intersectionality is how different types of discrimination create compounded negative impacts for each individual. Crenshaw recently explained, "One of the main points of intersectionality is that you can't just take the experiences of a Black man and a white woman and put them together to describe a Black woman's experience. A Black woman's experience is not the sum total."

I find it helpful to think of a swarm of invisible angry wasps out in the world, buzzing around looking for targets. Sexism, racism, classism, ableism, xenophobia, and homophobia are all angry wasps in the swarm. Some people are stung more often, and with more painful stingers, just based on their identity.

It's crucial to understand that we mostly tend to see and focus on the wasps that sting us as individuals. Because of this, we—but particularly those of us with fewer wasp stings, like white women such as myself—can never forget that no matter how hard or uncomfortable it is to talk about racism, sexism, and xenophobia, that conversation will never be as hard as it is to experience it.

To win, the modern women's movement must be intersectional. We must pay deep respect to everything that we each carry and bring as women into our worlds, both alone and shared. Many women have long known this. As the great feminist thinker Audre Lorde said many decades ago, "There is no such thing as a single-issue struggle because we do not live single-issue lives. Our struggles are particular, but we are not alone." We are stronger together.

We saw, felt, and heard how strong we are at the Women's March when millions of women took to the streets in the largest march in American history. We also saw that we are a beautiful cacophony of backgrounds, making a strong mosaic of a powerful movement together, and that the strands of all of us woven together are an unbreakable force. The fight for women's rights to succeed is a fight for our nation to succeed. All of us together will make America strong.

Full Disclosure

Each of us brings our individual world of experience, talents, hopes, dreams, and worries to this movement. Similarly, each of us also wears blinders to each other's worlds. In order for the movement to be successful, we must admit that we all wear blinders, open ourselves up to learning, and be as transparent as possible in order to lift all women up and win the fight for equality, equity, and justice.

So: As we begin this book, here's who I am (or at least partly). I am a white, blond, now upper-middle-class, cisgender, hetero married woman with two children and a dog. I live outside of Seattle. I play soccer. I am bad at tennis, can't figure out accessories, and am sometimes painfully awkward at small talk. I'm an imperfect parent of two. I'm a Democrat married to a former Republican state senator. I often work in my jammies from home, guzzling lattes and blue Gatorade as I type. I'll take whiskey over wine any day. I've worked as a house cleaner, waitress, freelance writer, political director, and now as an executive director and more. I sometimes do yoga when I'm stressed out. I also was born in Chicago and raised in Maryland. As a child, my cupboards weren't always full, my family of origin was never "nuclear," and the close people in my early life weren't all heteronormative.

I'm flawed—far from perfect. I screw up regularly but persist just the same.

And each and every day I fight for a modern women's movement that doesn't center around women who look exactly like me, knowing that our fight and movement must be different than it has been in the past.

What Woke Me Up

To be completely honest, I assumed that most of the fights for women's rights were over and that we had won, until I became a mom. I couldn't have been more wrong. When my son was born in 1996, he was diagnosed with an immune deficiency disorder that made it impossible for him to be in childcare with other kids.

A minor cold for other kids often meant a hospital trip and nerve-racking, wheezing weeks of illness. At the time, I didn't have access to any paid family/medical leave, so I had to quit my job to care for my son. In the process, I lost not only my income but also my employer-provided health care coverage.

I never expected to be an unemployed mom. My mom, who was single for most of my childhood, always said to never, ever, ever, ever rely on a partner in order to have food on the table. But there I was, relying on a husband for food on the table, a roof over our heads, health care, and more. It was lucky there were resources to get my son and, later, my daughter the health care they needed when I couldn't work. But an unplanned out-of-work situation like that could have been a flat-out disaster for my own mother or for more than three-quarters of moms who are breadwinners in our nation. Luck alone should never determine whether a woman, child, and family can thrive. Yet too often it does for too many. More than 80 percent of women have children in their lifetimes,[1] a quarter of families with young children in America are living in poverty,[2] and having a baby is now one of the leading causes of poverty. Being a mom is now a greater predictor of wage and hiring discrimination than being a woman, and the wages of moms of color take the biggest hits. These are all signals that the fight for intersectional women's rights isn't over.[3]

In truth I've had many wake-up calls (some at two a.m., eyes blinking in the darkness, baby crying) about how very much we need a new kind of women's movement. This new movement needs to center the voices, the power, and the leadership of moms, of women of color, of women with disabilities, of LGBTQ+ women, of women of all ages and religions, of women of all income levels, and of women who are often denied chairs at the power tables. It was these many wake-up calls that led me to co-found MomsRising in 2006.

I now serve as executive director of that organization and work with a brilliant team of women across the nation, and none of us are exactly alike. I am led by and learn from the women at Moms-Rising. Our team is Black, Asian, Latina, white, queer, Muslim, Jewish, Christian, and more. Together we've built an intersectional organization that works across multiple policy areas at the same time, within a core framework of justice for women, mothers, and families. We've pushed each other to grow our individual ideas about gender, racial, economic, LGBTQ+, and disability justice. Together we build campaigns that will make all women in America and families stronger. Together we rise.

How We Move Forward

To build a truly intersectional movement, we have to touch base with where we've been. Women of color have played major roles advancing the rights of women in our nation's history, and women of color have often led the way. But much of that work has, historically, been ignored or erased. Gloria Steinem recently reiterated this during an interview with Chelsea Handler. "It's condescending to say make the movement inclusive; women of color are the movement and have always been the movement."[4] Case in point, a 1972 national poll conducted by *Ms.* magazine—a magazine Steinem helped to launch—found that while over 60 percent of women of color supported feminism and women's equality issues at the time, only around 30 percent of white women supported those same issues at that time.[5] Women of color were leading the way in 1972 (before then, too) and still are today. In fact, the leadership of women of color has long propelled the entire women's movement forward.

Make no mistake: Gender justice is economic justice is racial justice. One doesn't happen without the others. It's time for all of us to stand together with each other and for each other's rights in a new kind of women's movement. When we speak about women's issues, we must speak to issues that impact every woman—not just the issues that impact able-bodied, middle-class, cis, and straight white women. We need to embrace that we don't all have to define things in precisely the same way, see ourselves reflected in all of other people's experiences, or be exactly the same in order to celebrate each other as we fight for the same outcome. And we must do this not just because this is the right thing to do, but also because we can't win anyone's freedom without fighting for everyone's freedom.

"It's the old thing of I'm not free until my sister is free," said Sarah Sophie Flicker of the Women's March. "Our role is to show up for each other and protect each other. We are kept separate to keep us all down. When we don't show up for each other and don't acknowledge each other, and when my privilege pushes down my sisters, we can't win. We can't win until we all show up for each other."

Sarah's right. Our goal is simple: We all win when we all win.

Anything that hurts one of us hurts all of us. In order to build a strong women's movement, we have to have one another's backs—especially when a discriminatory policy doesn't impact every single one of us in our daily lives, but impacts so many of our sisters. An intersectional approach, like the one in this book, covers many policies that have often been left out of the mainstream women's movement agenda in the past. For example, mass incarceration and the fair treatment of immigrant families are covered in chapters 12 and 10, respectively, right along with fair pay (chapter 11) and reproductive rights (chapter 7). The policy platform in this book isn't centered on a single issue, and neither are any of us in real life.

All of the issues in this book deeply affect women across our nation—along with everyone else. And, speaking of everyone else, it's high time people in power stop telling women that the issues that are destroying our lives and dreams aren't priorities in our country. The truth is, when this many people are having the same struggles at the same time, that's a national issue that we must solve together—*not* an epidemic of personal failings.

Mistakes Are Necessary

Building an intersectional movement requires being curious and compassionate about all the issues women face and how to break down those barriers. It requires us to imagine ourselves in one another's worlds. And it requires us to consider not only the issues we're dealing or have dealt with, but also those in the lives of people who have had very different experiences.

Building an intersectional movement also requires that we each make mistakes.

As a longtime organizer for women's rights, I've made many mistakes and had many failures due to my blinders along the way. Too many to count, in fact. I've said the wrong thing; done the wrong thing; been embarrassed; second-, third-, and fourth-guessed myself. I've also been thankful to have my mistakes pointed out so that I can do better—and this has helped me to play a role in more wins than I ever expected.

For instance, in 2009 I was onstage at George Washington University for the Feminism 2.0 Conference. During my talk I addressed the average wage gap for women overall and mentioned that moms experienced even more discrimination when it comes to pay. After I was done, Shireen Mitchell, founder of Digital Sisters/Sistas Inc. and Stop Online Violence Against Women, raised her hand and asked: "What about women of color? The numbers you shared don't reflect women of color. You left us out."

My stomach dropped. I was mortified. I'd hit one of my own blind spots. My own implicit, unconscious bias was center stage. I should have known better. I had inadvertently repeated history. My mortification in that moment was nothing compared to decades of women of color being forgotten or erased. (Historically, white feminists have often failed to incorporate how structural racism permeates everything that has to do with sexism as does classism, homophobia, and other isms, too, for that matter.)

This may seem like not a big deal: I left women of color out of my presentation. So what? But it was a big deal. Shireen Mitchell was rightly pointing out that women of color had even further to climb to achieve parity in pay with white men than white women did. Which means that I left an entire group of women out of my data, out of my presentation, and out of sight.

It wasn't Shireen's job to call me out that day in 2009, and while it was a moment of public failure, I'm forever grateful to her for it. The reason I share this story is because sometimes people tell me they're afraid to get involved because they may accidentally do or say something wrong. But it's important not to let fear stop us from joining in. Nobody is perfect in anything we do. It's time to give each other grace, lift one another up, and accept that if we're truly building the best kind of movement for our nation, then we'll be uncomfortable and make mistakes at least some of the time, and that if we listen, learn, and work together, we will rise together.

RACISM, SEXISM, AND XENOPHOBIA ARE REAL

—

As we work to do better, there's something that must be addressed: There's no such thing as reverse racism. I know, sometimes people have negative opinions about white people as a whole. That happens. But that's prejudice, not racism. Racism is power and prejudice intertwined. In our white-dominant culture, where structural racism and implicit bias is woven throughout our institutions, even if it doesn't always feel that way, white people have had structural power throughout the history of our country. So, no, reverse racism isn't real.

Racism kills, jails, injures, and closes doors to opportunity. Prejudice hurts feelings. There's a difference. And while we're on the topic of things that must be said: Racism today is real. It isn't a thing of the past. Sexism, classism, homophobia, and xenophobia aren't myths, either. It's time to call everyone *in* so we can work this out.

We have to say this out loud: Sexism is real. Racism is real. Why? Many people—again, particularly white people—often have a skewed view of reality and are caught inside our own bubbles, where we don't see what we don't personally experience. For instance, studies show that white women and girls are suspended less often from school for the same offenses,[6] are given higher levels of presumption of innocence by the police,[7] experience less wage discrimination,[8] are even more likely to be given free rides by bus drivers,[9] and the list goes on. Research also shows that white people are more likely to think racism is a thing of the past than Black people do, while Black people are more accurate in their assessments that racism is a part of the present. One study found that only 16 percent of white people believe there is "a lot" of discrimination in America today, a view which is held by 56 percent of Black people.[10]

The Internal Fight against Discrimination

Sexism, racism, and xenophobia have been part of our nation's culture since the beginning. This means that it's also part of each of us. Implicit bias in America is like toxic air pollution that we unconsciously breathe in often as we walk through our daily lives. This is no small thing. Sexism, structural racism, and a lot of unchecked implicit bias led us to elect Donald Trump, a noted sexist bigot. They're also key reasons we have the highest incarceration rate in the world, with people of color unfairly disproportionately incarcerated,[11] and that women still don't make equal pay for equal work. Moreover, there's been a 6 percent increase in hate crimes since Trump was elected.[12] Unchecked implicit bias can be costly and deadly.

The fight against all discrimination is as much an internal fight within each of us as it is also an external fight for legislative and cultural change. Rebecca Cokley, former executive director of the National Council on Disability, told me that "One of the critical pieces as white women in these spaces is making sure we use our privilege daily, minute by minute, to elevate the voices of women of color." I agree wholeheartedly.

While it's crucial to influence legislation, elected officials, corporate practices, our culture, and our unjust systems, including the criminal justice system, we as individuals—particularly white people like myself—also have to be a witness to our own internal implicit biases on a daily basis, even be in conversation with them so we can put them in check, tell them off, and even argue with them in order to be truly effective.

As we move forward, it's also incumbent that we listen to each other, especially when we come from different experiences. The co-founder of Black Lives Matter, Patrisse Khan-Cullors, has an important suggestion. "There's a great question we must ask ourselves about impact—whether white, queer, Latina, Black, etc. 'What have I learned from my family, my culture, what parts do I think are toxic that I don't want to continue, and what is beautiful that I want to grow?'"

The Best Kinds of Solutions

An intersectional approach leads to the best kinds of solutions—solutions that take all of our identities into account, that identify inequalities and fix them, and that can lift our entire nation. In fact, data shows that our nation's diversity—and people caring about one another—is what's played a large role in making us such a strong, creative, and prosperous nation so far. *Harvard Business Review* recently reported that companies with the most "ethnic and racial diversity in management were 35% more likely to have financial returns above their industry mean" and those with the most women in management "were 15% more likely to have returns above the industry mean."[13] In other words, companies are more successful when their management team is diverse and intersectional.

We all win when we all win, and when we all win, our country wins, too.

America has come a long way together as a nation, and we're not turning our backs on each other now. After all, our nation has been pursuing women's rights, and reaching for equity and equality, for generations. There's a long history of women marching across generations, across our nation, showing leadership across races and classes, to right wrongs in the United States.

Women have fought for and won rights in the past, and we're still fighting for our rights every day. We're fighting to keep our reproductive choices, for the right to be treated equally, the right to be free from police brutality, the right to have our very lives respected, and much more. We've taken more than a few steps forward. But we've taken many steps backward, too.

History has shown us that when women lead—together—our nation succeeds. By raising our voices, by sharing our truths, by amplifying each other, and by being truly intersectional, we can build an America that lifts all women, our families, and our country.

So let's stand, let's march, let's all rise for each other—together.

How to Believe

The first rule of #KeepMarching is to believe in yourself. Remember, this book isn't about a literal march, but about building a movement. Believe in the women, men, and people around you. Know that the calls, letters, texts, meetings, gatherings, marches, rallies, social media shares—and all the tactics that are described at the end of every chapter in this book—add up and make a difference. The difference may not be apparent overnight, but if you persist, if you organize and strategize, then change will happen bit by bit, moment by moment. Know that if you—and thousands of others—believe that something is possible, then that something becomes very possible.

That's right: Believing in yourself—knowing at a cellular level that you can make a difference—is a powerful tactic, a core part of change, and is essential to developing your personal power. In fact, believing in yourself is such an important tactic that it's the first advocacy and organizing tip in a book where tips close each chapter.

This isn't a platitude. It's not an empty promise. I've seen it happen more times than I can count.

The first win I saw happen was in 1992 when underground testing of nuclear devices stopped in the United States. That happened after several years when thousands of people spoke out. Some, including myself, literally walked out onto the nuclear testing grounds so the bombs couldn't be detonated. All these actions, all these people rising up, added up to real change. Many people walked out into the hot Nevada desert nuclear testing grounds in the early 1990s, putting their bodies on the line for what we believed in. Yes, we were arrested then. But so were the nuclear bombs.

Your body is powerful. Your mind is powerful. Your voice is powerful.

The next wins I saw came in a cluster, working after college for Washington Conservation Voters (WCV). We recruited, trained, endorsed, and ran environmentally responsible candidates at the city, county, and state levels. Some years over one hundred endorsed candidates with several targeted candidates received extensive assistance from WCV on their campaigns—and one great year the win rate was 76 percent. Some of those wins were by a margin of a single handful of votes. A handful. Literally how many people you see in a coffee shop on a busy morning have changed the outcome of elections, especially locally—and it still can happen. But sometimes handfuls of votes can even change national elections, depending if that handful is voting in the right state at the right time. (The outcome of the 2000 presidential race was essentially decided by just 537 votes in Florida, which tipped the entire national electoral college toward George W. Bush instead of Al Gore.)

Your vote is powerful. Your support is powerful. Your belief in yourself is powerful. The lengths that you have already gone to and will continue to go to in order to care for, provide for, defend, protect, and empower the ones you love is powerful.

I've witnessed many, many wins due to individual and collective masterminding at MomsRising. I've been blown away. I came into MomsRising already a believer in the power of change, but I seriously underestimated the power of women sharing their experiences and speaking out. The members and team of MomsRising have helped advance more wins than I can even count over the last decade: from helping to get healthier foods in every elementary, middle, and high school in the country; to helping to pass the Lilly Ledbetter Fair Pay Act and the Affordable Care Act through Congress in the first place (and then rising to protect it again and again); to helping to protect Medicaid many times over (which covers the health care of one in four children and half of all child-births); to helping get a special prosecutor in New York for cases of police brutality; to helping to advance earned sick days, paid family leave, childcare, and protection for pregnant and nursing women in cities and states across the nation, as well as fair pay policies, and so very much more. As a group, we're pretty powerful.

And so are *you*—your voice, your story, your experiences, *you* are powerful.

More powerful than you think.

The actions you take—even the actions that don't take a lot of time, like clicking to sign a petition from an organization you respect or joining a Twitter or social media campaign—have an impact, whether you directly see that impact happening in real time or not.

Remember, tiny drops of water create waves. And when we take individual action—big actions like organizing a human resources policy change at work or visiting an elected leader, or small actions like taking five minutes to click in an email to sign an open letter to Congress—a wave of change is created.

This doesn't mean we'll instantly win every fight. In fact, persistence is the name of the game. So believe in yourself. Stand up. Put on your imaginary superhero cape and infuse that belief that you are powerful into every step, call, action, you take as you invite others to also believe in themselves, in the power of us together.

Because if we, together, believe in something strongly enough, we can make change happen. That, my friend, is the first rule of change.

PART I

OUR MONEY

2

The Benjamins

A couple of years ago, Cynthia shared something that happened to her at an office party. She was at an event for an advertising firm where she worked, looked around the room, and suddenly realized that the vast majority of people who worked at the firm were women. In a party setting, it was obvious. Cynthia asked her boss why. He told her, "I can pay them less."

"I was twenty-three and shocked," Cynthia shared. "I hadn't yet learned I was less valuable than a man."

This is not right. Obviously the contributions of women aren't any less valuable than contributions from men. Not even a little bit. In fact, study after study show that businesses tend to make *higher* profits with women in leadership and that better decisions are made when there are diverse decision makers. For instance, one study found female hedge fund managers outperformed men by 8.95 percent to 2.69 percent, respectively, on returns.[1] A nineteen-year study of all Fortune 500 companies by Pepperdine University found a direct correlation between high levels of women in leadership and higher profits—and that promoting women meant outperforming the competition.[2] But despite those facts, women are still treated unfairly: Women are judged more harshly, paid unequally, and discriminated against in the labor force.

When it comes to pay, the Benjamins go to the Benjamins, quite literally. I'm not sure when I first got the gory details on the wage discrimination women face each and every day in the United States of America. All I really remember is thinking, *Oh, $hit*, accompanied by a sinking feeling that women still had a lot of work to do. More than I ever imagined before looking at the numbers, in fact. If you haven't heard the wage gap numbers yet, apologies in advance if what you're about to read makes you a bit nauseous and then more than a little bit irate.

THE WAGE GAP
COMPARED TO WHITE, NON-HISPANIC MEN

$1	87¢	80¢	75¢	71¢	63¢	57¢	54¢
MEN OVERALL	ASIAN AMERICAN & PACIFIC ISLANDER WOMEN	WOMEN OVERALL	WHITE NON-HISPANIC WOMEN	MOMS OVERALL	BLACK WOMEN	NATIVE AMERICAN WOMEN	LATINA WOMEN

The U.S. Census reports that women, on average, earned just 80 cents to a man's dollar in 2017 for all year-round full-time workers. That being said, both moms and women of color experience increased wage hits.[3] More specifically, the data shows that white, non-Hispanic women are earning only 75 cents;[4] Black women only 63 cents; Native American women only 57 cents; and Latina women only 54 cents for every dollar earned by white, non-Hispanic men. Asian American and

Pacific Islander women experience a smaller wage gap on average,[5] but still make only 87 cents on average for every dollar made by white non-Hispanic men, with some subgroups of Asian American and Pacific Islander women experiencing much bigger wage gaps.[6]

Transgender women also receive unequal pay,[7] with one study finding that the earnings of transgender women dropped by nearly one-third following their transition.[8]

Laura found proof of the wage gap in her marriage. She and her husband met at Columbia University and graduated with the same degree. They both got jobs at the same agency in the exact same position. However, they were dumbfounded by the difference in their salaries. She made $5,000 less than he did. When Laura asked the agency about the discrepancy, she was given the runaround. Basically she was told to accept the pay or they would give the job to someone else.

Though Laura's example is pretty clear, the wage gap women face is often more complicated than it first looks. For instance, Asian American and Pacific Islander women seem to be doing better than women overall, earning on average 87 cents to a white man's dollar. But that doesn't tell the full story. Broad categories don't give the whole picture. This is especially true for Asian American and Pacific Islander women. Miriam Yeung, co-founder of We Belong Together and former executive director of the National Asian Pacific American Women's Forum, explains that the ethnicity of Asian American and Pacific Islander women includes a tremendous number of diverse countries. A closer look at the numbers reveal that Burmese women are earning only 44 cents to a white man's dollar, Fijian women are earning 45 cents, and Nepalese women are earning just 51 cents.[9] "There hasn't been enough attention to build a strong women of color analysis yet that fully includes Asian American and Pacific Islander women in it," Miriam revealed.

It Gets Worse

Sometimes I feel like Alice going down the rabbit hole into Wonderland, White Rabbit–style, when I start digging into the numbers behind the numbers. Or, if I'm up working too late at night, images of myself as a data detective, pipe in mouth and an intriguing hat tilted jauntily on my head with a Nancy Drew–like obsession for solving the mysteries hidden in Excel files, have come to mind.

Put on your imaginary detective hat, because our dive down into numbers isn't over. That's because for the 81 percent of women who become mothers, the wage gap is even bigger, and it's bigger still for moms of color. The truth is that right now, in the United States of America, being a mom is a greater predictor of wage and hiring discrimination than being a woman. Our country, which claims to love, adore, and respect motherhood, pays moms just 71 cents to every dollar that dads earn.[10] To get a real picture of what's going on, here are the specific numbers: Asian American and Pacific Islander mothers are paid 85 cents; white, non-Hispanic mothers are paid 69 cents; Black mothers are paid 51 cents; Native American mothers are paid 49 cents; and Latina mothers are paid just 46 cents for every dollar paid to white, non-Hispanic fathers. Furthermore, mothers in low-wage jobs are paid just 66 cents for every dollar paid to fathers in low-wage jobs.[11]

THE WAGE GAP FOR MOMS
COMPARED TO WHITE, NON-HISPANIC DADS

	$1	85¢	71¢	69¢	55¢	51¢	49¢	46¢
DADS OVERALL	ASIAN AMERICAN & PACIFIC ISLANDER MOMS	MOMS OVERALL	WHITE MOMS	SINGLE MOMS	BLACK MOMS	NATIVE AMERICAN MOMS	LATINA MOMS	

Felicia experienced blatant wage discrimination while working at a technical support center for a large retail corporation. She was hired to work the exact same job as her brother-in-law, and after talking to him discovered that she was being paid about $4 an hour less to do the exact same job. She went on to find out that all of the men at work, working the same job, with the same amount of experience, were making $4 an hour more than her. And, as it turns out, all the women were making the lower wage. The wage gap hurts women, families, and our economy.

Singled Out

Moms in general—whether minimum wage earners or beyond—earn just 71 cents to every dollar that dads earn, but the discrimination in pay is compounded for single moms and their children.[12] Paid just 55 cents for every dollar paid to all fathers,[13] single mothers are among those who face the worst wage discrimination in our nation.[14]

When Tara was growing up, her family was barely able to get by. Tara and her mom (who was single) lived with Tara's grandmother, which was the only way that her mom would have enough money to get gas to go back and forth from work and to purchase essentials. After a while, Tara and her mom moved into a place with her uncle. If it was not for her grandma and her uncle, they would have had a hard time keeping a roof over their heads and getting food to eat.

The wage discrimination that single moms like Tara's face is impacting a tremendous and growing number of women and children. A study from Johns Hopkins University found that 57 percent of babies born to millennials were not born within a marriage. Technically these are "single mothers" by many people's definition, but that doesn't mean there isn't a partner.

Family structure and our culture is changing.[15] Currently, 69 percent of American children live with two parents (down from 88 percent in 1960) and 23 percent live with a single mother (up from 8 percent in 1960).[16] It's important to note that even though the number of children who live with single mothers has nearly tripled since 1960, it doesn't mean that there isn't a same-sex partner involved, and it also doesn't mean that dads or other partners aren't involved. For instance, while Black families have some of the lowest marriage rates in our nation[17], studies show that Black fathers, regardless of marital and cohabitation status, are the most involved with their children's daily lives of any group of fathers in our nation.[18]

The numbers demonstrate that family structure and the story of families has changed, but our workplace structures and public policy are outdated. Our economy and our families are both negatively affected by the fact that many of our key public policies have fallen behind the realities that numerous women and families in America are living in right now. It's on all of us to catch up.

Mia Birdsong, co-director of Family Story, is one of the few people focused on the incredibly important work of combating the racism, sexism, and classism that's permeated much of our culture's view of families. Among other things, Birdsong and her organization are hard at work updating our country's outdated picture of the typical family in America. Birdsong was inspired to help launch Family Story because she noticed that there is greater system-wide support for "nuclear" families than other family structures. In other words, our national policies, workplaces, and culture often discriminate against families that don't match a 1950s imaginary vision of one mom, one dad, and two kids—even though that family structure is becoming the exception, not the rule. The change Birdsong wants to see is an end to a hierarchy of family structures so all types of families are able to access the resources they need without prejudice regardless of gender roles, race, and class. I couldn't agree more. It's long past time to update outdated ideas about families in our nation.

The Double-Wage-Hit Whammy

Lani, a working mom, shared that the wage gap makes it nearly impossible for her or her wife to stay home with their children—despite having "good" jobs as attorneys. Both moms went back to work when their baby was only three months old. It was just basic math. Lani says, "When my wife and I sat down and figured out how much we each made and the cost of childcare, we found that between rental prices in our region and student loans, there was no way for either of us to be out of the labor force."

Lani and her wife ended up delaying plans to have a second child because childcare prices are so high. There's no way they could afford to have two children in childcare, so they have to wait. At the same time, the clock is ticking: They can't wait too long and risk fertility issues. Two moms face a double-wage-hit whammy, but two dads get a double boost, and that has an impact on the options open to them as parents. The *New York Times* reported that couples with two dads are the most likely to have a stay-at-home parent, a heterosexual couple is the next most likely, and two moms are the least likely even if they want to because it's often simply unaffordable.[19]

Clearly, sexuality also needs to be front and center in any discussion of the wage gap as it intersects and adds up to be a double or triple whammy on the pocketbook. In our nation, 4.2 percent of people between the ages of eighteen and forty-four identify as lesbian, gay, or bisexual, with 62 percent of that cohort being female. Further data find that 71 percent of all those who identify as bisexual are female, and 49 percent of all those who identify as lesbian or gay are female. In addition, a recent study found that 1.4 million individuals identify as transgender.[20]

When marching for equity and equality, discrimination based on sexuality and gender identity absolutely must not be forgotten.

Busting the Myths

Let's take a minute to discuss some reasons why women *are not* being paid less. For instance, many people cite that the wage gap is due to women taking lesser-paying jobs. Not true. Wage differences within the same occupations account for much of the pay gap between men and women in *many* job categories, whether a doctor or a clerk. While women are, on the whole, concentrated in lower-wage job areas, this doesn't explain away the wage gap; it just makes the economic pressure greater because unfair pay pushes many women and families into poverty.

Women are actually graduating from college in higher numbers than men.[21] But after only one year in the workforce, young women are already earning less than equally qualified young men in many occupations.[22]

Claudia Goldin, a labor economist at Harvard University, has found in studying age, race, work hours, and education that people working in the exact same sectors experience wage gaps. For instance, female doctors and surgeons earn 71 percent of men's wages. Female financial specialists earn 66 percent of men's wages.[23]

Wage and hiring discrimination has been a major hurdle for women since we joined the workforce.[24] This is discrimination against women in real time. This is what happens when inadvertent implicit bias against women runs unchecked, even though studies show that the work women do is far from inferior. Of course, there's not a secret committee of people deciding to pay women less, but the subconscious negative assumptions about women and work add up to a massive amount of money lost for women over time.

To be clear: No one is proposing that everyone gets paid the same thing for doing different jobs. This fight is focused on equal pay for equal work. No more, no less. Women also experience increased unfair pay pressure because we are more likely to be concentrated in fewer types of jobs, notes Sarah Jane Glynn in a paper for the Center for American Progress. Furthermore, those job types are also more likely to be dominated by women—a fact that often leads to lower wages for that job sector as a whole. (Interestingly, studies also show that when women start to be a high percentage of any profession, the overall pay levels of that profession often get lower. That's exactly what's happened with the veterinarian field. As the percentage of women veterinarians rose, salaries decreased.[25]) This trend leads to female-dominated industries paying lower wages than male-dominated industries that require similar skill levels. These trends have also played a role in women making up the majority of minimum-wage workers in the United States.[26]

But it's not just low wages that are impacted. The effect of wage discrimination is strong in jobs that require higher levels of education and pay higher wages, too.[27]

Naysayers—who are usually a medley of corporate CEOs, conservative legislators, and media pundits—often ridiculously (and insultingly) argue that the wage gap doesn't deserve attention because women just aren't negotiating enough, aren't equally qualified, are trading pay for benefits,[28] or other ludicrous excuses.[29] But the wage gap can't be blamed on women for a supposed "lack of confidence" or a lack of leaning in. That particular blame game raises my blood pressure, particularly because it often comes in the form of self-help advice gone awry. For instance, Claire Shipman and Katty Kay's viral article several years ago in *The Atlantic*, "The Confidence Gap,"[30] has been repeatedly used—whether Shipman and Kay intended it or not—to argue that women's lack of confidence is responsible for gender barriers in the workforce. One *Forbes* article, directly following their line of reasoning, put the blame squarely on women's shoulders for not reaching top management positions. The article said, "Women, we aren't taking action often enough and that's crucial. We don't have to be perfect. Men are confident about their ability at 60%."[31]

Balderdash. (Yes, that's the word that came to my mind.)

The truth is that women ask for raises just as often as men, but women are granted raises less often—and to make matters worse, women are also regularly penalized for asking.[32]

Unfortunately, many people believe the balderdash because it seeps out into our communities and workforce. In fact, in 2017 (yes, 2017, not 1917) an all-male panel of notable public relations professionals at a *PRWeek* conference demonstrated a moment of pure balderdash in action. When the panel was confronted with the fact that women PR professionals earn an average of $36,000 less than men in the field, several shared the opinion that women need to "speak up more loudly" about unfair pay. Ironically the panelist who said that the loudest, Richard Edelman, the CEO of the largest independently owned PR firm in the world, had just proved exactly how and why speaking up isn't always a solution for women. At the panel, Edelman said that when women in his firm spoke up to him about wage gaps, he told them, "You speak up first."[33] Uh, first? These women were *already* speaking up first by bringing up the issue of unfair pay directly to the CEO of the company. This was a true #HeadDesk moment.

What we're seeing is flat-out discrimination. The wage gap isn't the result of women's lack of confidence, quietness, or bad choices—and it's also certainly not a reflection of men being "more motivated by money" than women, as New Hampshire state representative Will Infantine said as he argued against the New Hampshire Paycheck Equality Act.[34] (The word *balderdash* just came to mind again!)

There is very real wage and hiring discrimination going on— and it hits moms and women of color the hardest.[35] One series of studies painted a stark picture. Moms were hired 80 percent less often than women with equal résumés who didn't have children. And when moms are hired, they're offered salaries that are on average $11,000 lower than what's offered to non-moms. On the other hand, dads with equal résumés were offered $6,000 more than non-dads,[36] proving that the antiquated idea that only men need paychecks large enough to support their families is alive and well (not to mention, keeping many families poor and hungry). Studies have also shown that employees who identified as mothers are perceived to be less competent, less promotable, and less likely to be recommended for management, despite having the same credentials as non-mothers.[37] Still today, women have to think about whether to hide their status as mothers during job interviews.

All told, this is a big deal. A major study found that men receive a wage bonus of 11.6 percent when they become fathers. But moms, on the other hand, get a wage penalty for motherhood of 4 percent per child; that, Michelle J. Budig, writing in *Third Way*, reports, "Cannot be explained by human capital, family structure, family-friendly job characteristics, or differences among women that are stable over time...This motherhood penalty is larger among low-wage workers while the top 10% of female workers incur no motherhood wage penalty."[38]

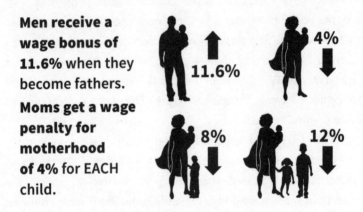

Men receive a wage bonus of 11.6% when they become fathers.

Moms get a wage penalty for motherhood of 4% for EACH child.

11.6%   4%   8%   12%

The Wage Gaps Add Up

Often when books are written and stories are told about the fight for women's equality, the main focus is only on highly paid professional women breaking the glass ceiling and the hurdles women face in those sectors. That's an important conversation to have, and one that's included in the next chapter, but it's time for a reality check: The hourly wage gaps are adding up into annual earnings gaps. Here's what that looks like:

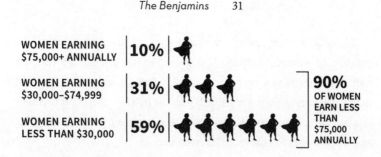

That's right: Only 10 percent of all women in the labor force earn $75,000 or more annually, which means 90 percent of all working women earn less. In fact, 31 percent of women are in the next lower wage bracket, earning between $30,000 and $74,999 annually, and the majority of working women (59 percent) earn less than $30,000 annually[39]—while only 40 percent of men earn less than $30,000 annually.

Christy shares that in her life, the wage gap, coupled with low wages, caused her to have two or three minimum jobs at one time when her sons were young in order to make ends meet. Even with that extra work, Christy often still couldn't get her young children proper dental care, tutoring, or clothing when they needed it.

Men and dads, on the other hand, don't face the same levels of hour by hour wage discrimination that women and moms face each day; and it all adds up to men and dads having higher annual wages than women and moms:

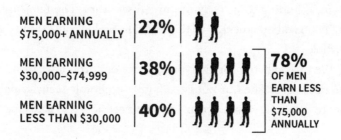

There are many negative rippling repercussions to a full 90 percent of women earning less than $75,000 a year, more than half of whom are earning less than $30,000 a year. One is that too many women are working hard, playing by the rules, and still falling below the poverty line—and are struggling to raise families and open doors for their children to thrive.

Paying Women Unfairly Hurts Our Economy

Wage discrimination against women and moms needs to stop. It's hurting our economy, our businesses, our families, and our communities. It's not just me who thinks this. Economic studies show that equal pay for women would boost our entire national economy. A recent analysis of data over time by the Institute for Women's Policy Research found that if women received equal pay for equal work, it would cut poverty by more than half for women and families and add $513 billion to our national economy.[40]

Having pay parity, studies find, would increase our gross domestic product by at least 3 percent.[41] Why? When women don't have funds to spend in our consumer-fueled economy, businesses have fewer customers and there is lower economic activity across our nation on the whole. And the lower wages don't just reduce economic activity now. Reduced wages also reduce retirement savings, leading to poverty in our sunset years. The Benjamins really do add up quickly—both personally and for our country as a whole.

We can do better for everyone and for our economy. To start, we need to update our outdated family economic security policies to help fully close the gap. Families need access to paid family and medical leave, earned sick days, and affordable childcare. We cannot close the gaps between moms and women without children, and between women and men overall, without these policies. Of course, we also need pay transparency legislation like the Paycheck Fairness Act so that apples-to-apples comparisons of pay can be made and outright discrimination can be stopped in its tracks. It doesn't take rocket science to move these policies forward. We've already seen a lot of forward movement at the state levels because of people reaching out to elected leaders. It takes as many people as possible raising their voices and demanding that change happen.

Make no mistake: Together we can march our entire nation forward, not just for women but for everyone. To do that we work for pay transparency policies, raising the minimum wage, fair pay, and family economic security policies like access to paid family/medical leave and affordable childcare, all of which lower the wage gaps. When women win, America wins—and women can lift our nation.

How to Make Positive Change

Huge, systemic issues like the wage gap can seem impossibly large to tackle. But an important thing to remember is that change starts at an individual level. So let's talk about *you*. What's your passion, which skills are yours to share, and what type of volunteer work do you love? How can *you* create real change?

No matter where you are in terms of experience, I want to make something clear: *You* are needed. The voices of women are powerful. Here are five easy steps for getting your voice heard by getting involved.

- **Find out what you care about fixing.**

    Want to make a difference, but not sure where to start—or what policy or issue area to start on? Don't worry. Our first step is to figure out what issue or policy area you want to focus on helping advance. This may seem like a simple task, but it's often complicated by the fact that more than a few policy areas and issues are in need of action. So how do you choose?

    Maybe the last chapter about the wage gap angered you and now you want to take action. If so, great! But if not, ask yourself: What draws my attention in the news, on social media, in conversations, in this book? Is it getting better candidates elected? Think for a moment. Still not sure? Keep thinking. Ask yourself this: What keeps you up at night? What is the one thing you want future generations to *not* have to fix? What breaks your heart? Is it the fact that moms are financially penalized for having children, while fathers are rewarded?

If you're still having trouble, ask yourself this question: If my possible future grandchildren ask me what in the heck I was doing when _____ was happening, will I be embarrassed to tell them I stood by silently? Now *that* question can let you know exactly what area you want to work in extremely fast. I know it's gotten me out of my chair more times than I can count.

■ **Uncover the type of activism that brings you joy.**

Are you ready to find out what type of work brings you joy in the fight for equity, equality, and justice? Figure out what skills you have up your sleeve and, importantly, what you have fun doing that could benefit where you're volunteering.

What secret—or not-so-secret—superpower skills do you have? Are you really great at talking with people? (Volunteers are always needed at phone banks and doorbelling.) Are you crafty? Are you a great writer? (Organizations often need help creating and packaging content.) Do you love research? Do you like to do activities like serving food, building houses, cleaning? Are you a spectacular event planner? Database expert? Do you like children? What type of work makes you *not* look at the clock to see when it's time to go home?

Not sure yet? Try a few activities and see what feels fun! One goal in fighting for change is that the work is fun for you, feeds your soul, and sometimes makes you laugh, because we need you for a marathon and not a sprint. Another goal is to use your skills to add capacity to an organization or cause. In order to keep marching, it has to bring you joy at least some of the time.

■ **Find the right place.**

There's a lot of work to do, and it's often easiest to do it with a group of people and/or an organization supporting you. Now that you know what issue you want to work on and what skills you bring to the table, the question is, where do you want to do it?

If you aren't already involved in an advocacy project or organization, don't worry! There are lots of places you can engage and multiply your impact by working with others: a national, state, or local advocacy organization; a city, county, state, or federal political campaign; a service organization; a local school; a church; a shelter or food serving location; a union; a hospital—the list goes on. Take a moment to figure out what type of place you can work on your top issue area using your secret superpower skills.

There's a lot to choose from. Did you decide what type of place you're interested in connecting with yet? Done? Okay, let's go to the next step. Find some to try!

Use any search engine to find a place to volunteer. For instance, I just googled "fair wage women Washington State" and several organizations popped up.

But don't stop there. Ask your friends, family, and neighbors in person and via social media what organizations they see having the biggest impact on the issues you care the most about right now. Here's a sample post: *Friends!—I'm looking for a way to volunteer to advance _____ (fill in the blank for the policy you like) in _____ (geographic region). Have any advice? Who's doing great work?*

After you've picked one or two (or three, four, or five!) places to check out, do a bit more research. Check out their Facebook page and Twitter presence. Go to their website and read their mission and check out their "About" page. Ask around a bit about their reputation. Find out what wins they've helped make happen. See if they are listed on any of the nonprofit review sites. Start your short list of two to five organizations or places you want to lend your time and get ready to take the next step. (Check out the lists of highly recommended organizations throughout this book, too.)

- **Be open-minded.**

As you make your list of organizations and places you want to volunteer, be open-minded. For instance, an organization with a solid online and on-the-ground presence and regular opportunities (which you can choose to ignore when you're busy) might be a good fit for you rather than a more classic brick-and-mortar organization.

Many organizations know you're busy and do the hard work for you. They'll contact you whenever there's opportunity to make your voice heard and have an impact on a top issue. Most offer easy ways to take action online and in person, on the ground. Organizations are at your service! For instance, when you are signed on with MomsRising, every week at least five possible actions are delivered directly to you that you can choose to do or not. With each action, you can choose if you have time (and inclination) to do it or not, your choice. You can even start a local #KeepMarching Circle and connect with other leaders via MomsRising.

For many organizations, you don't necessarily need to reach out with a call or email. You can just go to their websites and sign up, and then you'll be kept up-to-date about when your voice is needed in real time.

■ **Connect and create change.**

Once you have the issue you want to advance and have identified the skills you have to share and a short list of places you want to volunteer, it's time to make some calls or send some emails. One thing: Sometimes the busiest organizations will need you to reach out more than once. Make it easy all around by calling or emailing and saying something like: *Hi, I'm* _____ *[name]. I'd love to volunteer doing* _____ *(insert your superhero skill) or another activity to help. What volunteer opportunities do you have right now?*

Keep in mind that you don't need to get married to the first organization or place that you try out. Volunteer at a few places. See where you feel like it's the right fit for you. See who is making a real difference. And then keep volunteering in that best-fit place—even bring friends. Keep marching!

....

3

The Invisible Glass Ceilings

Cheryl Contee has never been someone to mess with. Once, in first grade, Cheryl broke the nose of a bully on the playground with a roundhouse kick. Hers was a righteous fight. She was bullied all year and had racist insults hurled her way; the teachers looked the other way when Cheryl stood her ground. Those boys never messed with her again.

I know the adult Cheryl Contee as a warrior. She is also one of the kindest people I know. She's the co-founder of Attentive.ly with Roz Lemieux, which is the first tech company with a Black female co-founder on board to be acquired by a company listed on NASDAQ.

Only about 10 percent of all women even get into a room where there might be a glass ceiling in the first place like Cheryl did. How do I know this? Only 10 percent of all women in the labor force earn $75,000 or more annually,[1] so it's the women in this top 10 percent of earners who are the ones that usually have a shot at making it rain glass. Just like women face a wage gap, women also face an opportunity gap. Wage and hiring discrimination go hand in hand with advancement discrimination. Not that many women have an opportunity to break through. But some do. Their stories shine a spotlight on the hurdles that we need to break down so more women can break through the many glass ceilings we all face. They also give insight into the intense ways in which women have to fight inequality in every space and workplace.

The barriers women face start when we are very young, including harassment, which forms a million different glass ceilings above our heads, not only at work but literally everywhere we go. Harassment starts at an early age and continues as we grow into women. You better bet the high levels of harassment women face play a role in strengthening the glass ceilings, making it harder for women to break through it.

I cheered when Cheryl broke through the glass ceiling as her tech company was acquired by a NASDAQ company—and I also smiled big when she shared that roundhouse kick story with me. I won't lie. I admire a girl, a woman, with a good roundhouse kick when necessary. I shared with Cheryl that I, too, had an early history of fist-fighting boys, complete with fat lips and black eyes from standing my ground and literally fighting back as they tried to grab my ass, chased me on the playground, chased me home from school, chased me at the pool—basically everywhere, it seemed some days.

Cheryl said, "I'm so sorry you had to go through that."

You know what? No one has ever said that to me in my life. It was a sobering moment. I replied, "Cheryl, I'm so sorry you had to go through what you did, too." No woman should have to run a gauntlet of sexist and/or racist harassment in order to move forward through life. We can do better as a culture, as a nation, as a world.

The sheer level of harassment that all women face calls for a moment of pause, of talking to our male friends and our sons, of sharing that each moment of harassment is causing harm and strengthening that glass ceiling—and it's got to stop: A full 65 percent of all women experience street harassment, and for 85 percent of these women, the first occurrence happened before they were seventeen years old. Even more disturbing, 67 percent of women report that their first experience of street harassment occurred before they were fourteen years old.[2]

Drilling down in the stats on street harassment is alarming: Of the 65 percent of women who experienced harassment, 77 percent of women under age forty reported being followed by a man or group of men in the past year in a way that made them feel unsafe; 57 percent under age forty felt distracted at school or work due to street harassment; half reported they have been groped or fondled during the past year.

How is this part of forming the glass ceilings above our heads? More than half of women experiencing harassment report having changed their clothing, refusing a social event, or choosing a different transportation option as a result; and more than a third said they were made late for school or work due to street harassment. It's sadly important to note that contrary to what more than a few people of the male persuasion think, close to zero women reported finding street harassment flattering.[3]

Of course the harassment doesn't end on the street, and there's more than one kind of harassment that women face. For instance, one in four women report that they've experienced sexual harassment in the workplace.[4]

It's no wonder that #MeToo, a hashtag and movement, first sparked by Tarana Burke many years ago to support survivors of sexual harassment and assault, went viral in 2017.[5] A request went out that year, passed from person to person, for all the women who have ever been sexually harassed or assaulted to put #MeToo in their social media status in order to give people a sense of the magnitude of the problem. Eyes were opened. It turns out it's not just #MeToo. It's #MeUs. It's nearly every woman I (and you) know. The additive negative impacts over time can't be underestimated.

Harassment is often one of the many contributing factors—along with outdated workplace policies related to becoming a parent, a lack of economic security, structural racism and flat-out discrimination in hiring, pay, and advancement—that helps make the glass ceiling bulletproof. #MeToo is just the beginning of a larger conversation about the epidemic levels of sexual harassment and assault that negatively affect the lives and the careers of women. The partial reckoning for those who harass and assault women is a positive step forward. But, as a nation and as a world, we still have a tremendous amount of work to do.

Our 30 Percent

In very few sectors of our economic, political, scientific, and business arenas have women broken through the glass ceilings. Even though women make up a little more than 50 percent of the American population, and more than half of the advanced degrees are awarded to women, women have yet to break through being more than 30 percent of leadership across sectors. You read that right. We occupy fewer positions of power despite holding more college and graduate degrees than men.[6]

Want to see what the glass ceiling looks like? Currently:

- Women are only 6 percent of Fortune 500 CEOs.[7]
- Women are only 19 percent of all members of Congress.[8]
- Women are less than 30 percent of funded research scientists.[9]
- Women are less than 14 percent of the experts interviewed on Sunday TV talk shows and a tiny subset of radio hosts, and

male-authored front-page newspaper bylines outnumber those bylined by women by a 3 to 1 margin.[10]

- According to the most recent data available, just 9 percent of the directors of top U.S. grossing films are women, and female characters are only 12 percent of protagonists, 29 percent of major characters, and 30 percent of all speaking characters in the U.S. top 100 grossing films in 2014.[11]

Obituaries of men even outnumber those of women, despite the fact that women are slightly more than half our population, as if the life of a man is more newsworthy than that of a woman.[12] *It isn't.* The list goes on. Somehow, most of our nation has subconsciously decided that 30 percent is equality. *It's not.* Women are 50 percent of the population, so we're 20 percent short.

Why are we 20 percent short? Well, to start, disdain for women, including harassment and misogyny, is a consistent aspect of our culture. The best example of this is President Donald Trump, who always seems to have something demeaning to say about women, including leaders on the international stage. Trump even once told the First Lady of France, Brigitte Macron, "You're in such good shape,"[13] as if it were appropriate to comment on a woman's body. But Trump's behavior, and the fact that he was elected president in spite of his reputation for openly demeaning women, is a symptom of a far bigger problem in our nation than just that one person, even if that one person sits in the Oval Office. The persistent idea that women are less than men will exist forever if we don't stand up, break through, keep marching, and speak out. Women and girls need to be treated with respect, listened to with open ears, paid and advanced equally to all other genders. Full stop. But we have a long way to go to get there.

Our culture has become relatively numb to harassment and sexism directed at women. Too often it's normalized background static. That normalization is part of why it starts to feel like a victory when women reach 30 percent of the leadership in any field, even though we're still 20 percent short of parity and women have higher levels of education than men on average. It's part of why it's hard to break through the glass ceilings in the first place. And it's part of what we need to address in order to make it rain glass.

As my close friend Kirstin Larson says, "We have been conditioned to believe that we deserve less parity and told that because we have made gains (from 0 to 30 percent), we should be happy that we have made some gains at all. This is akin to telling women that they should be flattered when being catcalled." We have work to do, women and men alike, to open the doors to success, because, as you'll see on the pages that follow, we all lose out when women are locked out. The data is clear in every field from business, to science, to politics, to the media: When women succeed, America succeeds. Women have a tremendous amount to offer, but too many are trapped under a solid ceiling of glass, unable to break through.

But some women do break through—building a road for others to follow. The rest of this chapter is about breaking through, persisting against the odds, and what we can learn from the experiences of women who do break through to use in our own lives.

Breaking Through

Cheryl broke through that 30 percent barrier in business and has become a powerful and highly respected voice in our nation. But before she made a mark on her own, Cheryl had to leave the international public relations firm FleishmanHillard, where she'd been working. The firm refused to promote her, even though her original job offer letter stated that she would become a senior vice president. "I was working eighteen to nineteen hours a day, bringing in hundreds of thousands of dollars," she told me, "but they didn't give the promotion to me."

Doing her own calculations, Cheryl realized she could more than support herself if she could bring in just a percentage of the business she'd been managing and bringing in for the PR firm. So she set out and paired up with her business partner, Roz Lemieux. But, like many women and particularly women of color, Cheryl and Roz had to do double, triple, quadruple the work of their male colleagues in the same industry. It turns out that Cheryl had taken for granted basics like people taking her phone calls or meeting with her. People ignored her and were curt and condescending.

In fact, Cheryl says, "It was hard and completely humiliating." As someone who had launched a successful media platform (Jack and Jill Politics), was well known in her field, and had been a high-level executive, Cheryl was used to people at least treating her with some level of respect. Cheryl had come face-to-face with the glass ceiling.

One of the big tasks that business owners, particularly those in technology companies, need to do is raise capital to bring an idea to full fruition and scale. Cheryl and Roz had to do that, too. Once, Cheryl gave a demo for a well-known fund that specializes in minority tech entrepreneurs. A person who was younger than her, white, and male said, "This is a really a great product. I just don't know if *you* can pull this forward."

Cheryl was infuriated. "At that point I had a successful multimillion-dollar business. I was like, are you serious?" she said. Unfortunately, Cheryl's experience is not unique. Because she is a woman of color, Cheryl faces barriers that others would not.[14] Eventually, Cheryl and her business partner, Roz, broke through not just the barriers related to their race and gender, but another barrier that the majority of women face: being moms. Cheryl and Roz both were pregnant during the lifecycle of their company. Studies show that motherhood triggers a tremendous amount of bias, but Cheryl and Roz didn't let that stop them, either. Instead, they addressed it belly forward.

"We were starting to raise capital for our startup and had a big pitch in Atlanta in front of six hundred people," Cheryl told me, adding that most in the audience were men. "Roz was maybe eight months pregnant at the time. She was going to make a self-deprecating joke about her pregnancy. But I said, 'Roz, you should not make fun of yourself in front of these people. Most of that audience would never be brave enough to do what you've done, let alone stand on that stage and talk about it. Let's make a joke that builds you up as the hero you are.'"

So they did. Roz got up in front of the crowd and said, "In full truth, I have two startups: One is in my belly and has an eighteen-year runway and the other is Attentive.ly." The room roared. Cheryl adds, "That was a big moment for our company and for Roz as an entrepreneur. She did great."

But is it really possible to break through when so few have done it? Cheryl tells people that it's not impossible to be a successful female CEO; it's just that you're going to have to be more persistent, give it more time, knock on more doors, and provide more proof. It's so much more time, in fact, that women in fields like tech often have to add that time into their business models. "For example, if the funding raised for a company run by men will last six months, then women may have to make it last twelve months, because it's so much harder for women to raise money," Cheryl told me.

And then she said something that has stuck with me. "I see racism and sexism as market distortion. It introduces irrational factors that create noise in the system, which means good ideas and women, and particularly women of color entrepreneurs who have them, either need extra time or don't get funding at all even if they have an incredible product or amazing app that could change the world as we know it. Sometimes it will take too long to raise the capital or they won't be able to raise any at all. This is a market distortion factor that our economy must confront in order to succeed in the twenty-first century."

A mountain of data echoes Cheryl's assessment.[15] A *Harvard Business Review* article reported that venture capitalists talk very differently about women and women of color entrepreneurs, which adds up to significantly less funding, concluding, "This isn't only damaging for women entrepreneurs; it's potentially damaging for society as a whole."[16] One of the many reasons the funding gap is damaging for society as a whole is that women often build more prosperous businesses. For example:

- *Harvard Business Review* reported a study finding: "If a group includes more women, its collective intelligence rises."[17]
- A study by Pepperdine University found a direct correlation between higher levels of women in leadership and higher profits—and that promoting women meant outperforming the competition—for all Fortune 500 companies.[18]
- A study by the accounting firm Rothstein Kass found that female hedge fund managers outperformed men, earning an 8.95 percent return in 2012, compared to a 2.69 percent index return, when the market took a dive.[19]
- A Credit Suisse study found that companies with at least one woman on their board had a higher return on investment than companies with no women on their board. And a Catalyst report on S&P 500 companies found a correlation between women's representation on boards and

a significantly higher return on equity, a higher return on sales, and a higher return on invested capital.[20]

▪ Research on private firms found that managerial diversity is related to positive performance outcomes.[21]

These are just a few studies from a huge stack of research demonstrating the positive impact of women, and women of color, as entrepreneurs, hedge fund leaders, managers, and more. I could fill the rest of this book with just that list of studies and their findings. One of the most compelling studies I came across is that businesses with female CEOs during the Great Recession were less likely than their male peers to lay off staff (14 vs. 6 percent), which led to better community outcomes.[22] Women have long been outstanding colleagues in the workplace and continue to be outstanding today.

Despite all of this data, the glass ceilings remain completely solid. As noted above, only 6 percent of CEOs of Fortune 500 companies are women. And there are *zero* Black women heading Fortune 500 companies after the departure of Ursula Burns as CEO of Xerox in 2017[23]. Black, Asian, and Hispanic women make up less than 3 percent of board directors at Fortune 500 companies.[24] And then of course there's the wage and hiring discrimination that most women, particularly moms and women of color, face each and every day in our nation in every job sector.

Cheryl's story shows a glimpse of what happens when women aren't advanced in corporations. I'm not talking about her story of success here, but what came just before that—the moment she was denied a promotion, despite having that promotion be part of her initial job offer. It turns out that not only had Cheryl met the criteria for a promotion and been overlooked, but she had actually executed additional work and *still* was ignored. "I created a plan to bring in

$1 million in revenue (with appropriate staffing). My bosses thought it was hilarious. So I left. Then in our first year launching Fission immediately after that, Roz and I brought in over $1 million in an even more challenging social enterprise–focused business. At the company I had worked for, it was clear that their thinking was too narrow to imagine success for female entrepreneurs." It's time to broaden perspectives for the good of women, business, and our economy. It bears repeating: We all lose out when women are left out.

Parity Is a Win for Everyone

It's time for parity. Parity is a win-win. To be clear, I'm not suggesting that women become 100 percent of CEOs, 100 percent of leaders, 100 percent of anything. That's not what this is about. I'm simply suggesting that women have parity in all sectors—and parity is when our representation in these fields matches our representation in the population as a whole. We are at least 20 percent short of parity right now. And one of the first steps to getting to parity is realizing that having women make up only 10, 20, 30, or even 40 percent of any sector of leadership is leaving the contributions and talents of too many women on the table, locked out, stuck below a glass ceiling.

That being said, the work positions covered in this chapter are all relatively high-paying positions that only women in the top 10 percent of earners usually hold. But the majority of women are in low-wage positions—which means that far too few women even get a shot at getting into a room with a glass ceiling in the first place. Let's change that.

How to Organize People

Don't be afraid to ask for help, to ask for a political contribution, to ask for someone to join you in volunteering on a campaign, or to ask someone for help on an advocacy project. Most people will be delighted that you asked and thankful that you've opened a way for them to have an impact. The very worst that could happen is that someone says no.

A colleague, Anita Jackson, shared this: "One of the wisest things I was ever told when I needed help, but didn't want to ask for it, is this: 'Asking for help is a generous act. Allowing others to step up and be their best, most helpful selves is a gift to them as much as it is for you.'"

While this might sound like a cheesy Hallmark card, it's actually one of the best advocacy tips around, and I've experienced the truth in Anita's words time and time again. Inviting people in to help fix a problem is pretty much the definition of the word *organizing*. Respecting and empowering people while helping to open avenues for a legislative, cultural, or corporate change that will lift every woman is a generous act.

One of the biggest hurdles in organizing is making sure the organizers (that's you now!) aren't fearful that they're bothering people, putting unwanted work on people, or, worse, annoying people when they invite them to take action on planning, implementing, or attending a project.

Trust me, you're not being annoying. What you're doing is letting in the sunlight. You're giving someone the opportunity to breathe a sigh of relief that, yes, something can be done to fix this problem. You're opening doors for people to feel their power.

Think of it like this: You have a delicious appetizer, say a plate of cheese and crackers, to share. The only polite thing to do is pass it around the room and see if anyone is interested. Some people will think it's delicious and want to eat the entire plate. Some people will be allergic to blue cheese, or just not enjoy cheese at all, and will pass. You don't demand that people eat the blue cheese and crackers even if they don't like them, but you also don't refrain from giving people the option to take a taste.

That, my friends, is organizing.

You invite as many people as possible to work with you on your project because some people might find it simply spectacular and have been waiting for a way to help. You can invite people via email or social media, a phone call, in person, and the list goes on. Be sure to go to where people are already hanging out in your community to invite people to be a part of the project that you're working on and invite them in a way that they're already familiar with; you don't have to snail mail a formal invitation on a piece of paper, but you can if that's how your community regularly gets together!

Just like I've advised not to be annoyed if people say no, don't take it personally, either. If people or friends aren't interested in your project this time around, then they might be interested in another project you do sometime in the future.

I'm here to remind you that there's a special place in America for women who help other women, women who invite other women in across our differences, and women who lift each other up. In fact, that's the exact way that many of our most important economic security and justice policy advances have happened. So this advocacy tip is for you to invite people in, make it a party, and always think of it as offering an opportunity—whether it's to make phone calls to save health care or fundraise for a candidate who supports women's issues. Get to organizing!

4

Sound the Alarm

In 2013, Barbara found herself in a situation no one wants to be in: suddenly and unexpectedly out of a job. Receiving only $1,000 from Social Security to pay her rent and bills, as well as to eat, she temporarily relied on the Supplemental Nutrition Assistance Program (SNAP), also known as food stamps. "No one really wants to go on this program," she shared. "You have to hit rock bottom before you sign up. But it helped temporarily until I started working again."

Barbara is not alone. Women's economic opportunities related to jobs, income, professional development, and wealth have never been more at risk. That's a strong statement, but there are facts to back it up. As two-thirds of all minimum wage earners,[1] women not only face wage and hiring discrimination but are also at the epicenter of a huge crisis in our nation related to wealth inequality and our rapidly shifting work structures. In the last chapter, we covered the top 10 percent of earners who are hitting glass ceilings. Now we draw our focus to the 90 percent of women in our nation, many of whom are struggling to get by in a changing economy where wealth inequality is expanding and the fastest growing job sectors in our national economy are in low-wage industries.[2] These include retail, food service, and direct-care industries (which employ domestic workers and the people taking care of our homes, children, and elders). In addition to this rapid expansion of low-paying jobs, the "gig economy"—the rise of short-term contract work instead of full-time positions—as well as disruption across industries, automation, and a shift from holding one or two jobs in our lives to many, all demonstrate how work has changed for most Americans.

Because of these shifts, fewer and fewer women have access to economic protections like job-based retirement, health care, and other traditional employer-linked benefits that play a role in stabilizing economic security. Addressing wealth inequality will be crucial in the next wave of the women's movement. The need for universal protections and benefits that stay with the worker instead of being tied to a specific workplace, which everyone—at every wage level—can access, is becoming increasingly urgent. This urgency is partly because jobs within the growing "gig economy" are largely missing these crucial protections. It's also because today, the lower the wage someone earns at their job, the less likely that person is to have access to necessary workplace protections like earned sick days, paid family/medical leave, adequate health care coverage, and affordable childcare. These protections are a given in most other industrialized countries. We are in a perfect storm. Shifting work structures and a damaging lack of workplace benefits and protections are happening at the very same time that the incomes of women are increasingly needed to fuel the family budget and as female-dominated, low-wage jobs are among the fastest growing employment sectors in our economy.[3]

Fast. Growing. Those sound like good words. Working in one of the fastest job growth sectors could sound positively great until you have to rely on minimum or low wages for things like feeding kids and putting a roof over your family's head. Pricilla is a good example of how this plays out in real life. A mother of four, Pricilla works in the direct-care industry as a home care worker in North Carolina. Five days a week she's on the late shift, taking the bus at three p.m. to care for as many as twenty people each day, often not getting home until after midnight. Pricilla earns only $12 per hour after five years on the job and doesn't have paid sick days or vacation. As a leader with We Dream in Black (a program within the National Domestic Workers Alliance), Pricilla has been raising her voice so the work she and other home care workers perform is valued. She said, "We should be treated for the quality of the work that we perform and get paid for that quality as well."

But that's not happening. The average pay for domestic workers, including those in home care like Pricilla, is low and discriminatory. Domestic and farm workers have long been unfairly excluded from critical worker protections established by the Fair Labor Standards Act. That's largely because, when the law was passed in 1938, members of Congress from Southern states didn't want to include farm or domestic workers, who were primarily Black. This is a big deal because the Fair Labor Standards Act established the forty-hour work week and mandated that employers pay the minimum wage and overtime pay. But domestic and farm workers still aren't fully protected by the Fair Labor Standards Act. This has got to change.

Women are now the majority of workers in these job sectors, and it is these job sectors that are expected to have the most job growth in the coming decade. Specifically, direct-care and in-home occupations such as in-home direct-care aides to elders and people with disabilities, as well as in-home childcare providers, are expected to grow 53.2 percent, compared with a much lower 14.3 percent growth for other occupations.[4]

Though this job sector provides ample opportunity for people to find work, it's on us to make sure that this sector provides economic security to the people who hold these jobs and fosters our economy at the same time. There's a lot of work to do. To start, the wages in this sector are unethically low: The median hourly wage for a non-agency–based direct-care aide worker, which includes in-home health care aides and personal care aides,[5] is $12/hour for a white worker, but only $10.37 for a Black worker and $10.53 for a Hispanic worker in that same profession.[6] It also can't be ignored that direct-care and domestic workers, and workers in many other fast growing low-wage job sectors, often don't have workplace protections or family economic security policies, and are also regularly hard hit by wage theft, which means not being paid at all for some or part of their work.

The key factor driving this fast job growth in the direct-care sector is the "Silver Tsunami." In 1930, seniors over age sixty-five were about 5 percent of the population, but today they make up 15 percent. In 2050 they'll make up 22 percent; and by 2060 seniors will make up a full 24 percent of our population.[7]

THE "SILVER TSUNAMI"
PERCENTAGE OF SENIORS OVER 65 YEARS OLD

1930	2015	2050	2060
~5%	15%	22%	24%

The Silver Tsunami means that a lot of eldercare is going to be needed, and much of this work is carried out by domestic workers as well as by home care aides, home health aides, personal aides, and certified nurse assistants.

Ai-jen Poo of the National Domestic Workers Alliance is deeply involved in raising workers' voices and won a MacArthur "genius" grant for her work. She dove into this area of advocacy after visiting her grandfather in a nursing home with substandard care. "He begged me to take him out of there. But I couldn't," recalls Ai-jen. "Through my grandfather, I found out that our care system is dehumanizing and problematic all around. I knew that the lack of dignity my grandfather faced was also experienced by the care workers. These jobs are some of the most vulnerable and also undervalued in our whole economy. But this situation isn't impossible to fix. There are better solutions than what we're doing now."

Domestic workers aren't the only women being underpaid for hard work. Though nearly 70 percent of our GDP is based on consumer spending,[8] job growth in the United States has mostly occurred in low-wage jobs that barely allow people to pay their bills. If people don't have funds to spend at local stores, to buy kids that new pair of shoes, to see a movie, then both businesses and our consumer-fueled economy will falter.

Raise the Wage

At just over half of our population, women hold up more than half the sky. But our half weighs more, costs us more, and is the heaviest. In fact, women are 30 percent more likely than men to live in poverty.[9]

WOMEN ARE **30%** MORE LIKELY TO LIVE IN POVERTY THAN MEN

On the whole, one in seven people in the United States is living in poverty right now. But when you dive into the numbers, it's clear that the sky isn't only heavier for women, it is also heavier for people of color.[10]

The total number of white people who are living in poverty—27 million—exceeds the total *number* of people in any other race or ethnicity who are living in poverty. But that 27 million number only represents 11 percent of all white people. In comparison, a total of 11 million Hispanic people (19 percent), 9 million Black people (22 percent), and 2 million Asian people (10 percent) are living in poverty.[11] It's easy to see the compounded impact of discrimination over time in the *percentage* of people of each race and ethnicity living in poverty.[12]

THE PERCENTAGE & NUMBER OF PEOPLE LIVING IN POVERTY BY RACE AND ETHNICITY

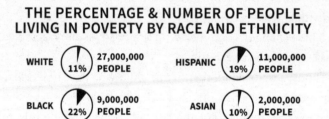

WHITE 11% 27,000,000 PEOPLE   HISPANIC 19% 11,000,000 PEOPLE

BLACK 22% 9,000,000 PEOPLE   ASIAN 10% 2,000,000 PEOPLE

Increasing the minimum wage for everyone, including direct-care and domestic workers, is absolutely necessary to combat poverty. This would have clear benefits for millions of low-wage workers as well as for the strength of our overall economy, especially since our economy and workforce are shifting quickly. In fact, it's safe to say that raising the minimum wage is now a bigger deal than at any time in recent history.

David Rolf rose up the ranks of union organizing to become

president of SEIU Local 775 and vice president of the national SEIU. To say that David pays close attention to labor force trends is an understatement. After working in labor policy for several decades and doing a tremendous amount of research, David observed that raising the floor for the minimum hourly wage has become even more critical as many protections for workers have eroded or been outright abandoned. This erosion ranges from moving to defined contribution pensions (retirement plans that an employee pays for) instead of defined benefit pensions (retirement plans the employer pays for); to offering high-deductible health care plans (which places a higher financial burden on the employee) instead of employer health care coverage (which places the financial burden on the employer); and also includes eliminating collective bargaining. All of these changes—and more—transfer the cost of doing business from the actual business to the individual worker.

These changes, combined with low or stagnant wages, create a crisis for women and families.

Cindy, a married mother of one child who lives in Florida, has experienced this crisis firsthand. Her husband works at a temporary job that he's had for the last two years, making minimum wage (just under $8 an hour), and she works for Red Roof Inn, also at minimum wage. In order to pay basic health insurance, car insurance, and have food for their daughter, Cindy and her husband went into debt paying for their home and, ultimately, were evicted. They now live in a three-hundred-square-foot room at the hotel Cindy works for, which deducts $300 every two weeks from her check. They had to go on the Special Supplemental Nutrition Program for Women, Infants, and Children (WIC) to be able to provide enough food for their daughter, and both Cindy and her husband eat only one meal a day.

Cindy remarks, "When people say the minimum wage is enough to live on, I don't know what cost of living they are looking at, but to me it seems impossible to surmise that it would come even close to being able to meet even the most basic of needs. We're not the only ones in this hard situation. In the hotel I work at there are over a dozen families (single or both parents with children) trying, and failing, to make a life for themselves, many of whom are making *more* than the current minimum wage. Is this the new American Dream?"

The majority of people who earn the minimum wage are women—28 percent of whom have children.[13] Many do critical work in our communities like preparing and serving food, cleaning offices and schools, and caring for the elderly.[14] More than half are working full-time and still living below the poverty line.[15] This is destructive for a whole host of reasons. One of the most important reasons is that, in our consumer-fueled economy, women and moms make nearly three-quarters of purchasing decisions.[16] That's a lot of consumer power. But it also means that when women and moms aren't paid fairly and don't have funds to spend, our entire economy is negatively impacted.

The minimum wage is far too low for women, for families, and for our economy to thrive. In 2017 the federal minimum wage was still stuck, as it has been since 2009, at the deplorably low rate of $7.25 per hour,[17] or $15,080 per year for a person who works full-time year-round with no breaks. And the federal minimum wage for tipped workers is just $2.13 per hour. Nearly half of all current minimum wage workers have had some college experience or an associate's degree. One in ten minimum wage workers has a bachelor's degree or higher. Only 20 percent of minimum wage workers are teens.[18] The scale of the income inequality crisis overall is illustrated by the fact that 50 percent of all working people in our nation make $17.81 per hour or less each year,[19] which means that a large number of people are holding low-wage jobs.

Think about those low numbers. Remember that women are currently 42 percent of all primary breadwinners for families and that three-quarters of moms are in the labor force contributing to the family income.[20] Particularly with women making up nearly two-thirds (64 percent) of minimum wage workers,[21] raising the minimum wage would be a good start on the road to addressing the disproportionate income inequality and poverty that women face and to boosting our economy.

But hold on to your hats, because the data gets even more troubling: The federal minimum wage for tipped workers is just $2.13 per hour, and over half of tipped workers are women, disproportionately women of color, and over a quarter are moms. Tipped workers haven't seen a raise since 1991.[22]

Victoria worked for tips for over twenty years while her kids were in school so she could be home when they were awake and they could spend more time together. She notes: "$2.13 an hour is not only horrible wages, but most people do not understand that tipped workers are taxed based on a percentage of their sales, not how much they make in tips. This often means they are paying income tax on tips they never received." In addition, when a tipped worker gets laid off their unemployment benefits are based on the $2.13 an hour and *no tips* are included!

When Victoria got laid off from her full-time job as a waitress at a three-star restaurant, unemployment insurance only paid her $46 a week because of this unfair formula. She was taxed on her full earnings, but the restaurant only had to pay benefits based on the $2.13 an hour wage—not including whatever tips she might have received for working hard and doing well at her job. This subminimum wage for tipped workers is, in effect, legislated pay inequality for a majority female workforce, perpetuating the gender pay gap. To make matters worse, there's rampant sexual harassment in the restaurant industry, which leads all industries in charges filed by women with the Equal Employment Opportunity Commission.[23]

That being said, restaurant workers are organizing and speaking out, with the Restaurant Opportunities Centers United leading the charge to increase the federal and state minimum wages for tipped workers. Seven states have stepped up and eliminated the lower wage for tipped workers, including California, which has the nation's largest restaurant industry.[24] Studies are showing that by offering one fair wage, these states are faring as well, if not better, in terms of sales and job growth in the restaurant industry, higher rates of tipping, and comparable menu prices.[25] The poverty rate among tipped workers is lower by one-fifth in states with higher minimum wages, and the reduction is most significant for workers of color—a full 18 percent of tipped workers of color in states with a subminimum wage live in poverty, compared to 14.5 percent in states without a subminimum wage.[26]

It's time for a little more myth busting in order to help raise the wage. Raising the minimum wage boosts the economy, not the other way around. Before we dive into this further, let's get one thing clear: We're aren't talking about more than doubling the minimum wage tomorrow; we're talking about an increase over time. Gradually raising the minimum wage to $15 by 2024 would directly lift the wages of 22.5 million workers and affect another 19 million workers who would benefit from a spillover effect. All in all, raising the minimum to $15 in 2024 would directly or indirectly lift wages for

41.5 million workers, or 25 percent of the projected labor force in 2024,[27] which is a significant boost to our consumer-fueled economy.[28] Multiple studies show these ripples would lift businesses and our economy in major ways.[29]

Because low-paid workers have to spend much of their extra earnings fairly immediately on the necessities of day-to-day life, this injection of wages would increase consumer spending, which would help stimulate the economy and spur greater business activity and job growth.[30]

In fact, a study from UC Berkeley Labor Center found that the poverty-level wages paid by employers cost U.S. taxpayers $152.8 billion each year in public support for working families who otherwise would not be able to put food on the table. By raising workers' wages, fewer people will have to depend on programs like SNAP.[31]

Unemployment would also be affected in good ways by raising the wage. One study showed that raising the minimum wage would create 140,000 new jobs (or more).[32] The Federal Reserve Bank of Chicago says a raise in the minimum wage would help our economy by increasing household spending nationwide by roughly $48 billion. That's enough to move the needle on our gross domestic product.[33] It's clear that raising the minimum wage boosts families and our economy. It's no coincidence that Seattle, the city with the highest minimum wage in the country (approaching $15 per hour), also has the nation's highest job growth.

Our Economy Has Changed; Our Policies Must Change Too

The minimum wage needs our close attention, particularly because our economy has changed. We used to be more economically based on manufacturing, but today, our economy largely depends on consumer spending. Jobs in the manufacturing sector have declined, due to globalization and a variety of other factors (including automation across multiple job sectors[34]). It also means that the job growth that does exist is often focused in industries that have low wages, offer few if any benefits, and are often in female-dominated sectors. This combination of economic and human factors is the reason many tech, union, and industry leaders along with politicians are pushing to not only raise the minimum wage and protect existing safety net programs but also to move forward innovative policies to boost our economy and families alike, like a possible universal basic income, which is a set amount of money that everyone would receive each month.

We need to work to create a better economy full of better jobs, and we also need to make sure that there are supports in place for people right now—not in the future, not when Democrats win back Congress and the presidency, not when we solve all of the problems we currently face, but *right now*. This means looking into innovative solutions that affect women and their families and also ensuring the strength and continuation of our social safety net programs—like SNAP, WIC, the earned income tax credit (EITC), Temporary Assistance for Needy Families (TANF), Head Start, Medicaid, and more—that immediately inject funds into our economy as they allow people to buy the groceries and other basic goods and services needed to thrive and survive. For instance, for every $1.00 that goes into funding SNAP, our economy gets back $1.70.[35]

WHAT WE CATCH IN OUR SAFETY NET

———

Sometimes, people get mad when women need to use programs like WIC. I don't. Ever. I'm mad that too often the pay people get is too low to be a living wage, making WIC a necessity.

Knowingly paying someone an unlivable wage is actually a corporate handout, because paying people low wages shifts the costs from the corporation to the taxpayer, hurts the economy, and hinders families. Something has to change—and that something isn't taking away WIC.

It's flat-out ridiculous that those working full-time at minimum wage in big box stores, those serving in the military, or those working full-time and playing by the rules anywhere aren't able to earn a living wage.

Theresa's husband was serving in the navy in the submarine service during the Cold War. As an E4, he didn't bring home a lot of money. Military housing wasn't available to Theresa and her husband, so buying basic healthy foods for their family was a struggle. A friend heard of WIC, and it made all the difference in the world. Theresa and her husband gained a sense of calm knowing that their daughter would have the nutrition she needed without them having to decide which bill not to pay so they could afford it. As their daughter got older, they had the milk and cheese and healthy foods their daughter needed to grow. Now, more than thirty-five years later, Theresa is still grateful to the WIC program for the help they provided to her young military family.

WIC is just one of several life-saving and economy-lifting programs in our nation. Medicaid, SNAP, the EITC, Head Start, and Social Security are all crucial. Even so, these programs have been continually under attack. In truth, they lift our economy and families—and as such should be enhanced, not destroyed.

Safety net programs fuel our economy. Don't let anyone tell you otherwise. For instance, Social Security provides vital economic security to American women. Since women, on average, are family caretakers, receive lower pay, are less likely to have private pensions (retirement), and live longer, Social Security is particularly important to our lifetime well-being. "Social Security is a women's issue," explained Nancy Altman, president of Social Security Works. "Social Security has transformed the nation, allowing dignity and independence when wages are gone."

Women fuel our economy, too. Our buying power is one of the biggest drivers in our economy overall, not trickle-down economics, as some elected leaders have erroneously asserted. In fact, the whole idea of trickle-down economics, where the ultra-wealthy and corporations are given tax breaks that are usually funded by cutting safety net programs with the supposed idea that this will fuel our economy, has been proven time and time again not to work. It's a fantasy that doesn't materialize in the real world. In the past, both wages and productivity have grown substantially faster in decades where corporate tax rates were higher, not lower. Neither the Reagan-era tax reform nor the cut to taxes on dividends in 2003 increased wages or productivity.[36] Look at it this way: A billionaire can only buy and eat so many burgers, and then the rest of their funds often get locked away in investments or savings accounts, where they aren't doing much to fuel our consumer-driven economy. On the other hand, a woman who buys groceries and essentials using the money from a safety net program puts those funds to work in our economy and our communities immediately. We need to change the way we think about our safety net programs. Instead of being viewed as handouts, it should be understood that these programs actually lift and boost our entire economy.

We, as women and as a nation, are facing some extreme challenges. We must protect and advance programs that we know work, like those that build our safety net. We must also explore and advance innovative new programs to match our modern economy. I don't have all the answers here; I'm not sure anyone does. But a ton of conversation and research is going on in response to the fact that as our economy is rapidly transforming, so are the job opportunities, the ways that women work, and the overall workforce.

Wealth Inequality Is a Crucial Women's Issue

Roll up your sleeves and put on your data detective hat: It's time to dive into the subject of income, wealth inequality, and women. Income inequality is how income—which includes wages and salaries—are distributed across a population. Basically, this is the gap between people who make a lot of money and people who don't make a lot.[37] (For example, if everyone made $50,000 a year, we wouldn't have income inequality.) In the United States, income inequality—the gap between the amount people are earning at the high and low end of the incomes scale—has been rising steadily since the 1970s. Partly, that's because the wealthiest Americans have been earning more of the overall total available income in the United States.[38] This is a relatively new trend. One hundred or so years ago, the wealthiest people got their income primarily through the wealth of prior generations. In the United States, we now have a category of working wealthy.[39]

Women are particularly hard hit by income inequality because we are facing wage, hiring, and advancement discrimination, all of which directly impact our income. But that's not all: There's also a trend of growing wealth inequality.

Wealth inequality is the unequal distribution of assets among people across a population—the gap in overall wealth between the rich and poor. This can include things like readily available cash in a savings account, but also reflects assets like retirement accounts such as 401(k)s, home equity, and investments like stocks and bonds. The United States has a higher wealth gap between rich and poor people than any other developed nation.[40] This wealth gap is largely fueled by the super-rich (the "1 percent"), with a significant rise in the wealth gap taking off in the 1980s.[41]

The nexus between income and wealth inequality is where it gets particularly tricky for women: Due to the income inequality and opportunity gap that women are facing, as well as other intersectional discrimination, wealth inequality often hits women the hardest. Single women, in particular, are negatively impacted in this way. This is not a small group of people: 49 percent of women over eighteen are unmarried at any given point,[42] and nearly half of all marriages end in divorce.[43]

Let's dig into wealth inequality through the lenses of gender and marriage for a moment, too. Most wealth in our nation is held at the household level, many of which are mixed-gender households and benefit from the relative lack of economic discrimination that men face. Unmarried women are less likely to hold just about every kind of asset than unmarried men. Divorce also negatively impacts women's economics more than that of men. For example, single women experience:

- Higher debt-to-income ratios
- More wealth tied up in housing, which can be volatile

- Lower overall savings
- Less access to credit (women-owned businesses are more likely to fail at least in part because of this)
- Greater likelihood of labor market uncertainty[44]

It turns out that tricky isn't even the half of it. Inequality in all its forms is a too often silent, persistent, and pernicious crisis—and it's a crisis that has a disproportionate impact on women, particularly women of color, single women, and moms. For instance, because of wealth inequality, one recent study found that a middle-class income doesn't directly correlate with middle-class economic security for everyone. For instance, white households earning an annual income between $37,201 and $61,201 owned eight times as much wealth as Black people in that same income bracket, and ten times as much as Latino people in that same income bracket.[45] The racial wealth gap is much bigger than the wage gap, and this impacts whole communities being able to pay for things like college, times out of the labor force, retirement, starting a business, buying a house, passing down resources to children, investments, sabbaticals, and much more.[46] This is a big deal. This is one example of why our fight for equity and equality must always be intersectional—and it is part of why addressing wealth inequality will be crucial in the next wave of the women's movement.

Few people realize that wage inequality and wealth inequality aren't the same thing, assuming that everyone starts at the same place on the same playing field. But we don't. We have to fight for both equality and equity, so at least we can all start equitably on the same field. It's only fair. Some forms of inequity and inequality are rarely discussed but have a tremendous impact on women, families, and our overall economy, and wealth inequality is one of those.[47] The United States is a wealthy country overall;

it's just that the wealth is extremely unequally and inequitably distributed.

The net wealth in the United States is over $84 trillion, according to the Federal Reserve.[48] But there is an enormous problem within that $84 trillion: The wealthiest 10 percent of U.S. households hold an astonishing 76 percent of all the wealth in our country, and the bottom 40 percent of U.S. households have *negative* wealth. What does this end up looking like for families? A full 44 percent of adults say they could not easily cover a $400 emergency expense, and 47 percent say their spending was higher than their income last year.[49]

Angela shared that she spends $400 per month more for food and gas than she did just a few years ago because the minimum increase in salaries that Angela and her husband received hasn't kept up with the rising prices on necessities. Rising wealth inequality is playing a role in Angela's financial worries. Partially due to unfair wages, partially due to investments like real estate and the stock market, and partially due to inherited funds, wealth inequality is a constant in most of our lives. And at the end of the day, very little of the wealth in our nation is going to the majority of people who work (and who spend the most money fueling our economy). The problem isn't just what income we're earning; it's also that with the wealth gaps that already exist many women and people of color are starting way behind.

Starting from behind can happen in a multitude of ways. So can starting ahead. People from wealthy families often don't face college debt, they get assistance with a down payment for a home, and they even make contacts with other wealthy families for jobs and internships—not to mention that people from wealthy families often have the option of doing unpaid internships when most others don't have that option because income is a necessity.

In short, wealthy people have more resources and can more easily set up the next generation to also be wealthy—without having to open any doors for additional people to work their way up the ladder of the American Dream. The playing field is far from level. We need equity and equality. We need the same starting line for everyone. We all need access to the American Dream.

The Current State of the American Dream

We're a country that self-identifies as dreamers, a people filled with hope. But the level of income and wealth inequality in our nation right now is closing the door to the American Dream for too many. While 40 percent of people in the United States may think that it is common for people born into poor families to work their way toward the top, the sad reality is that, right now, 70 percent of those born into families at the bottom of the income distribution never even make it to the middle.[50] This isn't an arbitrary thought: Many experts have been researching this area, including two Princeton professors, Anne Case and Angus Deaton. As they've researched the impact of income inequality combined with lack of access to education and advancement opportunities at work, they've found that the crisis of inequality is also a crisis of hope and health that has rippling negative repercussions for people across every race and ethnicity.

Too many women have to walk uphill both ways through life. Too many of us are working hard, but not earning a living wage because the minimum wage is insufficient to fuel our families or our economy. Too many of us, again and again, face tax policies that regularly give breaks to the wealthy and piles on the rest of us, which sucks the wind out of the economy.[51]

The United States isn't doing well when it comes to income inequality overall. We rank far behind many other nations. In fact, the United States of America is now the third worst nation in terms of income inequality—after Chile and Mexico—among the Organisation for Economic Co-operation and Development countries.[52] The high level of income inequality in our nation led MIT economist Peter Temin to assert that we're regressing to developing nation status. In 2017, Temin noted that the United States has largely become a two-track economy, with roughly 20 percent of our population educated and in good jobs, and 80 percent working in the low-wage sector with little hope of advancement.[53]

This situation can't be ignored. Wealth and income inequality are important for everyone to address, regardless of where you are on the income spectrum. That's because data shows that the bigger the gap gets between the rich and the poor, the lower overall economic growth will be, the fewer the jobs will be, and the less economic security and hope there will be for women and families. As I'll discuss further in the next chapter, many women are hitting an economic wall when they become moms and begin to raise a family. In other words, even when women work hard and play by the rules, many struggle to put food on the table or advance up the career and wage ladder. Essentially, the ladder up is broken at the same time as the waters of economic inequality are rising at the feet of America.

Those waters are rising the fastest at women's feet.

How to Take Action

I've been doing some form of community engagement, policy, or politics work since I was nineteen years old. My organizing started with many failures. I *love* failures! I'd go out in the rain trying to drum up attendees to an event, struggle with wet tape on wet surfaces, water dripping down my nose, only to find that I'd postered the wrong part of campus and would end up with an empty event. I'd learn what I'd done wrong, change tactics, and try again until I got it right. (Or at least until I got a better result!) I started organizing before the Internet, email, or social media even existed. But while the tools for organizing have changed, the strategies remain the same.

Due to my many failures, I now have some tricks up my sleeve that have helped win some significant battles. One of those tricks is beginning any activism project by using a simple outline, which I call an action sketch. Over the years I've used this technique on the back of napkins to help plan more than a few high-impact advocacy projects. You can also do this on a computer or on regular piece of paper, of course! But sometimes using a napkin-size piece of paper helps to simplify your planning.

An action sketch starts with answering four key questions:

1. What is your focused priority area for this project?
2. Why is it important for your voice to be heard right now?
3. What change do you want to make?
4. Who has the power to make that change? (This is who should be contacted to make the change happen.)

Here's an example of a roughly completed action sketch using protecting the safety net as an example to give you an idea of how it can be used in real time. (Here's a big hint: You should be able to do your action sketch on the back of a napkin over coffee. If it takes more time than that or more than a page of writing, you're not doing it right.)

1. **Focused priority area for this project?**
   Making sure that women maintain access to safety net programs like SNAP, Medicaid, and WIC.
2. **Why now?**
   Recent tax proposals include big cuts to these important programs in order to fund tax breaks for the very wealthy.
3. **What change?**
   Protect and increase access to these safety net programs and boost our economy.
4. **Who has the power?**
   Congress has the power to move policy for all in our nation forward (or backward). So I should contact my members of Congress.

When you put these items together, you have a plan of what you're doing, when you need to do it, and who you need to reach to make the change you seek. It's easy. Each policy area has specific leverage points and outcome goals, so each should get its own action sketch. Don't combine them.

I promise it's not rocket science. Just practice. And have fun!

5

The Maternal Wall

Leaving the hospital, my 7½ pound tiny daughter snapped into her navy blue car seat and wearing what I called at the time her Secretary Madeleine Albright outfit, I couldn't stop smiling. A mini salmon-colored matching top and bottom set, it looked to me like she could rule the world, baby style.

But my husband, toddler son, mom, and I drove home to a tricky situation. Like the majority of people in the United States, I didn't have any paid family/medical leave after my daughter arrived. Only 13 percent of all people in our country—and 6 percent of low-wage workers[1]—have access to paid family/medical leave through their employer.[2]

To say becoming a mom was complicated for me is an understatement. I'd unexpectedly left the salaried labor force when we realized that our infant son couldn't be in childcare due to his immune system deficiency and anaphylactic allergies. So, after my daughter was born, I was working from home on contract for nonprofits doing policy analysis and advocacy strategies. I thought I'd finally figured it out.

I thought the gig economy, contract work, was the way to work and raise kids on my own terms. I knew for sure that I was lucky—and extremely privileged—to even have the option to do work at home on contract. In one moment, I actually thought: *"This is THE way!"* I didn't realize then that this was just my duct-taped solution to a national problem.

I picked up the phone and called Ann Crittenden, author of the bestselling book *The Price of Motherhood*. I gleefully boasted into the phone: "Ann—I figured it out. The way to raise kids and also work is to do contract work!"

Ann replied: "Kristin, do you have any health care coverage on your own?"

Ummm…"Nope," I replied.

"What about sick days and paid family/medical leave? Have any of those?"

Ummm…"Nope again," I had to confess.

And, Ann asked, "Retirement? Is there a retirement plan with your current solution? What are you going to do when you're older?"

Ummmmm…

That moment remains in my mind as one of many important wake-up calls. My conversation with Ann was a reality check. I was parenting without a safety net. No one can solve this current untenable situation on their own.

Many women are working in the "gig" economy or stuck in jobs that offer few or no basic benefits like health care coverage, paid family/medical leave, or retirement savings plans. This is why we need national social insurance programs like paid family/medical leave, where the business doesn't foot the cost all at once because it's paid via small paycheck deductions over time and the coverage stays with the person, not the workplace.

Access to paid family/medical leave for everyone is a crucial part of the women's movement agenda and of boosting our national economy. In fact, enacting a national paid family/

medical leave policy that covers all parents in our country absolutely must be addressed in order to advance equality (the lack of paid family medical leave is a major contributor to women's lower pay), improve infant health, boost businesses, and save taxpayer dollars.

So what are we talking about here? Paid family/medical leave is a defined amount of time off in the moments when people need it the most: birth and medical crisis. It's time to heal, to bond, to be there when you're truly needed. It's paid time off after a new baby arrives. And it's the time women need to heal from childbirth and establish breastfeeding and bonds, or to take care of themselves, a spouse, domestic partner, a parent, or child if a significant medical crisis strikes.

But here's the full truth: When the baby comes home, so does the impact of living in a country that says it worships moms but is far, far behind other nations in terms of passing policies that allow a woman to actually be a mom and have economic security in a way that the entire family (and the national economy, by the way) can thrive. There are only two countries in the world without any national maternity policy: the United States and Papua New Guinea.[3] (Without this workplace protection, one in four new mothers in our nation has to go back to work within ten days after giving birth.[4])

Most women don't realize they're walking out of the delivery room into a space without basic workplace protections for moms and right into a maternal wall, which is the high level of wage and hiring discrimination that moms in particular face. Implicit bias against women, moms, and moms of color is strong—so strong that it pulls our paychecks down even though the work we do is proven over and over again to be far more than adequate. There's not a committee of people saying, "Pay women less," but the subconscious inaccurate assumptions about our work add up to a massive amount of money lost for women. The wage discrimination that builds the maternal wall is sexism in action. But we don't often hear about the maternal wall. Instead, the message women often get from society is that all of this stress—all the ways in which we fear we might be failing our children in one moment and falling down on the job the next—is a result of our own personal inadequacies. We don't often hear that this madness is no one's personal problem and that we have a systemic, outdated public policy problem that we can fix together. Well, I'm here to tell you we can fix this.

The good news is that it also doesn't take rocket science to break down this wall. By moving forward long-overdue policies like access to paid family/medical leave, affordable childcare, health care, and earned sick days, the maternal wall can be broken. Other countries have done it. And the United States can, too. In fact, studies show that countries with these policies in place have less hiring and wage discrimination than we do.

The maternal wall hurts children, women, and our economy. It hurts us all. It's no accident that fewer Fortune 500 CEOs are women,[5] that there's a shortage of women in Congress, and that of the last six Supreme Court nominees, all the men had children while none of the women did. This wall hurts moms. Many moms are working full-time, playing by the rules, and still struggling to make ends meet and put food on the table. This wall hurts kids, too. One in five children in the United States experiences food scarcity due to family economic limitations[6] and a quarter of young families in this country are living in poverty.[7]

The first step to change is realizing that a maternal wall exists in the first place so we can stop accidental implicit bias in its tracks by calling attention to it.

Paid Family/Medical Leave: A Win-Win-Win Solution

Advancing a national paid family/medical leave policy does more than allow time for new families to heal, bond, and thrive. It raises our economy and lowers wage gaps. Crucially, in order to be effective, it needs to cover all parents, not just birth mothers. In fact, paternity leave in particular directly helps reduce the wage gap between men and women. The World Economic Forum found that the countries that offer paid parental leave for moms and dads are the most successful in closing the wage gap between men and women.[8] So once we finally pass a national policy in this area—and I firmly believe that will happen within this generation—we also will have to work to change our culture so people of all genders use this policy when a new baby arrives or to care for seriously ill family members. Breaking down gender walls breaks down the maternal wall, too.

Roxanne shared, "In our family I work and my husband stays home with our children. We would not be able to survive without paid family leave as my husband's job is staying home with our four-year-old (and now nine-month-old twins), yet I still needed to recover from the birth of our twin boys. Without paid family/medical leave, we would have no income while I recovered from the birth. With culture changing and both men and women being stay-at-home parents, it's even more important to have paid family leave for situations like ours, where the mom works and the father stays home."

The reality is that our labor force and many of our families have changed. For the first time in history, women are now half of the labor force,[9] and moms are now the primary breadwinners in more than 40 percent of families.[10] Yet our public policies—like access to paid family/medical leave for all parents, affordable childcare, fair pay, access to sick days, and more—haven't caught up to our modern-day workforce, even though the vast majority of women in our nation become moms at some point in their lives. The wages of moms aren't pocket change; they put food on the table and fuel our economy.

But this isn't just about moms. Access to paid leave also benefits dads. Studies show that fathers who are able to take paid leave to care for their children are more involved in their kids' lives nine months after they are born, and their families are less likely to need public assistance.[11] It also helps families balance the distribution of unpaid labor. Fathers who take paternity leave are more likely to take an active role in childcare tasks. According to a study of four rich countries—the United States, Australia, Britain, and Denmark—fathers who had taken paternity leave were more likely to feed, dress, bathe, and play with their child long after the period of leave had ended. Danish men were the most diligent: 77 percent of them play with their children regularly. And, in Britain, dads who took time off at birth were almost a third more likely to read books with their toddlers than those who hadn't.[12] Paternity leave is good for women's careers, too. When men shoulder more of the unpaid childcare burden, the effect of parenting on women is lessened.[13]

The additional unpaid work women do at home is a big deal. Even when there's a partner involved, women still bear the brunt of the load when it comes to tracking family needs, like who has to go to the doctor and when the coffee is going to run out,[14] as well as performing the vast majority of household chores and caregiving.[15] All of this takes time and is work. According to one UN Human Development Report, if all the tasks women do for free were paid, even at low wages, the total would be $11 *trillion*.[16] To put this figure into perspective, the official estimate of total paid wages around the world is $23 trillion.[17] Women's unpaid labor (whether full-time or part-time) takes physical and mental space and time. It also puts a tremendous amount of money into the economy, but too often that work is invisible and disrespected—and that deep level of disrespect leaches over into the paid labor force, where it becomes part of the gender pay gap.

Unpaid work should be respected and distributed more evenly across genders. Access to paid family/medical leave helps make that happen. Having both parents be able to access paid family/medical leave immediately after a new baby arrives allows new family task patterns to be established more evenly between genders.

Babies, the future leaders of tomorrow, benefit from paid family/medical leave policies, too. Infant mortality decreases up to 25 percent when parents have paid leave compared to unpaid leave.[18] Parental bonding is strengthened, and infants have improved brain and social development. Also, women who take paid family/medical leave breastfeed for longer,[19] which is universally recommended by pediatricians because breastfeeding has a positive effect on their overall health and the overall long-term health of the babies.[20]

Lia explained, "I have two daughters and I work full-time as a teacher. When we decided to plan for a second child, we had to save for over a year. I took off the twelve weeks afforded to me through the FMLA, but it wasn't nearly enough time to fully bond with my daughter. When I returned to work, I was still breastfeeding my baby. My school did not have any reserved space for pumping, so I had to pump in a bathroom twice a day. Instead of feeling the joy of motherhood, I felt as though I was being penalized for being a working mother. I would love to have another child, but I do not think my family could afford to have another period like this in our lives. Mothers, fathers, and children deserve more than this."

MOMentum

Moms, dads, and babies all benefit from paid family/medical leave. So do women without children who encounter a medical emergency or who have a spouse, parent, or domestic partner in a medical crisis. Women's rights are advanced. But that's still just the tip of the iceberg. Businesses, employers, and our economy benefit, too.

Fortunately, several states have stepped up to move this policy forward, with excellent outcomes and data to prove that this policy walks the talk when it comes to benefiting businesses, families, and our economy. In fact, a 2011 study of California's Paid Family Leave program found that most employers reported that providing paid family leave had a positive effect on productivity, profitability, performance, turnover, and employee morale.[21]

Good for Businesses

The majority of proposed—and all passed—paid family/medical leave policies at the state and federal level are paid for as social insurance programs. That means that the cost of the program is paid by some form of small employee and/or employer paycheck deduction and not directly by the business when an employee takes leave. This actually lowers the cost for many businesses because the compensation of people who are on leave is covered through funds from a state or federal program instead of directly from the business itself. So passing paid family/medical leave programs at the state and federal levels actually lifts the direct cost off businesses because they don't have to pay wages during the time the employee takes for leave in order to care for a new baby, a seriously ill close family member, or their own serious illness.

Rachael is the owner of a small business and agrees that we need a national paid family/medical leave program to lift the cost off individual businesses like hers. Many of her employees have taken paid time off, saving vacation, personal, and sick time to use after they became parents. Scheduling hasn't been a problem. But because we don't have a national paid family leave program, Rachael reports that she's challenged by the outflow of funds for their employees' paid time off while also paying for someone to take their place. Without a national program, when someone takes leave Rachael has to pay twice—once for the employee on leave and once for their replacement. A national program would solve this cash flow issue. She notes: "In order to smooth all this out, *and* give more time, like twelve to sixteen weeks for a postpartum stretch—a business would benefit from payments made into a paid family leave program much like their unemployment account that could cover the cost when people take time out. This is just good planning for businesses."

In addition, businesses that have paid family/medical leave policies save on recruitment, retention, and retraining costs. In one poll, 77 percent of respondents indicated that the amount of parental leave offered by a potential employer affects their decision when choosing one company over another, and 50 percent said they would rather have more parental leave than a pay raise.[22] Many companies are using this policy to lure and retain workers—and it's working! When Google lengthened maternity leave from three months to five and offered full pay instead of partial pay, attrition decreased by 50 percent.[23]

As the changes at Google demonstrate, access to paid family leave also stabilizes the labor force—thus helping businesses with retraining costs. Studies have also found that moms with access to paid family leave were more likely to be in the labor force one year after having a child and significantly less likely to rely on government programs, saving taxpayer dollars.[24]

Boosting the Economy

When Terry's mom passed away suddenly, her dad, who had rapidly progressing metastatic cancer, was left behind. As an only child, Terry had sole caregiving responsibility. "When I approached my bosses for a leave of absence to be at my dad's bedside, I was told they would 'consider it,' but that I would lose all of my accounts during my absence." As she waited for the company's decision, her dad got sicker. Terry was working, taking her dad to the doctor, and trying to juggle it all. The juggle wasn't working. Terry recalls that because she couldn't get time off, her "ability to effectively manage dad's care was greatly impeded." She then requested to work from home, but was denied that option, too. Then, just hours after her dad died in her arms, Terry's boss phoned to finally say they would grant her a short leave of absence. "When I told my boss my dad died, the phone went silent. I will forever be haunted by that experience."

Terry is not alone. When women (and men, too) have access to paid family leave, they are more likely to stay in their jobs, be able to continue to pay taxes, and also to get the wage increases that go along with longer employment histories—no matter what is going on with their personal or family lives. The economy as a whole also benefits when workers have access to paid leave.

Jennifer shared her story. "In 2006, I was living in California and I was fortunate enough to be able to use California Paid Family Leave after my son was born. It allowed me to take the time to bond with my newborn and stay home for three months with pay. My husband was then able to use Paid Family Leave when I returned to work for six additional weeks (paid through PFL). The amount taken out of my paycheck to support this program was not even noticeable! I love being a parent and I love being an employee. (I'm a social worker and love my job!) I am glad that

I did not have to choose between one or the other, like so many families are forced to do."

The benefits of paid family leave are real and palpable. Twenty-six weeks of paid maternity leave would increase U.S. women's labor force participation to the tune of a 5 percent increase in gross domestic product, which is $900 billion per year.[25]

Despite that, only 13 percent of U.S. workers overall and only 6 percent of low-wage workers have access to paid family leave, even though more than half of all new mothers work outside the home for pay. As a result, many take unpaid leave, quit, or even lose their jobs when they face a major health issue or have a baby.[26] No family should face the prospect of poverty because of the birth of a child. I'm not the only person who thinks this.

The majority of voters in our nation strongly support paid family leave policies. California, New Jersey, and Rhode Island all have paid family leave insurance laws.[27] As of the writing of this book, five states have passed paid family/medical leave and nearly fifty cities have moved forward some type of paid family/medical leave policy, even if just for city workers.[28] But access to coverage shouldn't be dependent on geography or winning the job lottery.

Right now, the only policy we have at the national level is the 1993 Family Medical Leave Act, which provides unpaid leave but doesn't cover all workers. We need to keep pushing and bringing these policies forward in cities and states across the nation. The momentum is already growing and must continue right on into Washington, DC, so we can change legislation at a national level. Women have fueled many of these wins by making phone calls, sharing their experiences, writing letters, signing online petitions, attending meetings with elected leaders, holding events, sharing information on social media, and more. It all adds up.

Women's Workplace Justice

There's more than one policy in the women's workplace justice mix that we can't afford to overlook. You see, paid family/medical leave is for the birth or adoption of a new child, your own very serious illness, or to care for a close family member having a health crisis, but it's not for when you catch a regular bug like the flu. That falls under sick days.

When Miranda was working for a major retailer, she and her co-workers could take a sick day, but would not be paid for any time missed. Instead, she told me, "Everyone would come in to work because we all needed the money. We'd pass around the same cold for weeks. Once, someone came in who had meningitis."

Similarly, Barbara, like 54 percent of all mothers, didn't have access to any paid sick days, so she had to postpone taking her daughter to the doctor.[29] One time, this resulted in her daughter having a serious untreated ear infection that permanently harmed her hearing.

For all women and all people, sick days are crucial. More than 70 percent of low-wage workers—like Miranda and Barbara—don't have access to a single paid sick day to care for themselves or a family member (like a child), and 40 percent of all private sector workers don't, either.[30] This is *not* okay.

Earned sick days are a few days per year that people can receive with pay based on the total hours that they work. This allows employees to have paid time off when they have the flu, an ear infection, a bad cold, or any other regular illness. This is important because everyone gets sick from time to time, but not everyone has a chance to get better. It's time to change that.

Paid sick days are also a big win for businesses because they reduce employee turnover cost, boost workplace morale, and help stop the spread of illness among workers.[31] As Miranda's story demonstrates, employees coming to work sick because they don't have access to paid sick days costs the national economy more than $155 billion annually because of lost productivity.[32] It's no wonder so many businesses support paid sick days.

We're also the only developed nation in the world without a national paid sick days law. It's hurting our global competitiveness, and we're overdue for a change.[33] Over 160 countries have passed this type of policy—and we can and must, too. This is a critically important policy for families, businesses, and our economy. Without the ability to earn paid sick days, working women and families are faced with impossible choices: sending a sick kid to school or going to work sick, versus staying home and losing an invaluable day's pay, or sometimes even losing a job.

In these uncertain and tenuous times, it's more important than ever to fight for the 41 million workers, including more than half of all working moms, who can't earn a single paid sick day to stay home when needed—and women are rising to do exactly that.[34]

I have good news to share (and some bad news, too).

First, we're winning these fights. City by city, and state by state, people are rising up (including many volunteers from MomsRising) and urging elected leaders to pass local paid sick day policies, and change is happening in real lives. Thirty-one jurisdictions (cities and counties), seven states, and the District of Columbia have already passed paid sick days for their residents and workers.[35] As of March 2017, 68 percent of private sector workers now have access to paid sick days compared to 64 percent in 2016, and 61 percent in 2015.[36] When I started working on this policy area over a decade ago, only 40 percent of private sector workers had access to this policy, so this is a big jump in coverage.

I actually did a little happy dance when I saw these new

numbers. Each city and state that passes this policy adds up to a higher overall percentage of real people who are covered. Real people who can take the time needed to care for a sick child, or to take care of themselves. (Thank you to all the people and organizations who played a role in these many wins across the nation.)

But while we're winning at the local level and gaining momentum, we still need a national sick days policy to cover 100 percent of people—particularly because hidden in those stats is the fact that low-wage workers are the least likely to have access to sick days.

So it's time to pump up the volume.

For an average family without paid sick days, just three and a half days of missed work is the equivalent to an entire month of groceries.[37] And nearly one in five low-wage working mothers have been fired for needing time off because they or their child is sick.[38] Without the opportunity to earn paid sick days, the realities that Donna shares are unfortunately all too normal. "I work in a factory where people come into work even when they are sick because they can't afford to stay home. You can't get well that way!"

Unprecedented support for paid sick days is building across the nation in no small part because women are raising their voices. But access to paid sick days shouldn't depend on your zip code— we need a national policy that makes paid sick days standard.

Paid family/medical leave, earned sick days, and equal pay together help ensure the economic security of women across our nation, especially women in the most vulnerable communities, including communities of color and Muslim, immigrant, and LGBTQ+ families, as well as families in rural communities. These are fights we can win.

How to Draw Attention

There are influential people in your community, often with the power to make the change you seek. It may seem surprising, but you can often draw attention to a topic or a policy—and essentially talk directly to them—by writing a letter to the editor of a local newspaper.

After all, who reads the editorial pages of newspapers most closely?[39] Elected officials, decision makers within your community, and local media. That's right, writing a short letter to the editor is a powerful and often underutilized way to help create change. Elected leaders often figure out what to prioritize by reading their local editorial pages, so getting your voice in those outlets can have a big impact. Since these letters must be short, writing a letter to the editor is fun and relatively easy. Here are some tips:

- **Do your research.**

  Do a little online search to see which local papers in your area accept letters to the editor. This can include daily newspapers, weekly newspapers, and neighborhood papers, too. Search online to find their submission criteria, including the maximum number of words and how to submit your letter to the editor. If the information isn't obvious online, find their main phone number and call to ask. (Many papers also print short responses to letters to the editor as well, so this could be another option for you to ask about.)

- **Brevity is beautiful.**

    Typically, effective letters to the editor are roughly 150–200 words. Be sure to check with your local paper for their word limits and submission guidelines.

- **Think before you type.**

    Decide on one main point you want to get across, and find one fact as well as one short story to back it up. A personal experience is powerful if you can fit it in. If you're having trouble with your draft, contact an organization that works on the policy area that you're writing about, and they'll likely be overjoyed to help you with finding a fact, reviewing your draft, or assisting with anything else that you may need.

- **Be concise.**

    When you start writing be sure to make one point, at most two, in your letter. Use an active tense and try to start with a catchy opening.

- **Keep it current.**

    Mentioning something that's been in the news in the past couple of days significantly increases your chances of getting published. You can also mention a recent specific article or letter that appeared in their paper, and refer to the title, date, or author.

- **Back up your facts.**

    If you use a fact, share where you found it. I always like to keep the links to the facts handy so I can easily find the fact again—and I usually share the link to the fact with the paper, too.

- **Be nice.**

    Avoid attacking reporters or the newspaper. It's fine to refute specific statements, but do so politely if you want to get printed. This is especially important when responding to a previously published letter to the editor from an opposing viewpoint.

- **Be relevant.**

    Connect the issue to the community. If you're writing about a national issue, then share what it means to your local area.

- **Be inspired.**

    You only have to write 150–200 words, so don't put too much pressure on yourself. Have fun with it! To get an idea of the tone and length of what's being published, take a quick look at the letters to the editor that the paper has printed in the last month. It'll give you ideas and inspire you to put your own words to paper.

An effective next step is to get a writing group going. Hold a writing party, host a writing circle, or make letters to the editor part of your monthly #KeepMarching agenda. (There are tips on how to start a #KeepMarching Circle in the conclusion.) Often local papers limit the number of letters to the editor that they'll print from one person per year, so getting others to also write is not only fun but also a highly effective way to amplify your impact. In order to help encourage people to write, you can share the talking points and facts you pulled together to write your letter to the editor.

Writing a letter to the editor is a great way to get your point across, be heard by leaders at the top, sway public opinion, and have an impact with a very small number of words. I highly recommend it.

PART II

OUR BODIES

6

Saving Lives

Four of us squished into the back of a cab with coffees balanced precariously in our hands headed for Capitol Hill—me; Ashley Boyd, the then health care director of MomsRising; Felicia Willems, a volunteer at the time; and Felicia's five-year-old son, Ethan. That day was March 23, 2012, the second anniversary of the passage of the Affordable Care Act (ACA). The law had been under constant attack since it passed. Our message that day to Congress in Washington, DC, was simple: We're standing strong for the consumer protections we've won through the Affordable Care Act.

Felicia, Ethan, Ashley, and I were "taking the Hill" that day to deliver books of stories about how women from every state in the nation had benefited from the coverage and protections in the ACA. Some women shared their relief that because the ACA passed, they no longer had to worry about exceeding an annual or lifetime limit on coverage. Others expressed how grateful they were that they could now stay on their parents' health care plans until they were twenty-six years old. And so many women wrote us to share how glad they were that just being a woman was no longer a preexisting condition.

We had tens of thousands of signatures on an open letter to Congress from women across the nation supporting the ACA. It's not surprising that large numbers of women responded to protest the repeal of this critical legislation. After all, women make 80 percent of health care decisions—not just for themselves, but for their loved ones, too.[1]

Our heels clicking on the marble floors, the four of us visited office after office reminding members of Congress that women are paying attention to what they're doing inside the Beltway bubble, that everyone gets sick, and that everyone should have a chance to get better. We walked so many miles on those hard marble floors that Ashley, Felicia, and I started trading shoes among us midway through the day so that we'd rotate where we were each getting blisters on our feet.

But we kept on.

The content we were delivering that day was important. We were holding pure political power in our hands and delivering it directly to elected leaders to help shape the direction of health care policy as we literally walked in each other's shoes. Sometimes women think that the actions they take online, the petitions and open letters they sign, the experiences they share in glowing text boxes on their computers late at night, don't make a difference. I'm here to tell you that you are more powerful than you think. I've been part of nearly countless deliveries like this to elected leaders at the local, state, and national levels on a wide variety of policies, and every single time I've been humbled to witness an incredible impact.

We saw that impact on March 23 as we delivered the long list of signatures along with a book of stories from women around the country about the positive, life-saving impact of the ACA to members of Congress. We didn't stop there, though. We went on, in our now traded shoes, to share those stories later that day at a press conference alongside then House Minority Leader Nancy

Pelosi, and then we hopped in another cab. This time our stop was the West Wing, where we worked on a joint Tweetchat with the White House (led by President Barack Obama at the time) to help spread the word even farther about why health care still needed to be protected.

Women helped hold the line that day—and on many days after that one. As of the writing of this book, there have been more than fifty attempts by Republicans in Congress to overturn the ACA, which covers tens of millions of people. Access to health care for tens of millions of people has been on the line more than *fifty* times during my tenure at MomsRising alone. But together with other organizations and the over 1 million members of MomsRising, we've held the line every time. That line is strengthened with each of us sharing our personal stories so leaders can better understand the true impact of the proposed policies on their desks. When thousands of women across the nation share their stories and experiences with elected leaders, it all adds up to a big impact.

Our personal stories hold more power than any pinstriped suited corporate lobbyist will ever hold. On March 23, 2012, Felicia and her son Ethan shared their story. At meeting after meeting, Felicia straightened her back, centered herself, and shared what happened in her life in 2006. Ethan was born with a serious medical condition and needed to start chemotherapy at six weeks old to treat a life-threatening tumor. Round-the-clock care was essential, so Felicia had to quit work to care for him, which meant she also lost her employer-sponsored health insurance and her income.

Ethan qualified for Medicaid, which saved his life.

But the trouble wasn't over. Once Ethan was in remission and Felicia started to get back on her feet financially, she found out that she was uninsurable.

Crisis.

Felicia was one medical issue away from poverty, living without health care coverage while caring for a young child with a serious medical condition. Not being able to afford to go to the doctor is an untenable situation. Everyone should have a chance to get better when they get sick. But too often before the ACA, people missed out on the basic care they needed to be well, to contribute to our society, to thrive.

After the ACA went into effect that changed for the better—not just for Felicia but also for tens of millions of moms, dads, children, and single people too. Felicia's family, like many others, was finally able to buy affordable health insurance coverage on the ACA marketplace, and she was able to buy it despite her preexisting condition. The ACA includes consumer protections so insurance companies can no longer discriminate based on preexisting conditions or put lifetime limits on care.

And while Felicia has since gained employer-sponsored coverage, her family still benefits immensely from the peace of mind knowing that the preexisting conditions she has—and the one that Ethan was born with—cannot prevent them from getting health insurance in the future.

For now. Repeal of the ACA would be devastating to Felicia, to her family, and to tens of millions of other families. In total, more than 20 million people gained health insurance since ACA's implementation, and 11 million people gained access to Medicaid, which was expanded in thirty-one states and the District of Columbia.

The ACA is vital. It includes consumer protections like young people being able to remain on their parents' insurance plan until they reach twenty-six years old. Other protections include that insurers can't deny coverage, charge higher premiums, or refuse to cover care related to those preexisting health conditions. Insurers are also prohibited from imposing lifetime or annual dollar limits on coverage.[2] The ACA also expanded mental health and addiction coverage, including preventative services like depression screenings for adults and behavioral assessments for children, at no additional cost.[3]

But that's not all. The ACA significantly transformed access to reproductive health care and women's health care in general. The law forced insurers to cover maternity care and contraceptives. It prohibited insurance companies from charging women extra for gender-specific services and allowed many women to get contraceptives (as well as a variety of preventive services, like Pap smears and mammograms) at zero cost.[4]

Overwhelmingly, the ACA has benefited millions of women, saving dollars and lives. Because of that, it's hard to believe that there are still human beings who don't believe that every human being should have access to health care—and that some of these people are elected leaders. Frankly, it boggles my mind.

The fight over health care in recent years is a reality check on where we are now and where we need to be. In terms of health care, as we look ahead in this area, it's absolutely clear where we need to be as women: marching toward quality health care and comprehensive coverage, including access to reproductive, mental, and dental care coverage. The ACA is far from perfect, but it's a giant leap forward. As things stand now, the United States is the only industrialized nation in the world that doesn't guarantee health care for all.[5] So we still have some catching up to do.

There is urgency in our need to do that catching up. Lives are literally on the line. Access to health care is a human right, and that access should never be turned into a political football as too often happens in our nation. Needing health care is ingrained in our common humanity because everyone gets sick. It isn't a weakness. It can, however, be a lifesaver, a money saver, and a way to strengthen our families and economy.

Being Alive Is a Preexisting Condition

I've needed health care. My daughter and son both struggled with health issues when they were young. Thankfully both are now healthy today because they had access to health care professionals. This is no small matter.

I'm sure you've needed health care, too. Everyone gets sick, ends up in the ER with an injury, or experiences a condition that requires medicine. That's life. Being alive pretty much is a preexisting condition for needing health care at some point or another. And the fact that even with the ACA in place, 11.3 percent of the U.S. population is still in need of health care coverage is a big deal.[6] We still have work to do.

Living without insurance makes life harder. George told me, "I grew up without insurance. Every time one of us was sick was a time of great worry, not just for our recovery but for the eternal question, 'How are we going to pay for the doctor?' My parents had to max out their credit cards, bills were paid late, and sometimes we had to make trips to the pawn shop."

Lack of access to health care is an area where it's easy to see the compounded impact of income and racial inequality. Twenty-one percent of Hispanic people were uninsured in 2015 (down from 26 percent in 2013), 17 percent of American Indian or Alaska Native people (down from 25 percent in 2013), while 12 percent of Black people (down from 17 percent in 2013), 8 percent of white people (down from 12 percent in 2013), and 7 percent of Asian people (down from 13 percent in 2013).[7]

UNINSURED RATE BY RACE/ETHNICITY

	2013	2015	
HISPANICS	26%	21%	↓ 5%
AMERICAN INDIAN/ ALASKAN NATIVE	25%	17%	↓ 8%
BLACK	17%	12%	↓ 5%
WHITE	12%	8%	↓ 4%
ASIAN	13%	7%	↓ 6%

In addition to income and racial inequality in health care access, there are also compounding impacts in the LGBTQ+ community. The uninsured rate for LGBTQ+ people was 11 percent in 2015 (down from 22 percent in 2013).[8]

There's good news and bad news in these numbers. The good news: If you look closely at the numbers, the rate of people in every group who are uninsured fell fairly significantly between 2013 and 2015. That's the ACA, which passed in 2010 under President Obama, at work. That's lives saved.

The bad news: There's still inequitable access to health care in our nation. Here again inequality costs lives. It's at this point that I want to shout from the rooftops that health care is a right, not a privilege—and those who are denied that right too often pay with their lives.

Death rates are another window into the impact of compounded inequalities. Life expectancy data from the Centers for

Disease Control and the Kaiser Family Foundation show that Black people have the lowest life expectancy in our nation, 76 years, followed by a life expectancy of 76.9 among Native Americans and 79 years for white people. Hispanic people have the highest life expectancy in our nation, 82 years.[9]

Yes, you read that right. And, no, that isn't a typo. Hispanic people as a group have the lowest access to health insurance coverage, but the highest life expectancy. The CDC report that was released along with this data shares that there are several possible reasons for this: "People who migrate, particularly immigrants, are often very healthy; people who weren't born in the U.S. but live here often go to their place of birth when seriously ill; and, importantly, the family structure, lifestyle, behaviors and social networks in the Hispanic community may counter the negative effects of a lower socioeconomic status and minority status."[10]

Racism in Our Health Care System Must Be Addressed

Our nation's enduring legacy of systematic racism against Black people in particular has deep roots in virtually every sector of society—including health and life expectancy. And the fact is that most of these health disparities are rooted in health problems that are easily preventable and treatable, like diabetes and heart disease, the latter of which is not only the leading cause of death in the United States but also is a leading contributor to racial disparities in life expectancy.[11] As of 2014, death rate among Black people was 1.2 times higher than among white people. Though the death rate among white people has recently gone up and made news, the overall death rates in the Black community still remain 17 percent higher than those of whites.[12] These disparities in health and life expectancy aren't a coincidence: A study from as recent as 2016 showed that a shocking number of medical professionals polled hold wildly racist views about their Black patients, such as the false beliefs that Black people feel less pain than whites and that their blood coagulates faster—resulting in lack of proper treatment and care.[13] This is ridiculous, harmful, and wrong.

It's time to make sure that our health policies and practitioners are lifting every person in every community.

Medicaid Is a Lifesaver for Many Women and Children

We need to double down to move access to health care forward, not backward. Health care access must be expanded, not restricted. But don't worry—there is hope. We have a superpowered health care policy that hardly ever gets the spotlight, makes the news, or ends up in late night comedy sketch in our toolbox: Medicaid. And it's constantly at risk of being defunded. As of the writing of this book, 39 percent of all children in the United States receive health care coverage through Medicaid. Remember Ethan, Felicia's son, from the beginning of the chapter? He qualified for Medicaid and had his life-threatening tumor treated as a result. In some states the number of children who would have *no* health care coverage were it not for Medicaid is extremely high. In Maine, it's 47 percent of all children; in Arkansas, 47 percent; and in Arizona, 46 percent. And in our nation's capital, where Congressional leaders regularly play political football with health care, a full 49 percent of all children living in Washington, DC, receive life-saving health care only because of Medicaid.[14]

Stephanie's daughter was born with schizencephaly, cerebral palsy, and epilepsy. She is legally blind, is nonverbal, uses a

wheelchair, and has a feeding tube. Her medications, feeding supplies, and medical equipment and supplies cost thousands of dollars every month. Her feeding supplies alone cost almost $2,000,
of which private insurance only covers a small portion. If Stephanie's daughter loses coverage and Medicaid is cut, she will die.

In total over 70 million people are covered by Medicaid, including 10 million people with disabilities.[15] Medicaid is lifting up
families, empowering them to be able to work while caring for
children with disabilities or elderly parents, allowing people who
were priced out of access to health care to finally get the medical treatment they need to keep them healthy and productive,
and boosting our bottom line as a nation. Medicaid is critical for
women and families and to our economy.

Medicaid also plays a crucial role in helping ensure our nation's
aging population receives the care and dignity that they deserve later
in life, covering over 70 percent of nursing home patients.[16] Marilyn
shared, "I do not know what my family would have done without
Medicaid when my mother was institutionalized with Alzheimer's
disease. We private-paid for three years, and when she was broke,
having spent everything she worked a lifetime for to sit wasting away
in a nursing home, Medicaid picked up the tab for the last five years.
What on earth would have happened to her without that support?"

Medicaid also covers nearly half of all births in the United
States, making sure new moms and their babies get the care that
they need.[17] Kelley told me, "Without Medicaid, I wouldn't have
been able to afford the birth of my daughter, or her health issues
early in life. As someone who has always struggled with poverty,
as well as everyone I know being impoverished, we rely on Medicaid for the most basic of medical care. Being unable to treat a
simple infection or get a checkup for your child is something no
one should deal with, especially in America."

The impact of cutting Medicaid would be particularly severe for families, women of color, people with disabilities, and women who live in rural areas. In fact, Medicaid has long played an even larger role in providing health coverage and paying for care in rural areas than in urban areas. Nearly 1.7 million rural Americans have newly gained coverage through the Medicaid expansion, many of them women. According to the Center on Budget and Policy Priorities, "in [Medicaid] expansion states overall, rural residents make up a larger share of expansion enrollees than they do of these states' combined population. The Medicaid expansion has also become a critical financial lifeline sustaining rural hospitals."[18]

There's a key point that needs to be made about how ACA has benefited people living in rural parts of our country and what has been happening in politics. In at least eight of the states in which Medicaid expanded under the ACA, more than one-third of the people who benefited from that expansion live in rural areas. Yet six of these states awarded their electoral votes to Donald Trump. In fact, almost twice as many rural voters supported Trump (62 percent) compared to Hillary Clinton (34 percent). It's now clear that many people voted against their own interests when it comes to health care.

We saw the impact of this in 2017, when many of the people who originally voted for Trump because they wanted to "kill Obamacare" later learned more about the ACA policy, thankfully did a 180-degree change on their stance, and rose up against the health care repeal efforts. Ultimately the majority of people in all fifty states opposed the main repeal bill for the ACA in 2017, even in states that voted for Trump.[19]

Unfortunately, there's often a tremendous amount of racism and sexism in how we think and talk about health care and government safety net programs like Medicaid, as a country and particularly among those who vote conservatively. The racist mythology about who uses government programs is contradicted by the facts: Among whites, 42 percent are covered by Medicaid—more than Hispanics (31 percent) and twice the rate of African Americans, only 19 percent of whom have Medicaid coverage.[20]

The Good News

It cannot be forgotten that the voices of women and moms are a major reason why our nation was able to get the health care access expansion and consumer protections under President Obama in the first place.

One of my favorite moments of political engagement was when, in 2009, hundreds of thousands of members of MomsRising across the country signed an open letter urging every member of Congress to pass the ACA, shared personal stories about needing health care for their families, and volunteers even decorated hundreds of clean baby diapers with flowers and colorful designs that had this central message: *Our current health care system stinks. We need a change!*

The decorated, clean, cheerful diapers were delivered to every member of Congress, along with the stories and signatures on the open letter, to show that women and families across the nation were closely following the health care debate. Our mission? To show members of Congress that even if their constituents couldn't be there in Washington, DC, we were paying attention at home and had a strong opinion: It's time to pass health care!

At MomsRising we work to find ways for women's voices to be heard and seen in innovative and powerful ways. For instance, to advocate for health care, we've also delivered Apple-o-Grams ("An apple a day doesn't actually keep the doctor away: We need health care") and passed out superhero capes to senators, asking them to be "superheroes for our family's health," and much more.

This approach works for three reasons. First, the women who volunteer with MomsRising are busy and often don't have time to advocate in person, so delivering a physical item that someone made is a way for them to "be there" without being there in person. Second, the media often love to cover campaigns like this, so we're able to educate the public and leaders at the same time. And third, humor is a powerful and effective strategic tactic on its own. Studies of the brain using MRIs show that when people are in a partisan mindset—and many policies in our nation are still unfortunately locked in partisan mindsets—then it's very hard to move someone out of that emotional nonlogical partisan thinking to a different perspective using logic. But one thing that can open up people's minds to think in a new way is humor. So, seeing toddlers running down the halls of Congress in superhero costumes really lightens up the mood and allows us entry into offices that we might normally be turned away from and to get past the partisan barriers to have real conversation about solutions.

And our approach is working—as of the writing of this book, efforts to repeal the ACA simply haven't worked. That's because people, primarily women and moms, raised their voices, signed letters, shared their personal experiences with members of Congress, made hundreds of thousands of phone calls, and spoke up. Women, moms, people, have been going in to meet with their members of Congress in their local districts and in Washington, DC. I've been there, too. Many times over. It's a beautiful thing to see—democracy in action.

One particularly powerful moment in that fight, led primarily by women like Anita Cameron, Stephanie Woodward, and Colleen Flanagan, was the summer of ADAPT in 2017. Hundreds of people with different types of disabilities put their health on the line to save health care by protesting in the halls of Congress. Rebecca Cokley, senior fellow for disability policy at the Center for American Progress, recalls: "While the media portrayed them as vulnerable victims of police brutality, anyone who knows ADAPT knows that this is the very kind of civil disobedience they've trained for.... Their actions were powerful, in the risk to their own health, in their intent to gather media attention to their cause, and their ability to reframe the debate."

Watching how people are empowered when they work on health care policy has been beyond inspiring. Just being a part of the effort to save, protect, and expand health care coverage has had a transformative impact on more women than I can count—finding, using, and raising their voices, and then using that new-found power to bring forward the voices of other women.

Donna Norton, executive deputy director of MomsRising, who leads our health care campaigns, said, "It's amazing to see how many of us have come forward and found our voices and then come through to speak with leaders when it comes to lifting up families' health care needs."

We need to continue to fulfill that role every time there is pressure to roll back health care coverage and other policies that lift women, families, and our economy.

We can't let up.

We're going to have to win on health care again and again until everyone in our nation has access to health care and access is no longer under threat. I'm in for that. I hope you are, too.

How to Share Your Experience

Sharing your life experiences with leaders, members of the media, and others who may not have had the same experiences can open minds and change votes.[21] Remember, fewer than 20 percent of people in Congress and in media leadership are women, and fewer still are moms, so when you bring your story forward you are truly often sharing information that the person may not know.

Sharing your story is easier than you think and has a bigger impact than it often seems possible at first. You are more powerful than you likely know. Your real-life experiences with health care (or lack thereof), as well as any of the other topics in this book, matter. You hold important information. Decision makers and the media need to hear stories from those who are impacted by health care legislation and other policies so they fully understand the impact of bills they're considering. The media also needs to hear these stories because they help shape the public dialogue and build momentum for change. And it's important, too, that other people hear your story, so they know they're not alone.

When we unite our voices, it becomes clear that that we have a structural problem on our hands that we can all solve together through policy advocacy and positive change.

Your words and your experiences are power encapsulated. At MomsRising, we work to open avenues for busy people to be heard by leaders. As part of that, we strive to bring forth the voices and real world experiences of women and the people who love them to leaders at the very top, so that people who are not pinstripe-suited lobbyists can have an impact on the issues that matter to themselves, their families, and their communities.

We collect stories and experiences from our volunteers in all the areas outlined in this book, including health care, and so much more through our website, via email, and on social media. We also often bring forward people to testify or to share their story with reporters when a particular issue is being debated. Interested? Think you might have a story but aren't sure yet?

Here are a few things to ponder when you are figuring out how to share your story:

- **How is your life affected by this issue?**

    Think about how a policy impacts you. Maybe your family is directly affected by an issue that's being debated in Congress or by a recent executive order. Perhaps you or a family member is afraid of losing health care coverage because of a preexisting condition, or has faced a huge emergency room bill.

    Perhaps you aren't directly affected, but you are concerned about how a policy impacts others. For example, perhaps your concern is that women in other states don't have coverage for birth control or routine reproductive care.

- **What do you want to say?**

    Take pen to paper, or fingers to keyboard, and write out your story. First, write down what your goal is for sharing your story (maybe your goal is telling an elected leader that cutting all health care is a ridiculous idea, for example). Then jot down some bullet points about your story that relate to your goal. Then write it up. The mission is to get your story down to just a couple of paragraphs (about 2 minutes of talking).

■ **Where do you want to share your story?**

You can share your story with an advocacy organization like MomsRising, elected leaders, and the media. You can write your story into a letter to the editor to your local paper. You can share your story on a Facebook or blog post. You have many options. Decide which is best for you.

■ **Don't be intimidated.**

Sharing your story can feel intimidating, but it shouldn't be. It's your story. You know it best. You are the absolute and final expert. You don't need to write a lot. Just a few sentences about how a particular issue impacts your life can be very meaningful. It helps lawmakers connect the people they are supposed to represent, and puts faces and names on the statistics being studied. And it helps media understand what they are reporting. Last but far from least, it lets people who are having similar experiences know they aren't alone.

■ **Protect your privacy.**

You should decide if you are comfortable using your last name or whether you want to keep your name confidential. You will need to decide the level of confidentiality you want to use for every place you share your story. For example, organizations like MomsRising provide the support, training/coaching, and help you might need with maintaining privacy. MomsRising members have spoken at the White House and in press conferences, and have been featured on TV, in print stories, and more.

▪ Pass it on!

Even if you aren't directly impacted by health care or another issue that you care about, you may know someone else who is. You can help by encouraging them to share their stories. For example, teachers and school nurses tell some of the most powerful stories about why parents need health care for their children. Encouraging others to share their perspectives and viewpoints is also a great way to build community and understanding on an issue. Plus, many people don't realize they have a story—and that their voice is powerful—until it's asked for.

7

The Choice Is Ours!

Sitting in the crowd at nosebleed level in the Wells Fargo Center in Philadelphia for the Democratic National Convention in 2016, high above the speakers, the roar of the standing-room-only crowd washed over me as I took it all in, the words, the ideas, the inspiration, the hope. A woman in a bright red dress walked onto the stage, waving to the massive crowd in the arena with her arm raised high over her head.

Then, Ilyse Hogue made history by saying what no woman had ever said on a national convention stage. Ilyse, the president of NARAL Pro-Choice America, stepped up to the mic and said, "I wanted a family, but it was the wrong time." She explained a decision that she made years ago, while she was in graduate school.[1] "I made the decision that was best for me—to have an abortion, and get compassionate care at a clinic in my own community." The crowd was riveted. Abortion stories are rarely shared in public.

"Now, years later, my husband and I are parents to two incredible children," Ilyse continued. "And I'm not alone." One in three women in our nation has had an abortion by the age of forty-five. "The majority are mothers just trying to take care of the families they already have."

After covering more facts about abortion and reproductive

rights, Ilyse brought down the house with one last comment. "You see, it's not as simple as *bad* girls get abortions and *good* girls have families. We are the same women at different times in our lives—each making decisions that are the best for us. If we want families to succeed, we start by empowering women. Give us accurate information and access to health care. Keep politicians out of our business when we're not ready to parent, and support us when we are."

The crowd jumped to their feet in applause, surprised and thankful for Ilyse's words. You see, despite the fact that a woman's right to reproductive choice is an issue that the vast majority of people in our nation support (57 percent of Americans are strongly pro-choice)[2] and that the U.S. Supreme Court's *Roe v. Wade* decision in 1973 said this right is protected by nothing less than the Fourteenth Amendment of the U.S. Constitution, a woman's right to choose has been under continuous assault. Ilyse's words in 2016 marked the first time a woman had *ever* openly talked about having an abortion at any nominating convention.[3]

But it's not the first time women have talked about abortion. We secretly hug it out. Sit in solidarity. Take each other to appointments and never talk of it again. We've been there for one another. We all know in our core that being able to choose if we want children, how many to have, and when to have them is core to our personal freedoms. But because abortion isn't a subject most people talk about in groups, and because these stories are so rarely shared in public, there are a lot of misconceptions about what's really going on with women on this issue.

To start, I have yet to meet any person who didn't take reproductive choice and the responsibility of making that type of choice seriously. It's not just me who thinks this. The data shows it's true. In fact, the reasons patients most frequently have the procedure underscores a deep understanding of the economic responsibilities of parenthood. The three most common reasons given for this procedure are a concern for or responsibility to other individuals, the inability to afford raising a child, and the belief that having a baby would significantly interfere with work, school, or care for other dependents.[4] One mom said, "Twenty months after my first child was born, my birth control failed. I found out that I was accidentally pregnant. I'd just taken a new job to help put food on the table, and we didn't have the financial or emotional resources for another child at that time. So together, my husband and I decided to terminate the pregnancy." With the average cost of raising a child from birth to age eighteen now at $200,000 (not including college), she simply couldn't afford to have another child at that time.[5] Most women who have an abortion already have children and choose not to have another child for the well-being of their existing family, just like this mother. Access to birth control, family planning, and reproductive health care is a critical part of economic security for women and families.

My Body, My Choice

The right to control and make decisions about our own bodies is fundamental to women's freedom. Seems simple, right? Logically, "My body, my choice" should be met with "Her body, her choice." But far too often it's not. Instead, "My body, my choice" is often met with a resounding wall of "Not really your body, not really your choice." And, yes this makes steam come out of my ears. My ears that are *in* my body, by the way. There's a good reason for this steam: A woman's right to access birth control, abortion, and reproductive health care has all been increasingly under attack in the past several years.

In 2017, as the Affordable Care Act and Medicaid came under attack, so too did a woman's right to choose and to reproductive health care. That year we saw our conservative government leadership further limit access to affordable birth control and reproductive health care—as well as reduce funding for programs that help families. These actions are a catch-22 of epic proportions that affect women and children, largely advanced by men in leadership positions who are working hard to move women's rights back in time. As Cecile Richards, president of Planned Parenthood, has said in *Glamour,*[6] "No mother in the world wants her daughter to have fewer rights than she did."

Many conservative politicians also have been part of relentless attacks on Planned Parenthood, one of the main sources of reproductive care in our nation. Over 2 million people would lose access to health care if Planned Parenthood was defunded and their health centers were closed as was proposed. This would be a critical loss to our medical infrastructure. In more than 20 percent of the counties where Planned Parenthood health centers operate, there are no other health care providers who serve the patients who rely on safety net programs like Medicaid. In fact, two-thirds of states report having trouble ensuring enough providers, including ob-gyns, who will take Medicaid as Planned Parenthood does. This is a big deal because millions of women get their birth control from Planned Parenthood, not to mention other services such as 320,000 breast exams and nearly 295,000 Pap tests per year.[7]

Eviscerating funding for reproductive health care as has been proposed at the federal level is a very bad idea. What's happened in the states that have imposed massive funding cuts for women's health illustrates what we can expect in the future if we don't stand up for our rights. For instance, pregnancy-related deaths doubled in Texas after the state stopped reimbursing Planned

Parenthood and making other funding cuts to women's health care services.[8]

This has been no small assault on women's rights. The Guttmacher Institute found that "As of January 1, 2017, at least half of the states have imposed at least one of five major abortion restrictions: Unnecessary regulations on abortion clinics, mandated counseling designed to dissuade a woman from obtaining an abortion, a mandated waiting period before an abortion, a requirement of parental involvement before a minor obtains an abortion or prohibition on the use of state Medicaid funds to pay for medically necessary abortions."[9]

As I type these words, 90 percent of all counties in the United States now lack a facility that provides abortions, which accounts for 30 percent of all women of childbearing age without access.[10] While abortion rates are the lowest they've ever been, there's no link between the drop in rates and increased restrictions. Instead, studies show that abortion rates are falling because of increased access to affordable, high-quality birth control, which has happened through the ACA because it made birth control largely free. The Guttmacher Institute shares the details: "Of the 28 states and the District of Columbia that did not have major new restrictions in effect, 10 states had larger-than-average declines [in abortions]. In addition, four of the 22 states with new restrictions actually saw increases in their abortion rates, compared with two states and DC in the group without new restrictions."[11] The facts are solid: If reducing abortions is the goal, then the way to do that is by increasing access to birth control and to reproductive health care for women, not by restricting it. A woman's right to get reproductive health care and make decisions with her doctor in a facility that can safely provide her the care she needs is essential on more than one level.

It's also deeply troubling that in areas where abortion is restricted, data shows that there are now more Google searches on how to do abortions on your own. This is a dangerous practice that history has shown costs women their lives. In a 2017 Vox interview, Seth Stephens-Davidowitz, an author and former Google data scientist, stated: "I'm pretty convinced that the United States has a self-induced abortion crisis right now based on the volume of search inquiries. I was blown away by how frequently people are searching for ways to do abortions themselves now. These searches are concentrated in parts of the country where it's hard to get an abortion and rose substantially when it became harder to get an abortion."[12] This is flat-out dangerous.

How to Prevent Abortions

Studies show what common sense knows: Access to affordable birth control lowers the abortion rate. After the implementation of the Affordable Care Act in 2010, which covered free birth control without a co-pay, the abortion rate was at a historic low.[13,14] Because birth control was seen as a vital part of women's health care, it was covered by health plans without co-pays or deductibles. But in 2017 President Trump overturned that birth control access rule, undermining this critical policy. This reversal of the free birth control access rule hurts low-income women the most. Low-income women who are among the least likely to be able to afford birth control have the highest abortion rates: 75 percent of abortion patients in 2014 were poor or low-income.[15] So when elected leaders are talking about rolling back access, they're really talking about rolling access back the most for women who are already dealing with disproportionate levels of discrimination, including wage and opportunity gaps. Unbelievably, the very same conservative leaders who oppose access to reproductive health care and birth control also often oppose policies that open the door for women to be able to work and be self-reliant while having children such as paid family/medical leave, affordable childcare, and health care. *This is not okay.*

Being able to determine how many children to have and when to have them is a key part of women's freedom and economic prosperity. Providing the basics for a child requires a lot of money. Just a year of childcare now costs more than college in most states. In fact, in 2010 it cost $226,920[16] on average for a middle-income, two-parent family to raise a child from birth to eighteen years old. That's not including college. This is the reality that women face today when determining if and when it is the right time to start or expand a family.

Fighting for Generations

Sometimes I've had to call my 101-year-old grandma for a reality check—and a pep talk. At 101 my grandma still vividly recalled when anti–birth control activists would protest at her house in the early 1900s. Her mom (my great-grandmother) was working as the president of the Rochester, New York, chapter of Planned Parenthood to increase access to birth control for women. My grandmother remembers small crowds protesting outside their home, with people banging on their front door, hoping my great-grandmother would open it so they could yell at her for educating women about birth control. The protests that my grandmother described happening in the early 1900s aren't all that different than the anti-choice protests that are happening today.

There are times when I have to remind myself that this assault on birth control and choice is happening now, not in 1917. In those times, my grandmother reminds me, the women who came before us didn't back down, so neither should we. Today's generations of women stand on the shoulders of many giants who came before us in this fight, who were able to open doors and who rely on us not only to keep those doors open but also to build entire new houses of freedoms for our daughters.

The truth of the matter is that many Republican leaders and a few Democratic leaders, too, have been—and still are, at the writing of this book—putting forward legislation that limits women's freedoms. These laws often not only block women's access to abortion but also regularly fund abstinence-only education (which studies show causes unintended pregnancies to rise),[17] cut access to affordable birth control, halt reproductive health care, and end funding to Planned Parenthood, which today helps limit the number of women who get unintentionally pregnant and thus limits abortions. It simply defies logic that many conservative elected leaders would want to put women's health and freedoms at risk in this way.

Logic-defying leaps are common in this policy area, and so are myths. For example, some people think the reproductive choice and birth control debates don't impact that many people. Think again. A full 99 percent of women, including moms, use birth control at some point in their lives.[18] There's also a ridiculous rumor that women are using abortion as a method of birth control. Not so. Most patients were using a contraceptive method when they got pregnant, most commonly condoms or a hormonal method.[19]

Last but not least, let's set the record straight when it comes to teenagers, who, despite what some ads might claim, don't seek abortions at high rates. Only 12 percent of abortion patients are teens. Sixty percent are in their twenties, and 25 percent are in their thirties. Further belying the myth of the promiscuous teenage girl, teen pregnancy rates are at historic lows.[20] In fact, studies show that more than half of women who get an abortion (59 percent) are already the mother of at least one child.[21,22]

Finally, as the statistics in this book show, the fight for access to affordable birth control and reproductive choice is not just a bunch of hot air being blasted by politicians with little consequence. Nothing could be further from the truth. Reliable birth control and reproductive choices that permit women to manage how many children we want and when we want them is nothing short of revolutionary— not just for women and mothers, but for our country as a whole. It has helped to narrow the gender pay gap, improved the health of women and their families, and led women toward access to economic and political power. This is no small improvement. According to an article in the *American Economic Journal*, "Estimates imply that the Pill can account for 10 percent of the convergence of the gender gap in the 1980s and 30 percent in the 1990s."[23]

Ilyse Hogue has said that "The right to access a safe and legal abortion is now a proxy for a portion of our society telling women that we can't have sovereign rights to our own bodies and lives, without which we can never be equal citizens....Anytime we see a shift to a more authoritarian culture, women suffer. It's not surprising because men who buy into that frame know that the best way to control women is through their fertility. Once you have children everything changes. So unless we do it on our own terms, then all of our other rights and freedoms become tenuous. Now is the time to say this is an inalienable right and we can't afford one other dent in the armor."

So we need to pay attention. We need to watch for rights being slowly taken away from us over time. And we need to watch closely. It's similar to the parable of the boiling frog where a frog gets into a pot of cold water and doesn't realize its body has been slowly warming up until it's pretty much cooked. That's what's happening in regard to access to birth control and reproductive choice. Our freedoms are coming under increasing fire in a big way and at a constant rate. This problem is bigger than any one president and started long ago. The Guttmacher Institute reports: "In the 43 years since the U.S. Supreme Court handed down *Roe v. Wade*, states have enacted 1,074 abortion restrictions. Of these, 288 (27%) have been enacted just since 2010. This gives the last five years the dubious distinction of accounting for more abortion restrictions than any other single five-year period since *Roe*."[24]

Birth control is and should be a vital part of women's health care, women's economic security, and of both women's and men's freedom. Birth control is as necessary as any preventative care and, as a result, *absolutely* should be covered by health plans without co-pays or deductibles, allowing a woman and her doctor—not extremist politicians in Washington, DC—to decide what's best.

No matter where you stand on the pro- or anti-choice spectrum, access to birth control is a good thing. I want to reiterate that at the beginning of 2017, after the implementation of the Affordable Care Act in 2010, which covered birth control without a co-pay, the abortion rate in our nation was at a historic low.[25] Again, it's common sense: More birth control equals fewer abortions. And the data backs up common sense.[26]

It's time to get fired up, to make some calls, to demand access to the full suite of reproductive health care for everyone—and to keep the march going so every single woman in our nation, in every single state, gets to choose what's best for her, her body, and her life. Access to birth control and reproductive choice was, and still is, revolutionary. We can't let any of those doors close. Together we won't only keep doors open, we'll open whole worlds of freedoms for those who come after us.

How to Leverage Power

You don't have to walk the halls of Washington, DC, to have your opinions about choice or other issues be heard.[27] You also don't have to be a paid lobbyist to be listened to by leaders at the very top. You just have to be you—persistent, creative you. In more than two decades of organizing and advocating for change, I've learned that we get the best results when we are creative, engaging, persistent, and sometimes even a little bit silly (humor breaks down barriers while logic often doesn't). I've also learned that carrying forward the voices of others is incredibly powerful.

And I do literally mean *carrying* petition signatures, books of stories from our members, member messages stickered on things like apples, and more into their intended recipient. (At MomsRising, we think of ourselves as the postal service of advocacy. Rain, snow, sleet, or sunshine, we deliver all the messages from our members directly to the leaders who need to hear them.)

In the following pages, you'll find some tips on how to have an impact with local member(s) of Congress close to home.

Make a Powerful Delivery!

Delivering educational materials to a decision maker's local office is an incredibly powerful way to have an impact. Don't worry. No storks are needed. This is simply dropping off materials at the office of your local member of Congress, state legislator, or city councilperson. It's such an effective tactic that MomsRising members regularly drop off storybooks (booklets of stories on one topic) and stacks of signatures on petitions or open letters at the offices of local elected leaders—and we often drop these materials off along with an item that makes people smile as it also hammers in the point. For example, right now, as I'm writing this, we have storybooks going to all of Congress on people's experience with needing access to health care along with Life Savers candies. We also have storybooks going out right now on early learning and pre-K, criminal justice reform, and more. You can make deliveries to members of Congress, mayors, city council members, state legislators—any elected leader. Deliveries are easy to do and make a big impact.

Here are the steps to doing a delivery:

- Pick the policy area that you want to focus on.
- Choose an elected official at the city, county, state, or federal level.
- Research where their closest office to your house is.
- Grab a friend or two to go with you if you want.
- Figure out what you're going to deliver. You can deliver something simple like a note along with a fact sheet or a news story on the topic at hand. You could also deliver something like a mini pot of flowers with a message glued to the outside like "Please do all you can to make sure every family can bloom." Your delivery could also be a petition from an organization that has many, many signatures. You name it, you can deliver it! Just be sure you have a clear, polite, one-sentence message about the issue at hand so the elected leader hears your top concern.
- Call ahead to let the staff in the elected leader's office know you're planning to drop off materials. You may not be able to meet with an elected leader on short notice, but the chances are higher that you'll get some time with them if you let their office know you'll be stopping by in advance.

Also, when you call, you can find out when their office is open so you don't have to make more than one trip.

■ Be prepared—you usually don't meet with the member of Congress when you deliver materials, so plan to leave your item with a staff person at the front desk. Be sure to leave a short note with one sentence on your main message, as well as how to contact you. Example: *Hello! I stopped by to deliver [insert item] in hopes that you will take immediate steps to [insert issue].—[name], [phone], [email]*

■ Take a moment to jot down what you want to say before you step into their office. This should be no more than three sentences. You can just write an outline on a small piece of paper. It's easy: Be sure to introduce yourself, let them know you're a constituent, and tell them what you're dropping off and why. Example: *Hi, I'm_____ and I live in _____, so I'm a constituent. I'm dropping off these materials because I hope [leader name] votes [YES/NO] on [name of policy].* Remember, keep it short. This is your elevator pitch. (See tips on how to perfect this technique—in Chapter 9.) And don't forget to say thank you!

■ Want some backup? MomsRising and other organizations often invite volunteers to help deliver materials to members of Congress or state legislatures. When that happens, all you have to do is RSVP and show up. The organization will provide all the materials you need and give logistical support. Often MomsRising invites members and volunteers who can't make a delivery in person to call and email the representatives to let them know a delivery will be happening. This amplifies our impact together and is an important way for people to make a difference who can't be someplace in person. (Bringing kids with you to deliver high-impact materials can be fun, and it's good for kids to see change in motion.)

Attend Town Halls and Community Forums

Another high-impact way to be heard without traveling to Washington, DC, is to attend a local town hall meeting. When you're there, you can share the top policies that you'd like to see the leader working on, thank them for working hard (if appropriate), and even hold elected leaders accountable. Town halls are usually held during Congressional recesses or when state legislatures aren't in session. In some places, local elected officials hold "coffees" or other local gatherings to hear from constituents. Want to find one? Town halls and coffees are often listed on your representative's website, or sign up for their mailing list to stay in the loop about local events when they're scheduled. Don't see a calendar? Call their office directly and ask what they have coming up.

Here are some tips to make your town hall experience a success:

- **Prepare two or three questions ahead of time.**

  Have two or three short questions ready. What kind of questions, you might be wondering. Very short, fact-based questions that refer to how an issue impacts you or your community work best. Also include a clear request for the elected leader to vote yes or no on a policy if applicable. These types of yes or no questions often have the biggest impact. You might also request that the elected leader share where they stand on a policy or ask what they're doing about a certain issue. You can also ask them for a commitment to vote a certain way or to co-sponsor legislation. Examples: *Where do you stand on access to free birth control? What are your plans to address unfair pay? Can we count on your support for the domestic violence bill? It's bill number [insert number here].* Sometimes organizations, including MomsRising, have sample questions you can use. Have fun!

- **Be a bit early if you can.**

  Pro tip: Get a seat near the front or on an aisle where it's easier to get your question recognized.

- **Always, always, always say thank you.**

  Elected leaders encounter a lot of unhappy people reaching out to them, so the power of a thank-you is magnified. Be sure to use it and say thank you. Sometimes even starting with *Thank you for being here today. I have a question...* is helpful.

- **Show your support.**

  Make your support for other questions known by clapping when they ask a great question and/or when the elected leader has a great answer.

Last but not least, thanks go to *you* for being part of a participatory democracy and fighting for equity, equality, and our democracy!

8

Women against Violence

Jessica knocked softly on my dorm room door. "Can you talk?" I opened the door to let her in. Something was very wrong. Very, very wrong. Looking down at the floor, her face puffy from crying, Jessica stood in the doorway looking smaller than I'd ever seen her. "Can you take me to the police station?"

Jessica had been raped, tied to a chair, and held for hours.

The police station had linoleum floors and air that smelled like dust, defeat, and cleaning supplies all at the same time. Jessica was handed a seemingly endless amount of paperwork to fill out as the police questioned and questioned her again. The repeated questions were another torture in and of themselves.

Jessica's experience was not uncommon. The police didn't believe her. Jessica was a college student. He was her boyfriend. But Jessica isn't the only victim police have dismissed, insulted, or turned away. This is an all-too-common experience for women who have been assaulted—so common that entire organizations and projects have been launched in order to deal with the crisis. Project Unbreakable was one of those projects. Founded by Grace Brown when she was nineteen years old, Project Unbreakable provided women with a forum to share what happened when reporting that they had been raped to the police:

"The investigating detective told me 'If you don't tell us how many people you've ever slept with, the Assistant District Attorney won't even consider taking your case.' I refused to answer and the interview was over."

"A police officer scolded me, saying, 'This is why we have underage drinking laws! This is your fault. If you hadn't been drinking this wouldn't have happened to you.'"

"Well, we asked him [her attacker] and he said he didn't rape you, so there's nothing we can do."[1]

There's no excuse for any of this. None. Sexual assault, violence against women, police intransigence, rape culture, domestic abuse—there are many forms of violence against women and girls in our society. It all has to stop.

Right now sexual violence and domestic abuse, including rape and assault, happen all too often. One out of every three women experiences some form of sexual violence in her lifetime. Almost 23 million women have been victims of rape or attempted rape in our nation.[2]

Let's pause and think about those numbers for a moment. Take some time to let them sink in. Then join me in asking how it is even possible that our country, and our culture, accepts this staggering level of terror. I feel sick just writing about it. Too many of us have experienced this form of violence. One of the ways to help end it is to talk, learn, write, and shine a spotlight on it; then we know we're not alone and so we can march together, work together, and fight together for more accountability in the courts, streets, schools, workplaces, and in our communities, as well as for legislative and cultural change. There's no other choice but to stand up. Violence against women is costly on so many levels, emotionally, physically, and psychologically. The costs in terms of dollars are staggering: According to the Centers for Disease Control (CDC), the direct medical and mental health costs alone associated with intimate partner violence are roughly $4.1 billion annually.[3] But the cost in terms of lives and serious health consequences is even more devastating.[4]

Change is needed yesterday, a decade ago, forever ago. Sadly, Jessica and the rest of us are all facing rape culture (where sexual assault and abuse are normalized) in America. We're experiencing nothing short of an epidemic of violence against women—often perpetrated by those we know. Half of all female homicide victims, across all racial groups, are killed by their intimate partners, according to a 2017 CDC study.[5] One-third of girls in the juvenile justice system have been sexually abused.[6] And women who enlist in the military sign up to put their bodies on the line on the battlefield, not in the barracks where they sleep. But 3,192 cases of military sexual assault were reported in the year 2011 alone, and fewer than half of these were deemed "actionable" by military officials and fewer than 8 percent of these cases ever went to trial.[7]

Not an Imaginary Fear

As we march to stop violence against women, we can't ever forget that there are often compounding impacts of violence on women of color. Take, for instance, what's happening now in many Latina communities to people with families that include people of mixed immigration statuses. After Donald Trump was elected president in November 2016, significantly fewer Latina women reported sexual assault and domestic violence to the police. Reports of rape dropped by 40 percent in Houston alone in the first six months after President Trump was elected, and reports of sexual assault dropped by 25 percent in Los Angeles.[8]

To be clear, this doesn't mean the instances of abuse went down. It means that with the increased ICE raids and amplified animosity toward immigrants by President Trump, many women, particularly women who are members of undocumented families, were worried that if they called the police, then someone in their community would end up being ripped apart from their family as collateral damage.

Jackie Vimo, an economic justice policy analyst at the National Immigration Law Center, shares details on how this happens: "When Immigration and Customs Enforcement [ICE] is sent into communities with threats of deportations, this makes people scared not just of ICE, but also of and for their partners. Some feel like they can't get out of the relationship because if they do something about the domestic violence that they themselves are experiencing, then they or a loved one will be deported. Intersectionality exacerbates the impact for a lot of people and there is a ripple effect."[9]

Being afraid of reporting assault isn't an imaginary fear for women. After her boyfriend repeatedly assaulted her, Irvin Gonzalez needed a protective order. So Gonzalez, a transgender woman, went from the domestic violence shelter where she was staying to the local courthouse in El Paso, Texas, to get one. But when she arrived, an ICE officer was waiting to arrest her. ICE had been tipped off by Gonzalez's abusive boyfriend that she was going in to report him. So at the same time as Gonzalez was granted the protection order by the judge, ICE arrested her, a person who was a victim of a crime who was in a courthouse for protection, for her immigration status.[10]

The experience that Gonzalez went through is nothing short of a human rights violation in the name of immigration enforcement. This is what the cage of violence against women looks like for some women in our nation. We can and must do better by and for women.

Locked In

Trapped. Controlled. Hit. Yelled at. Violence against women comes in many forms. One form of domestic violence that's often overlooked is economic abuse, where one partner keeps funds in their sole control so the abused partner doesn't have the funds to leave.

Kim Gandy, former president of the National Organization for Women and current president and CEO of the National Network to End Domestic Violence, shares: "Financial abuse is present in about 99 percent of all domestic violence cases. And, it is as effective as a lock and key in trapping a victim in an abusive situation. Financial abuse is the invisible hold."

Kim dove into work as a women's rights advocate when she was newly wed. Starting a new job in Louisiana, Kim ran straight into the kind of economic sexism that disempowers women and puts them in danger if they are tied to and in the grips of an abusive partner. On Kim's first day on the job in her home state of Louisiana, she was given a stack of forms to fill out so she could use the health care and other benefits like retirement that came with her new job. Going through the forms, she stopped cold at one that said, "If you are a married woman, your husband must sign here."

Kim remembers sitting in the chair, the forms in front of her on the table, thinking, "Why would I need my husband's signature to get employment-related benefits on my job?"

So she asked that question—and then she subsequently found out that there was a "head and master" law in Louisiana that said the husband is the sole controller of all of the joint property in a marriage and can make decisions about joint property without the wife's knowledge or consent. The legal subordination of wives to their husbands also meant that women had no right to claim that a husband had raped her.[11] *What!?* Also by that definition the wife's income is part of the joint property of the marriage, so in Louisiana at the time the husband legally controlled the wife's income and, therefore, could say whether or not the wife could do things like sign up for health care and put 3 percent of her pay into a retirement plan.

I've known Kim for over a decade now and can just imagine the smoke that came out of her ears when she learned about this law. In fact, what I imagined is pretty close to what actually happened: After finding out about the "head and master" law, Kim spent seven years working to get rid of it. She found some people who were already working on the issue and in her free time, outside of work, fought very hard to repeal that law and to pass a new law in Louisiana that provided for the equal management of community property by both spouses: the Equal Management Law in 1979.[12]

In other words: She won. And every other woman in Louisiana won, too.

It took seven long years to get that win, but Kim didn't rest on her laurels. You see, while Kim was working on that issue, she discovered all kinds of other problems that also needed fixing. So Kim persisted and rose through multiple leadership roles and organizations, eventually becoming one of the driving forces for passing the Violence Against Women Act through Congress with President Bill Clinton signing it into law in 1994, and then was also the driving force as it was reauthorized again and again in 2000, 2005, and most recently 2013 after long legislative battles aimed at repealing it. Kim's persistence not only was necessary, but eventually paid off—which happens often in this kind of legislative fights.

Of course, as Kim is always quick to point out, she didn't do it alone. A strong coalition of organizations and women across the country raised their voices to make this win happen that Kim still celebrates today: "It was the first federal legislation that provided significant funding to combatting violence against women. It established the Office on Violence Against Women, created a community-based effort that brought together local domestic violence agencies with law enforcement and judges, training and education, and created what they called then a coordinated community response to domestic violence, which had never existed before, and has made a tremendous amount of change across the country."

But it's not just the big, headline-grabbing, federal-level legislative wins that make a difference. There are also wins happening locally right now helping women get out of situations of financial abuse. For instance, the National Network to End Domestic Violence has established the Independence Project to provide microloans to help survivors of domestic violence repair their credit.[13] Even a small, $100, interest-free loan being paid back that's reported to all of the credit bureaus every month can increase credit scores. Gandy notes that for a survivor who's trying to flee a domestic violence situation, improving a credit score may be the difference between being able to get an apartment or having to return to her abuser. These days, with employers checking credit scores, being able to improve credit may also be the difference between getting a job or not getting a job, between getting out or remaining with an abuser. Every survivor who improves her credit score is a win, too. The little things are often overlooked.

Most Incarcerated Women Survived Domestic Violence

Marissa Alexander, a mother of three who had a Florida concealed-weapons license,[14] fired a warning shot at the ceiling in 2012, harming no one, when her abusive ex-husband, whom she had a restraining order against, threatened to kill her. Florida has a "Stand Your Ground" law, passed in 2005, that allows lethal force in self-defense. But coverage under that law was denied to Marissa Alexander, a Black woman, and she was convicted of aggravated assault with a deadly weapon. That crime in Florida, at the time, carried a mandatory minimum of twenty years.[15]

It's critical to put what happened to Marissa in context. Studies show that the majority of women in prison are survivors of domestic violence, 82 percent of whom suffered serious physical or sexual abuse in their lifetime.[16] Clearly, many of the laws of our nation are failing women.

Added to that is the chronic failure of our criminal justice system to offer Constitutional protection of equal justice under law. Consider another notorious Florida case, also in 2012, where George Zimmerman shot and killed Trayvon Martin, an unarmed young Black teenager. Zimmerman argued using the same Stand Your Ground law that was not applied in Marissa's case and was cleared of all crimes by a jury.

Zimmerman walked free after he murdered a child when evidence showed that there was no threat to his life. Marissa, who harmed no one, served time for attempting to protect her life and the lives of her children. Speaking to the *New York Times*, one of

Marissa's lawyers, Bruce Zimet, pointed out the obvious: "Here is a Black woman who had a history of abuse against her and tried to use Stand Your Ground and ended up with a 20-year sentence."[17]

Thanks to constant public pressure online via Twitter through the #FreeMarissa and #SelfiesForSelfDefense hashtags and also the efforts of Free Marissa Now,[18] Survived and Punished, Sister Song, and other organizations who organized rallies, sent letters, spoke out to the media, and more, Marissa was released after serving three years in prison and an additional two years of home detention.

There wasn't a day Marissa was in jail that her name wasn't lifted up by other women leaders. That's what it took to get her out of jail. Zimmerman, on the other hand, not only served zero time, but he received $200,000 in public donations for his legal defense.[19]

Now a leader in speaking out against domestic violence, Marissa is also working to make sure the uneven application of Stand Your Ground laws ends. And she's making strides and changing the national conversation by speaking around the country. Though some laws in Florida are changing, Marissa also notes that there's much more to do and is leading the way advocating for justice to this day.

Stand Up for Women's Safety

Do you know what else is a women's rights issue and part of the culture of violence against women in our nation?

Guns.

Women who are physically abused by current or former intimate partners are five times more likely to be murdered when one of the partners owns a firearm.[20] But current federal policy is not tight enough to effectively prevent all convicted perpetrators of domestic violence and other violent crimes from obtaining guns, nor do we have limits on high-capacity magazines that accompany military-style assault weapons. We also don't have a federal gun trafficking statute. There are holes in our entire gun safety system that we need to close to protect the lives of women, children, families, and people in general. This isn't to say that guns should be outlawed altogether, but that in a country where there are more guns than people,[21] there should be safety parameters for the responsible purchase of firearms. The United States has the highest rates of gun ownership in the world,[22] and we're also the top exporter and top importer of "small arms and light weapons."[23] And we also have very lax gun safety measures.

I'm not alone in the desire for increased gun safety. More than 80 percent of gun owners, including National Rifle Association (NRA) members, want stronger background checks on people buying guns.[24]

The movement for increasing gun safety policies is growing, and with good reason. Women and children are frequently caught in the center of this violence. In fact, women in the United States are eleven times more likely to be murdered with guns than women in any other high-income country.[25] Gun violence is all too commonly a part of domestic violence and abuse.

Cassandra said, "One of my best friends, a successful career woman in her early forties, was almost fatally shot when she tried to break up with her abusive boyfriend. He got angry, drove to the nearest gun store, purchased a shotgun despite a record of depression and mental health issues, returned within thirty minutes, and shot her and himself in front of her two young sons. She barely survived, losing a lung and a kidney."

Guns make domestic violence even deadlier. Guns are used to kill women in 53 percent of intimate partner homicides.[26] "I was sixteen years old when I first had a gun pointed at my head by a boyfriend," said Marie. "I was leaving the country and he didn't want me to go." Marie's boyfriend asked her to jump in a pond or be shot. She jumped in the pond immediately. She said, "You may say I was lucky that day. But what I had to endure for the next five years perhaps would have been easier if I had died that day out by the water." It's too easy for unstable people to possess a handgun, she concluded.

All told, 33,000 people in our nation lose their lives to gun violence every year, which on average means more than ninety people are killed by guns every day.[27] That's not freedom. Freedom is the ability to live without the threat of violence on every corner. It's safe to say that most of us, at heart, think our lives are a higher priority than unchecked access to firearms. Our country is losing sisters, brothers, moms, dads, sons, daughters, and other loved ones each day in preventable deaths due to gun violence.

This has got to stop.

The damage from unchecked gun violence especially touches mothers and children. Among U.S. children age seventeen and younger, firearms are the third leading cause of death and the second leading cause of injury.[28] The threat of gun violence terrorizes our communities.

Many of us have received a version of "that call" that no parent wants to get from their child's school: a call saying the school is in lockdown because of a nearby confirmed armed threat. The first time I got that call there was a shooting at a nearby café[29] in Seattle. Five people lost their lives, and the gunman had fled on foot, running toward the school building where my children sat studying. The second time there was an armed bank robbery just blocks away.

Parents shouldn't have to wonder whether our kids will be safe when we drop them off at school, the mall, a concert, or the movies. No one should have to worry about being the victim of gun violence. My daughter, Anna, long well aware of the threat of gun violence, reminded me of this after the second lockdown at her school in just a couple of months. She said, "Mom—remember: Both of our lockdowns happened because of guns." I remember.

My son, like many others, has also long been aware of the situation. He tapped me on the shoulder once while we were driving from basketball practice many years ago to share this fact and ask an important question:[30] "In all the years since the assault weapon ban in Australia, there haven't been any mass shootings. That was a big improvement. Why don't we do that here?" And he's right: After a mass murder that killed thirty-five people and wounded nineteen, Australia increased their gun safety policies by banning all rapid-fire long guns (this includes all semiautomatic rifles and all semiautomatic and pump-action shotguns) and requiring owners to sell them back at market price to the Australian government. At the same time, the government passed laws that created a national registry and tightened restrictions on purchasing guns.

There hasn't been a single mass shooting in Australia since then.

Why *can't* we do that, too?

Many people are asking that same question, and a movement for change is rising. Wins are happening in states all over the country. For example, in late 2015, MomsRising and the League of Women Voters in Florida came together to fight a bill that was winding its way through their state legislature that would legalize the open carry of guns in the Sunshine State. We knew parents would not want to bring their children and other loved ones to have fun in the sun where there could be guns everywhere, including on the beach or in line waiting to get on a ride at one of Florida's world-class amusement parks. We also reasoned that Florida's powerful tourism industry would also likely oppose open carry, and that we could support their efforts to fight it in a powerful way.

So MomsRising launched a petition against Florida open carry, urging the Florida tourism industry to do everything in its power to stop it if it wants to remain the world's number one family vacation destination. More than thirty thousand MomsRising members signed that petition, and six thousand members submitted personal comments. The comments were strongly worded and sometimes deeply personal.

Donna from Missouri wrote: "I have no problem with responsible gun ownership, but open carry is an infringement upon the safety of my family. I won't be bringing my grandkids to Florida."

Elizabeth in New Jersey said, "As someone who has lost a loved one who was shot to death by a stranger, I will not put my family at risk by coming to any location in a state where anyone can carry a gun in the open."

MomsRising distilled the most powerful comments selected from every state into a booklet. We then sent the petition signatures and booklet via special delivery to Florida's major tourism stakeholders, including Disney World, Universal Studios, and the Florida Commission on Tourism. The League of Women Voters in Florida made sure that our champions in the Florida state house who were fighting open carry all had a copy of the booklet so they could incorporate the stories from our members during the policy debate. Other elements of the campaign included a robust media plan and several call-ins to Florida lawmakers with family members from across the country expressing their public safety concerns about open carry becoming law.

And we won! In February 2016, the Florida Senate officially tabled the open carry bill, killing it for the 2016 session. A key Florida senator, Miguel Díaz de la Portilla, later said that the potential impact of open carry on tourism and the safety concerns of moms was why the bill didn't move forward.

Whole organizations are rising up to fight for gun safety, like Moms Demand Action for Gun Sense in America, and win after win is advancing at the state level for gun safety. But that's just the beginning. We've got to keep marching, raising our voices, voting, and moving more wins forward. The pressure is on. We're up against a powerful force. You see, as important wins are advancing at the state level and a movement is growing, NRA leadership is spending millions on lobbying. In fact, NRA lobbying expenditures[31] completely dwarf that of even the best-funded gun safety advocacy groups.[32]

But this doesn't mean the NRA automatically can buy their way into winning every legislative battle. They can't. The voices of women can be more powerful than any corporate-funded gun lobbyist. I've seen it happen in the past, and together we will see it happen again.

Lucy McBath has seen it, too. A leading spokesperson for Moms Demand Action for Gun Sense in America, Lucy lost her own son, Jordan Davis, in 2012 to gun violence. But Lucy is hopeful: "I know people across the country have become very disturbed by the rising gun culture and the nature of gun violence in this country. People have begun to say, 'Enough is enough.' I've never seen such a groundswell of people that are actively standing up and participating in gun violence prevention. So, there is always hope."

It's time for solutions. People are coming together to stand behind basic commonsense reforms that are straightforward and long overdue. These reforms include universal background checks for all gun purchases (including gun shows and on the Internet), an assault weapon ban (which also limits high-capacity magazines), a ban on "bump stocks" that turn guns into rapid-fire killing machines, limits on the use of gun silencers, and advancing a federal gun trafficking statute with real penalties to stop illegal sales of guns. We also need to advance gun violence restraining orders (also called extreme risk protection orders), like those enacted in California and Washington, which allow people to petition a court to remove a person's access to guns if he or she poses an imminent danger to him- or herself or to others.[33]

To be clear, the fight isn't about banning all guns; it's about advancing gun safety, community safety, women's safety, and responsible gun ownership.

There are 85 million moms in our nation.[34] Together, we are a powerful force. And together we won't let the leaders of our country forget that their job is to make sure that our families, all of those we love, and all of our nation's children are safe from gun violence.

Stronger Together

We know which policies are needed to protect women from violence. Now we just have to raise grassroots voices and pressure elected leaders to move forward smart policies that save lives. Make no mistake: Our work to take back the night, the day, and all the moments in between is having an impact. Activism over the last forty years has had a significant impact: The rate of domestic violence decreased by more than 60 percent between 1994 and 2012.[35]

Our work isn't done, however. Domestic violence, sexual assault, and other forms of violence against women are still all-too-regular occurrences in the daily lives of women, and homicides of women remain stubbornly high.[36] Violence against women is not yet a thing of the past. We know that all violence against women has to stop. And we know that together, we are a powerful force to make that change happen.

How to Be Heard

Your phone holds power.[37] Making a call is a high-impact way to let an elected leader know that you're paying attention to an issue, a bill, or their stance on a policy in order to help move forward structural change. Making a call is easy, doesn't take a lot of time, and can be very effective, especially at the state and local levels, where offices are less likely to receive a lot of calls. For example, even just a few calls at the state level can make a big impact.

Here's some advice from U.S. Senator Kirsten Gillibrand, a person who is often on the receiving end of those calls: "It helps that I get thousands of phone calls every day on an issue because then when I'm giving a speech on the Senate floor, I can talk about the passion of my constituents and I can talk about letters that people have actually written me and share those stories to millions of people. So, you are projecting your voice when you make those calls regardless of who you're calling."

Here are some quick tips to make your phone calls the most effective:

- **Go on the Internet and find your legislators and their office phone numbers.**

  You can always call more than one legislator on any single issue. In fact, please do! You have two U.S. senators who represent you and one member of the U.S. House. So you can call one or all three. Don't forget that you also have state legislators and city council members who represent you that you can call to share your views on legislation. Every call counts, so you don't have to call them all. But if you get in a groove, keep dialing!

- **Be patient.**

  Sometimes when an issue is in the news, congressional offices will receive a high volume of phone calls. People will have trouble getting through or will even find full mailboxes. This is a good sign! People are making important calls and our numbers are being counted, so keep calling! Also, remember that members of Congress often have multiple offices around the state where you can call, too, if their Washington, DC, number is busy.

- **Know that your call counts. Literally.**

  Elected leaders usually keep tallies of how many calls come into their office on each issue area, so be sure to call. You'll be counted even if you just leave a message. And, yes, legislators who you agree with appreciate positive calls, too—they use the high tally of supportive calls to lobby other leaders.

- **Plan what you're going to say before you pick up the phone.**

  Be brief. Jot down your three lines: *Hi, I'm [name] from [place] and I would appreciate it if [legislator name] would vote [YES/NO] on [bill name or issue area].* If you have a personal experience with the issue, let them know in a succinct way.

- **If you're calling about a specific piece of legislation, name it specifically.**

  Try to find out the bill number and/or the name so you can mention it in your message, along with how you want the legislator to vote, yes or no.

- **Ask for a response if you want one.**

  Be sure to give your phone number, email, or mailing address where you can be reached so they can give you that response.

- **Be polite.**

  Thank them for their time. Building a relationship with the staff and/or lawmaker can be important to pushing additional policies forward in the future.

Bonus tip: Gather a few friends for coffee, cookies, or a favorite food and make some calls together. Have everyone bring a cell phone. Write the script; for example: *Hi, I'm [name] from [place] and I would appreciate it if [legislator name] votes [YES/NO] on [bill name or issue area].* Share the script. And let the calling party begin. In one night you and your gathering could call the entire U.S. or state senate that way!

9

Maternal Mortality

Room spinning, tired, I didn't realize I was hemorrhaging. My daughter had just been born in a rapid birth spurred by Pitocin because my labor wasn't progressing. I went from being six centimeters dilated to giving birth in seven minutes flat. Too fast.

Having elected for natural childbirth, it felt something like a tsunami hit the room, I'd been pulled deep under the churning waters, and she was swept in on a wave. To say I was worried about her is an understatement. Hearing my tiny daughter take that first breath and then start crying was one of the most relaxing noises I've ever heard. Such sweet relief. She was fine.

But I wasn't.

Shortly after my daughter was born, I remember my doctor leaning over me with the light framing her head above mine, looking me in the eye, and saying something like: "You're not done yet, and what I'm about to do is going to hurt more than anything you've ever felt in your life. Hold on." Without hesitation, she pulled out the broken pieces of placenta that were causing hemorrhaging that I didn't even know was happening at the time. As she did this I possibly broke a decibel record, dropping an epically loud F-bomb. But quick action was needed. If not treated quickly, postpartum hemorrhaging can be a sneaky, silent killer.

In fact, it's the fourth leading cause of pregnancy-related deaths in the United States.[1]

There's already a lot of blood involved in giving birth, and pain, too, so the person in trouble—in this case me—can be clueless that there's an emergency until it's too late.

I lived.

But many—too many—women don't. Women of color, in particular, are losing their lives at alarming rates. Hemorrhaging, like I did when I had my daughter, is one of the most common ways women die in childbirth, and the situation isn't getting better. According to the World Health Organization, the maternal mortality rate in our nation more than doubled between 1990 and 2013[2]—and some places in our nation have truly appalling maternal mortality rates. For instance, in 2017, the maternal mortality rate in Texas is the highest not only in the United States, but in the entire developed world.[3] It's no coincidence that this surge in maternal deaths coincided with devastating budget cuts to health care and clinics that provide reproductive health care in Texas. Lack of access to health care services during pregnancy can determine if a woman and her child live or die during or after childbirth.[4] In 2011 alone, the Texas state legislature slashed its family planning budget by $38 million, and maternal deaths increased.

But maternal deaths aren't limited to just Texas. Two or three women die every day in the United States while they are in the process of giving life, and every ten minutes a woman nearly dies due to pregnancy-related complications. This gives the United States the dubious distinction of being one of the only countries in the world where maternal deaths and injuries have been increasing in recent years.[5]

It doesn't have to be this way. While our maternal mortality rate has more than doubled over the past twenty years,[6] deaths related to pregnancy and childbirth fell by more than a third worldwide,[7] including in many developing countries.[8] Behind these shocking numbers in the United States is the appalling fact that nearly 60 percent of all maternal deaths are entirely preventable.[9]

We can, and we must, do something about this.

More Women of Color Are Dying

The truth of the matter is as the rate of moms in America who die in childbirth has been rising, large groups of people have been more significantly more likely to suffer serious complications of birth or die simply because of the color of their skin.[10] In every state, women of color experience disproportionately higher rates of maternal deaths. Black women in the United States are more than three times more likely to die during pregnancy and childbirth compared to white women, independent of age, education, or other measures of parity.[11] For every 100,000 births, 43.5 Black women die, compared to 12.7 deaths among white women and 14.4 deaths among women of all other races.[12]

"I remember everything like it was yesterday," Patrisse Khan-Cullors, co-founder of Black Lives Matter, shared. "My water broke. It broke in the way like you see on TV and you yell, 'My water broke!' I was excited. I was nervous. Then after contracting for twenty-four hours at home, my uterus was tired and just stopped contracting. It was at this moment that I learned I had to have a C-section at the hospital."

She continued: "After my baby was born, doctors checked on me, but no one took the time to tell me about the possible consequences of having a C-section. And this was at a hospital that was thought to be 'good.' After I got home I was tired, busy feeding and caring for the baby, and I started to wheeze. My mom heard me and said, 'Something sounds off.' So I went to the hospital and found out that I had pneumonia. I googled it and found out that pneumonia was pretty common after a C-section, but I had missed the early signs because my doctors never took the time to talk with me about self-care. Although I survived pregnancy and childbirth, many Black women don't."

So what's going on here? And can we fix it? Three key factors have been found to be at the root of maternal mortality in our nation. The first is inconsistent obstetric practice.[13] In other words, one of the top reasons for maternal mortality in the United States is that some doctors and hospitals know how to spot and treat childbirth emergencies but some don't. Unbelievably, hospitals in America don't have a standard protocol in the case of emergencies during childbirth, so crucial early treatment is often missing. This also means that because of implicit bias and racism, some groups of women are consistently getting life-saving treatment and others are not.

The second factor is lack of access to health care services during pregnancy, which can determine if a woman lives or dies during or after childbirth. This is particularly important for women with chronic conditions like diabetes and hypertension, which are known to spark pregnancy complications. Access to health care during pregnancy is also critical for the health of the baby. There's been a surge in the rate of babies born dangerously early in the past eight years.[14]

It's also not a coincidence that at the same time maternal mortality rates have been going up there has been a drop in availability of qualified midwives, obstetricians, and family medicine physicians to deliver babies across the country.[15] To put this problem in perspective, according to the American College of Nurse-Midwives, nearly half of all U.S. counties don't have a single obstetrician-gynecologist, and 56 percent are without a nurse-midwife.[16]

This is no small thing.

In the United States, not only are the lives of babies on the line, but women without access to health care services during pregnancy are four times as likely to die in childbirth[17]—and of course low-income women are significantly less able to afford health care.

The last factor is particularly maddening: We don't collect consistent data across all states in our nation about how, when, and where women are dying—which means that we can't target fixing this growing problem in our nation.

Black Women Are 400 Percent More Likely to Die in Childbirth than White Women

I'm white, I was in the upper middle class when my daughter was born, and I lived. This is not a coincidence. For example, Black women in California are 400 percent more likely to die in childbirth than white women.[18]

This is a big deal. As stated previously, more than 80 percent of all women have children by the time they're forty-four years old. What's more, the numbers of women and babies born in the United States are projected to increase sharply over the next decade and beyond. So it's absolutely unconscionable that race, income level, access to health care during pregnancy, and hospital training protocol and location play such major roles determining if a woman will survive or die while bringing a new life into the world—especially when half of all maternal deaths are preventable.[19] Every woman should have equal opportunity to live. But too often that's not happening in our nation.

We have to start by fighting for solutions that lift the people who are most impacted first. In doing that, we can lift our whole nation and save lives as we also maximize our return on investment. In doing that we all rise.

Fortunately, we already know how to solve these problems. The World Health Organization has done the research and has a list of the top ways to save lives:

- All doctors and hospitals need equal access to best practices and shared plans for childbirth emergencies, along with training. Women shouldn't die in childbirth simply because they choose the wrong hospital.[20]
- Everyone must have equitable access to health care services before, during, and after pregnancy.
- We have to consistently collect data—across all cities and states—on the when, where, why, and how of maternal mortality in our nation.[21]

Two additional concrete solutions are supported by advocates, scholars, and medical organizations. The first is to ease state and federal restrictions on nurse-midwives, who attend to labor and delivery as well as provide routine primary and gynecological care for women of all ages. The second is to offer financial incentives to encourage more medical professionals to specialize in maternal health care and to encourage them to locate in regions with extreme shortages, particularly in rural areas.[22]

Together we can make these changes a reality.

All Pregnant Women Need Access to Health Care

When we fight for these changes, we need to make sure all women are covered—particularly because not all women get to choose under what circumstances and when or how they're going to give birth, and the impact of that can be deadly. Women in prison and their babies are particularly at risk. The United States has the highest incarceration rate in the world, so it should not be that surprising to find out that many incarcerated women are pregnant. According to the most recent data available from the Bureau of Justice Statistics, 4 percent of women who enter state prison and 5 percent of those who enter jail are pregnant. But this data is more than a decade outdated. Why does the timing of the data matter so much? Because things have changed. In the past decade, the number of women incarcerated in the United States has nearly tripled, and women are now among the fastest growing segment of the U.S. prison and jail population. We have very little information and data on what medical care is provided to incarcerated pregnant women.[23]

What we do have is way too many heartbreaking horror stories about giving birth in prison or jail. Imagine losing your baby because no one would respond to your cries of help when you went into labor. And it's not that they didn't hear you...they ignored you.

Nicole Guerrero was eight and a half months pregnant and alone in a Texas county jail cell in 2015 when she suddenly started having contractions. After screaming for help over and over again and being ignored for hours, someone finally came to her assistance, but it was too late.[24] Her baby was born on a jail cell floor, a deep shade of purple, with the umbilical cord wrapped around her neck. Sadly, Nicole's baby did not survive.[25] Reports from advocates in Texas have told me this wasn't the first time a pregnant woman in a county jail was denied access to medical care.

No mother should face this nightmare, and no baby should have to suffer a lifetime of health problems or even loss of life because his or her mother was denied access to health care. No mother should have to endure what Nicole Guerrero did.

After Nicole's tragic loss, moms stood up, spoke out, and reached out to organizations like the Texas Jail Project, ACLU of Texas, and Mama Sana, and to Rachel Roth, a MomsRising blogger who writes extensively on these issues. A campaign was born. MomsRising and the coalition crafted an open letter to the Texas Commission on Jail Standards, which quickly garnered over a thousand signatures. But the campaign didn't stop there. A mom gave a brief statement and delivered the signatures to the commission at their quarterly meeting along with other moms backing her up. As a result of their strong showing, the commission agreed to open a dialogue with MomsRising and our Texas partners on how to address the larger issue of pregnant women in Texas jails.

But the wins didn't stop there. During the outreach to MomsRising members, one of the moms who received an email through a local moms group happened to be the chief of staff to Texas representative Celia Israel.

Israel's chief of staff brought the issue to the attention of the Texas House of Representatives and introduced bipartisan legislation with Representative Marisa Marquez to begin to address some of the issues we discussed with the Texas Commission on Jail Standards, including requiring counties to share their plans for care of pregnant inmates and a mechanism to evaluate and enumerate the number of pregnant women in jails throughout the state. After the bill passed we got this letter from a member of the Texas state legislative staff: "MomsRising brought the care of pregnant inmates to our attention, and we owe you one for that! (Both as a Texan and as a mom.)"

In other words: We won.

Women are powerful, we're often more networked together than we often realize, and by speaking out and working together we can save lives and change policies.

Our powerful voices are needed. Solitary confinement of pregnant women, as well as shackling pregnant women during delivery (which continues in the United States despite the fact that it violates the United Nations Convention against Torture and Other Cruel, Inhuman or Degrading Treatment or Punishment and our own Eighth Amendment of the U.S. Constitution), are both still allowed by the federal government even as states work to update their policies.[26] Many pregnant women also don't get ob-gyn and other health care, and pregnant women in prisons face other human rights nightmares as well. So even though women won this fight in Texas, there's a lot of work still to do. Just bringing the problems to the attention of the public and elected leaders can have a bigger impact than most people think.

Never underestimate the power of your voice in simply raising the obvious.

How to Build Influence

In the previous chapters you've figured out what issues you care about and the type of work you want to do, and you've learned about a bunch of effective tactics.[27] Now we'll cover how anyone can talk to leaders, decision makers, and the media about advocacy projects—and influence their decisions.

Often, these types of conversations are called elevator pitches because you may have just a short time to pitch your message to an organization, elected leader, or member of the media—about the length of an elevator ride.

This section focuses on how to "do" messaging by using the example of how to effectively communicate with leaders. But is equally applicable to other areas of work and life where you need to build allies.

Whether you're trying to communicate with an influential leader about maternal mortality or simply trying to get your friends and neighbors engaged, it helps to spend a little time beforehand thinking about your message.

First: What is your message? If you got into an elevator with someone, what would you say? What would you ask the person to do? What do you want them to remember? So many questions! Oh, and you only have about 60 seconds to answer them all.

Defining what you want your audience to take away from your message and what you want them to do as a result will make everything from emails to meetings to letters to the editor more effective.

The Problem, Solution, Action Triangle

One effective approach to crafting messages that's used by many—including organizations like the Spin Project, Opportunity Agenda, Women's Media Center, and many more—is charting a Problem, Solution, Action triangle.

(Want to draw? Do it! Take out a sheet of paper. Make your own triangle now.)

The triangle works because your audience needs to know what the problem is, how it can be fixed, and what you want them to do about it. Ideally, you should be able to describe your message with no more than two or three short sentences in each area.

This two-sentence limit is real. I can't tell you how many times I've had to talk with elected leaders in a hall, even during an elevator ride, in an actual lobby (hello, lobbyists), while boarding a plane, or otherwise in literal motion and had their attention for only a couple of sentences. This is an important strategy to learn, and I promise it will be useful.

Problem Message: What's your problem? Put your problem message, two to three short sentences, in the first part of the triangle. That sentence should communicate the scope of the problem, frame it in a way that fits with your values, and makes a compelling case. You can include one key fact supported by a very, very short story if you have one top of mind—but only if you can keep it short.

Problem message example: Maternal mortality is rising and women of color are dying at disproportionate rates. We are the only industrialized nation where more women are dying in childbirth, not fewer.

Solution message: Now, what's your solution? Put your two-sentence solution in that part of the triangle. Remember, you need to quickly move from stating the problem to saying how it can be fixed—as well as who can fix it. Don't get stuck talking about the problem for too long; give hope for solutions fast, or you'll lose your listener.

Solution Message Example: It doesn't have to be this way. All doctors and hospitals need equal access to best practices and shared plans for childbirth emergencies, along with training, and all women should have access to high-quality health care.

Action message: This is *your* moment. Never end an advocacy conversation without asking someone to take a specific action. Put your one-sentence action message down in that part of the triangle now. Not sure what it is? Here are some examples: Ask an elected official to vote yes or no on a specific piece of legislation. Encourage the media to cover a story or report. Urge a leader to speak up about why change is needed by making a phone call to another leader or by speaking out in the media. Or ask someone in your community to share their story. No matter what your "ask" is, every message needs to end in action. People want to know what they can do!

Action Message Example: When making an ask of elected officials, it may sound like, *Can I count on you to protect all pregnant women by voting yes on* _____ *legislation?* If they say no or they aren't sure, make sure to ask what information or support they might need in order to take the action you requested, and then make a plan to follow up with them or their staff.

Fake it until you make it work. If you feel like an imposter, like you don't know enough, aren't dressed the right way, or are somehow less than, know you are *not* less at all. There are women across the nation standing with you from afar. You belong in the halls of power just as much as anyone else. So, shoulders back, chin up, and walk proudly.

If you can't shake that imposter feeling, know that a lot of people feel, or have felt, the exact same way. Pretty much everyone who has created change, actually. You're not alone. You're not imagining things if you find yourself in a sea of pinstripe-suited males. Only 20 percent of Congress are women, and the U.S. Senate only got a women's restroom in the last decade. Male dominance exists not only in Congress but in most American institutions, but that's what we're working to change. So keep on!

Be yourself. "Fake it until you make it" might sound like the exact opposite of "be yourself," but it's not. Body language accounts for more than 70 percent of all communication, so be comfortable in yourself. Take a few deep breaths and center yourself before you walk into a meeting. Know that you belong exactly where you are. Don't worry. Be human. And remember the person you're meeting with is human, too.

Know that when you share your message, people listen best if they make a human connection, and there's no better way to do that than by being yourself. There are already enough people mimicking robots in the halls of Congress and elsewhere—don't be another one!

Be sure to thank the person meeting with you (or hearing your message) for their time. Everyone is busy. A thank-you goes a long way.

Before we move on, one question I regularly get is: "What do people typically wear when meeting with elected or corporate leaders?" My answer: Wear what makes you feel confident and comfortable in yourself.

••

PART III

——

OUR COMMUNITIES

PART III

OUR COMMUNITIES

10

Lady Liberty

Words between strangers can be telling. On a recent flight, the person sitting next to me started up a conversation, wondering where I was flying to and from that day. After a few minutes, he started confiding in me. As he talked, I felt my blood pressure rise. I blinked and steeled myself for what I knew would be a difficult conversation.

Random confessional encounters of racist, sexist, Islamophobic, or xenophobic beliefs are a relatively new thing in my life despite the fact that I have lived and worked with people from a variety of locations and political backgrounds for many years. But some people have started to assume that because I am a white woman on a business trip and they are also white people on a business trip, I'll share their views.

I don't.

The conversations often start the same. They lean in close, but not too close—just close enough so other people can't hear—and say things like what the man on the airplane said to me that day: "Illegals are killing our nation." I took two or three quiet deep breaths, and imperfectly dove in. "Really?...You or a close family member must have been personally deeply hurt at some point. What happened?"

"Well, nothing" is the only answer I've invariably heard back so far. But I keep the conversation going: "Have you lost your job or has your local economy been hurt by immigrants?"

"No" is the only answer I've gotten so far.

Then, still in a conversational tone, I usually share: "Did you know that immigrants or the children of immigrants started 40 percent of Fortune 500 companies in our country and that immigrants are a critically important part of all aspects of our labor force, of businesses of every size, and of our communities? The diversity of our nation is exactly what has made us strong, innovative, and prosperous."

To be clear, I don't believe immigrants are only as important as their labor and contributions to our GDP; however, when I've been in a position where other white people are openly admitting their biases, I know I'm up against a mammoth myth about immigrants draining our economy, so a strategic economic argument is often the first line of defense to open their eyes and minds.

The conversation continues. The next thing out of my mouth is usually the thing my heart wanted to start with in the first place. "One important thing: A human being can't be illegal. When you get pulled over for a speeding ticket you aren't 'illegal.' Your action of speeding was illegal, but not you as a person. A desperate border crossing doesn't make a person illegal, either."[1]

Talking past the point of disagreement, past our filtered bubbles of news sources and social media groups, past the pull to conform with a group we belong to, can be terrifying, triggering deeply negative emotions, but it is absolutely necessary to move our nation forward. Of course, some of the conversations get weird, uncomfortable, and, honestly, a bit threatening. Even as terrifying as it can be, it's important that we all engage past our comfort zones and not just ignore those who express views that we find offensive. This is critical because the rhetoric that's being used to dehumanize immigrants in America and the world is truly frightening in its cause and in its effects both now and into the future.

Our Freedoms Are Intertwined

Standing up to xenophobia, Islamophobia, homophobia, transphobia, as well as racist, sexist, and anti-Semitic beliefs are a part of supporting equal rights for *all* people in America. The majority of people—roughly two-thirds—directly harmed by the rising tide of hate and the anti-immigrant sentiment, and anti-Muslim policies that often accompany it, are women and their children. Our friends, family, neighbors, teammates, and colleagues—as well as members of our communities—are experiencing hate every day.

Silence is not an option. Our freedoms and our communities are intertwined.

We've all heard the old saying "Sticks and stones may break my bones, but words will never hurt me." Well, that saying isn't true. Words really do matter. National data shows that following the 2016 increase in hate rhetoric, there was at least a 6 percent increase in hate crimes, most of which were crimes against people.[2] And in the past year, approximately eight thousand hate crimes were committed with firearms.[3]

This hate isn't just impacting adults. Young students are experiencing more direct bullying in schools, too. The Southern Poverty Law Center conducted a survey of teachers that revealed heartbreaking statistics. Since the 2016 election, 80 percent of teachers shared that they were seeing increased anxiety from marginalized students, including immigrants, Muslims, African Americans, and LGBTQ+ students, and 40 percent heard bullying directed at students of color, Muslims, immigrants, and people based on gender or sexual orientation, including disturbing incidents involving images like swastikas, Nazi salutes, and Confederate flags.[4]

Those hateful words and images are causing real harm.

Hate Hurts and Harms

One in five Muslim women say they have enough stress and anxiety due to our political climate to believe they need the help of a mental health professional.[5] That signifies just how much bullying, discrimination, and stress Muslim women face in our nation.[6]

Children, particularly girls who are dealing with the dual challenges of Islamophobia and sexism, are negatively impacted, too. Bullying of Muslim students in schools is up significantly: 42 percent of Muslims with children in grades K–12 reported bullying of their children because of their faith. This isn't just children bullying children. Studies show that adults are involved in about a quarter of the bullying incidents. Given this information, it's not surprising that polls show personal safety is a major concern for a high numbers of people of the Muslim and Jewish faiths. This fear turns out to be based in reality. Religious-based discrimination is at unacceptably high levels, with Muslims reporting the highest levels (60 percent) and people of the Jewish faith (38 percent) reporting the next highest.

Too often Muslims have inaccurately been framed as foreigners, but in truth Muslims have been an integral part of our nation for hundreds of years. The American Muslim population is incredibly diverse, with the vast majority being U.S. citizens.[7] In fact, Muslims are the only faith community surveyed with no majority race. American Muslims are 25 percent Black, 24 percent white,

18 percent Asian, 18 percent Arab, 7 percent mixed race, and 5 percent Hispanic.[8] Muslims are our friends and our neighbors. Muslims are the people we volunteer and play on sports teams with, our colleagues, and part of who makes our nation work. Despite this, some conservative national opinion leaders have fanned the flames of Islamophobia, making Muslims and those perceived as Muslim very unsafe. This acutely impacts Muslim women who are dealing with xenophobia, racism, and sexism at the same time each and every day.

More than 60 percent of people in our nation have said they've never had a conversation with a person who they know is Muslim. The result of this is that the majority of people in our country know little to nothing about the religion,[9] but many get swept up in the negative misinformation pushed out by hardline conservative leaders.

This is putting many people in the Muslim community in direct danger. In the last year, according to the FBI, anti-Muslim hate crimes have risen 67 percent. This high statistic is more than likely quite low because Muslim leaders report that hate crimes are often not pursued, tracked, or reported to the extent that they are happening.[10] One thing is clear: Anti-Muslim hostility is based upon and inextricable from xenophobia, and we must fight back against both together.

The Rising Yet Unwelcome Tide

Both anti-Muslim and anti-immigrant sentiment are rising at the same time—and that's not a coincidence. Wendy Cervantes, a senior policy analyst at the Center for Law and Social Policy, told me, "Xenophobia and Islamophobia are rooted in the same type of fear. In fact, Islamophobia is a form of xenophobia. It's all rooted in the fear of the 'other.' And until we can realize that there really is no 'other,' this vicious cycle is going to continue." Make no mistake, this cycle is vicious in the literal sense.

Wendy visited a classroom in North Carolina where a nine-year-old boy told her that he's trying to perfect making peanut butter and jelly sandwiches in case his mom and dad get deported. He told her that he's worried about his three-year-old sister because she doesn't like jelly.

And this boy is not alone. Five million children, most of whom are under the age of ten, live with the constant fear of being separated from their parents.[11] Already thousands of children have been separated from their parents as a result of recent immigration enforcement activities.

More than 5 million children are experiencing the toxic stress of constant fear and worry of separation, and the women who are moms in this situation are experiencing this toxic stress, too. This situation speaks to the unintended consequences of an unfair national immigration policy on our communities. Five million children are roughly as many people as live in the city of Boston. Imagine a whole city of only children and no parents. It's a nearly unfathomable number. Yet 5 million children and their moms wake up every day not knowing whether they or their families will be safe.

One mother in Arizona knows this scenario all too well. Her two tiny children were left alone in a car after she was taken away by deputies after a traffic violation. The local Arizona NBC station news report described the incident through the eyes of a witness. "The deputies were wearing ski masks and detained the children's mother for about an hour while her children watched, crying."[12] How could this even be legal and okay with the supervisor of the deputies?

It turns out that the person in charge knew exactly what was going on. Sheriff Joe Arpaio was the person in charge of those deputies at the time. Arpaio has been cited repeatedly for gross civil rights violations and racial profiling of both citizens and noncitizens in the name of immigration enforcement. When questioned about his tactics, Arpaio said that under his jurisdiction, "it was not unusual for law enforcement officers to wear ski masks while on duty."[13]

Regardless of where any of us stand on immigration policy, no one should be treated that way. Arpaio is an extreme example, but he's not the only one. Human rights abuses in the name of immigration enforcement are un-American and are still happening all too often.

There was a win for justice in Arpaio's case. With over 2,700 lawsuits against Arpaio and forty thousand felony warrants outstanding in his jurisdiction at one point, Arpaio had fostered a climate of hate and fear using virulently anti-Latino and anti-immigrant tactics. He and his deputies regularly crossed the line by using tactics that violate civil rights in the name of immigration enforcement.[14] This is not okay. MomsRising members joined with other organizations like the National Day Laborer Organizing Network and called on the U.S. Department of Justice to investigate Arpaio for his out-of-control inhuman behavior and human rights abuses.

And they did.

The U.S. Department of Justice got involved, investigated, and Arpaio's ability to go unchecked was checked. Then we—all of us who believe in Lady Liberty—won another battle: After twenty-four years in office as the most widely recognized anti-immigrant law official in the country, and despite raising $12 million from donors for his reelection bid, Arpaio lost his most recent reelection.[15] Even though President Trump later pardoned Arpaio, the fact that he is no longer a sheriff with the force of law at his disposal is a major victory for people who spoke up, who voted, and who took action.

The evidence is clear. Our voices matter.

The Stereotypes Are Wrong

Stereotyping of people is both harmful and dangerous, and stereotypes are wrong. For instance, immigrants pay substantial taxes and contribute to our communities, not the opposite. In fact, undocumented immigrants paid $11.8 billion in state and local taxes in 2012 alone.[16] And while many undocumented immigrants pay taxes through sales taxes, payroll taxes, and more, many do not (and cannot) take funds out. Money CNN reports: "The truth is that undocumented immigrants contribute more in payroll taxes than they will ever consume in public benefits."[17] Contrary to a ridiculous and harmful narrative pushed forward by many hardline conservatives over many years, immigrants are less likely to commit crimes than those who are native born.[18] According to FBI statistics, when you look at the total number of crimes, white people actually commit the highest total number of crimes in our nation.[19]

There are two key wrong ideas about immigration on our southern border that must be addressed and set right. First, despite what many hardline conservatives have been inferring, the net migration at our southern border with Mexico is negative, and it has been so since the Great Recession. From 2009 to 2014, more people left the United States to return to Mexico than came here.[20] That's right. The "wall" that President Trump repeatedly said he wanted to build is even more ridiculous and delusional than most people thought at the time. (Asians make up the largest share of recent immigrants, despite what has been insinuated to the public.[21])

Second, many of the mothers and children who are seeking safety at our southern border are fleeing what has become known as the Northern Triangle of Central America: parts of Honduras, Guatemala, and El Salvador. This region has among the highest rates of homicide in the world and is considered the most violent region in the Western hemisphere.[22] U.S. Citizenship and Immigration Services, part of the Department of Homeland Security, found that 88 percent of the mothers and children entering at our southern border had credible fear, including escaping extreme sexual and gender-based violence,[23] that meets the threshold for qualifying for asylum, which is an international human right.[24] Yet, almost none of these mothers and children have received adequate legal representation. Shockingly, 80 percent of all asylum-seeking children fleeing violence from Central America continue to face their hearings alone.[25]

Throw out the stereotypes. This is the real situation. It's heartbreaking. It's time to remember the promise of America that is written on the base of our Statue of Liberty: "Give me your tired, your poor, your huddled masses yearning to breathe free, the wretched refuse of your teeming shore. Send these, the homeless, tempest-tossed to me, I lift my lamp beside the golden door!" These words have in many ways defined our country. Bringing people together, caring for one another, and reaching out in times of war, famine, and natural disasters are part of our national heritage. Closing the door on others closes doors for our country and for ourselves. We can never forget: It's our diversity that brings innovative ideas, solutions, and prosperity. We are truly stronger together.

It also bears repeating that immigrant women, children, and families are vital and important parts of our communities, workplaces, society, economy, friendships, and country. We must march to stop human rights abuses from happening in the name of immigration enforcement. Our nation needs federal comprehensive and fair immigration reform so there's a line to stand in for legal status and citizenship for our friends, family, and neighbors who are currently undocumented—and we need it yesterday. We don't have a comprehensive national immigration policy, an application process, or even a road map to citizenship for the undocumented people who live in our communities. Quite simply, there is no line to stand in. We need to fix this.

Right now, too many women and families are in limbo, working hard, fueling our economy, and paying taxes but vulnerable to losing a friend or family member who has been part of our community for years and years without notice. In fact, millions of women live with this fear each and every day:[26] These women have children like Gabi, who is seven years old and shares: "I always cry when my mom is late for pickup. She might not pick me up one day."[27]

All Hands on Deck

Our nation is prosperous and innovative because of our diversity, not in spite of it. It's time to stand up for our neighbors, not stand silently by as they and we are torn down. The fact that we have stood for each other in that past is what truly makes America great.

If you see something, do something. Say something, persist. Start conversations and keep talking when it gets uncomfortable as long as you are safe. Take action in a way that works best for you. But just be sure to do something. It's time to stand united for liberty and justice for every woman in America.

Never forget that together, we are a powerful force—and one conversation, one bullhorn, one letter to Congress at a time, everything we do adds up. We've come a long way as a nation together, and we cannot and will not turn our backs on the American Dream or on each other now.

How to Build Bridges across Differences

The hateful rhetoric that dominated the 2016 election cycle and the Trump presidency has sparked a rise in hate crimes and created tension within many families, between friends, among co-workers, and basically in every social situation possible. We are a deeply divided nation—but that's all the more reason to have conversations to help bridge our divides. It's time to talk it out. The current divisions hurt our hearts, families, communities, and country.

As you talk it out, it's important for you to know that studies show that calling people out directly as racist, xenophobic, or sexist usually leaves them further entrenched in their original point of view.[28]

So what *do* you say?

- **A good way to start is to ask an open-ended question** so you get a sense of where the person stands and you don't accidentally open the conversation in an adversarial way. For example: *How do you feel about what's going on in our country?*
- **Next, you can follow up with a specific question** that dives in a little deeper: *What are you thinking about the rise in white supremacy/xenophobia/sexism/a recent hate crime/[pick a topic in the news]?*
- **Then listen.** When the goal is helping someone else see our perspective or hear our experience, one of the most effective methods is to listen first. Pause, and then try to understand where that person is coming from so you can

have a genuine dialogue that can elicit empathy and create change. Refraining from immediately arguing back doesn't mean you've lost your moral compass, just that you're listening.

- **Once you're finished listening, then you can (and should!) share your perspective.** It's always helpful to share a personal story of how you or a friend has been affected by whatever issue you are discussing.

- **Similarly, consider sharing how you've struggled** with addressing your own bias, because this helps bridge divides. For example: *I've realized that even though I work hard to be against sexism/racism/xenophobia/homophobia/ anti-Semitism, I have work to do. For example, one time, I did* _____ *and I learned/realized* _____. *Have you had similar experiences?*[29]

- **Follow-up questions can also be helpful** in moving the conversation along in a good way, particularly if you don't agree. Handy phrases include: *Can you share more about why you think this? Or What experiences have you had in your life to make you feel that way? Or Really? That's not my experience.*

It won't be easy, but don't give up. Be aware that one conversation is just a start. The goal is to open the door for long-term conversations that can help break down barriers to equity and equality over time. As my colleague Gloria Pan said, "We all need to try as hard as we can to reach outside our bubbles to understand other lives and experiences—to resist the gravitational pull of breaking into small social groups that are similar to us—if we want our country to survive let alone thrive. Having those hard conversations is reaching outside our personal bubbles."

Keep at it. Often the point of disagreement is where our

conversations stop and when we each go back to our differently filtered news sources. But disagreement is where true dialogue really begins, where trust is grown, where minds expand, and where leaps in ideas are made. So it's time to break the bubbles. To open hearts. To help move our nation forward with love, not backward with hate.

Big shifts in cultural change and understandings can happen one uncomfortable conversation at a time. We all can be part of breaking down barriers to moving our country forward one coffee conversation at a time.

White Women like Me, Let's Talk for a Moment

There's a rising tide of racism in our country that has deadly consequences. It's time to embrace our learning curves and to put fighting racism in our focus (if it isn't already) as a key part of fighting for women's rights. We've got to stand up and to speak out, particularly through reaching out to other white people who don't always agree with us. I've been listening and learning, and listening some more—and here are some tips on how:

Talk with Other White People

Most people of color are highly aware of racism and xenophobia in America. On the other hand, a recent poll found that only 39 percent of white people thought this was still a problem[30] even though the national statistics clearly prove otherwise. This gap in understanding is in part because white people like me don't experience racism and xenophobia on a regular basis, so we often don't fully see what's happening. Given this situation, it's important to stand up against discrimination so the burden isn't solely on people of color to educate white people as a community. So roll up your sleeves and talk with your friends, family, and neighbors. Share data. (There's a lot of data for use in your conversations in this book.) Share stories. Share your experiences. Talk. Be sure to take time especially with people who don't fully agree with you and to not let casual racism, xenophobia, and sexism go unchecked. One way to do this is to say something if you hear something. Handy phrases to dive in include: "That's not necessary." "Have you thought about what you're saying?" "Where is that coming from?"

Remind people that the advancement of one group of people absolutely doesn't come at the expense of other groups of people. That's not how our nation works. In fact, it works in the opposite way.

Remind Friends That White Women Experience Less Discrimination than Women of Color

Recent polling data show that there are many people who're still not sure white women experience less discrimination than women of color.[31] Here are a few quick facts to have handy in conversations if needed:

Women of Color Experience Intense Wage Discrimination

Women, on average, earned just 80 cents to a man's dollar in 2017 for all year-round full-time workers. That being said, both moms and women of color experience increased wage hits:[32] White, non-Hispanic women are earning only 75 cents;[33] Black women only 63 cents; Native American women only 57 cents; and Latina women only 54 cents for every dollar earned by white, non-Hispanic men. Asian American women experience a smaller wage gap on average,[34] but still make only 85 cents on average for every dollar made by white non-Hispanic men.[35]

It's Easier for White Students to Get into College

A Georgetown University Center on Education and the Workforce report[36] recently found that white students are still overrepresented in the nation's elite institutions. The study found that despite the fact that equal rates of white and minority students are unprepared for college, more white students are admitted to universities.[37]

It's Easier for White People to Get a Free Ride

One recent study found that when a bus rider didn't have money to pay the fare (or their fare card was empty), bus drivers let 72 percent of white testers ride free, but only 36 percent of Black testers.[38] On the whole, the study found that Blacks and Indians got fewer free rides than other Asians and whites.[39]

There Is Rampant Discrimination in Our Criminal Justice System

A whole chapter is devoted to that in this book. Please feel free to use the stats and stories from that chapter in your conversations.

Embrace the Fact That We Won't Have All the Answers

Clearly none of us, including me, are experts on racism and xenophobia or what it feels like to deal with everyday racism and xenophobia no matter how many books we've read or degrees we have hanging on the wall. So it's important to keep an open mind and to keep listening. Follow leaders who are women of color on social media and in the news to keep up to date on important perspectives. Also, not fully understanding the impact of racism and xenophobia doesn't mean we step back from speaking out against it.

Listen. Read. Learn. Know History. Follow the Present.

Much of the history taught in school curriculums leaves out the contributions of women, with women of color all too often entirely erased from the pages of history, and the fact that women of color have also faced sexism is also often erased, too. It's no small coincidence that Rosa Parks was a rape crisis counselor before she ever sat on a bus. There's a tragic history of unprosecuted sexual violence against Black women and other women of color from the founding of our nation. People tend to forget that Black women were lynched along with Black men. People also tend to forget all that women of color have faced throughout our nation's history. During a historic suffrage parade in 1913, Black women were asked to march at the back of the parade in a separate segregated group after white women. Black suffragist leader Ida B. Wells bravely marched with her state's delegation anyway.[40]

To learn more, read *The New Jim Crow* by Michelle Alexander, as well as writings by leaders like Audre Lorde, Brittney Cooper, Marisa Franco, Maria Hinojosa, Ai-Jen Poo, Angela Davis, Patrisse Khan-Cullors, asha bandele, Alicia Garza, Roxane Gay, Rinku Sen, Chimamanda Ngozi Adichie, Monifa Bandele, dream hampton, Jamia Wilson, Malkia Cyril, and many more in books and magazines and on social media.

Follow and Support Women of Color

Find women of color leaders who are doing great work (and there are many). Follow and support their work, agenda, and vision. Solidarity is laying it on the line and following at least part of the time. Find out who is leading on racial justice and immigrant rights advocacy in your community and our nation and follow their leadership.

Look Around

When you're working in a coalition or leadership group, look up to see who has a seat at the table. If everyone sitting at the table looks exactly the same, then that's a problem. Our nation is diverse, and to be truly representative and effective, our coalitions and leadership groups must also be diverse from start to finish. Bringing in organizations representing people of color or women (or any group) after the agenda and strategies have been set isn't really expanding the table. We need to set the table together as we listen to each other's contributions, priorities, and needs, and then dive into action.

Know That It's Okay to Be Afraid

Being brave means doing something even though you're afraid. Many people fear talking about racism and xenophobia. I know I do. As a white woman I know I live and breathe a culture that's packed with implicit racial and sexual bias each and every day. I know that I'm bound to absorb more than a little of that negativity, whether I intend to or not. I know I've messed up in the past, and that I will continue to mess up in the future. Messing up isn't a fun experience. But white people need to keep trying anyway, because the embarrassment of messing up is nothing compared to the experience of living with xenophobia, racism, and other discrimination.

There is no fight for women's equity and equality without also fighting against racism and xenophobia. Sexism, racism, heterosexism, xenophobia, and classism are intertwined. And as women who are white we must fight back against all the isms that are swarming around our children, woven through our culture, and part of the fabric of our lives and our nation. Intersectionality is real—and so must be our fight for equality, equity, and justice for everyone.

11

The Domino Effect

The hurdles women face can sometimes feel like falling dominoes. You know that game? You place each domino on its narrow side, standing one tile after another, and make a line or a figure eight out of the tiles. Then you stand back, tap the first domino, and each falls, one after another in a wave. There's a reason this game has survived generations. The tap on the first domino and the rush as each subsequent domino falls down can be mesmerizing.

Another reason people have been riveted by falling dominoes for decades is because the game imitates life. For example, consider the lives of the more than 80 percent of women who have children, about 40 percent of whom are unmarried when giving birth.[1] Each crisis is connected, one tapping the other. A woman has her first baby. If that woman and her infant don't have access to health care, the health and financial costs can be crushing for years to come.

Next, if that woman doesn't have access to paid family/medical leave after her baby arrives, she'll need to go unpaid for a while or may have to go back to work before everyone is physically healed and breastfeeding is fully established.

Then, it's likely that our new mom will find it difficult to afford childcare. Childcare now costs more than college in most states in the country. But childcare is essential—because parents need safe and enriching places for their children to be so they can work, as three-quarters of moms now do. Not to mention that young minds need high-quality early education so they can thrive, and childcare workers, most of whom are women, need fair pay.

We Are Failing Working Women

MacKenzie from New Hampshire knows what it's like when the dominoes you've stacked begin to tip. She and husband did everything they could to prepare for the birth of their daughter, including arranging for MacKenzie's mom to watch their daughter while MacKenzie was at work. But all their preparations went out the window when MacKenzie's mother had a stroke. Like many families, MacKenzie and her husband needed both of their paychecks to make ends meet. A missed paycheck wasn't an option. So when it came time for MacKenzie to go back to work, she was panicked by the cost of childcare and by the fact that none of the childcare facilities in her area accepted infants less than six weeks old. MacKenzie's only option at that point was to take her five-week-old daughter to work with her. It was an unbelievably difficult time for MacKenzie, who had also used up all her sick days after the baby arrived since she didn't have any paid family/medical leave. "I was not well. I was tired, stressed, and sick to my stomach worrying about my mom, money, childcare, and how my son was taking to having a brand-new sibling."

The dominoes had fallen. MacKenzie didn't have childcare or paid family/medical leave, yet couldn't afford not to work. And MacKenzie isn't alone. Most people don't even realize that there are this many dominoes waiting to fall until they have children.

We have an entire system that's out of whack in America, and it's hurting women in particular. And because the whole system is out of whack, no one is experiencing hardship because of just *one* policy area in crisis at a time. In real life, the same people who are facing unfair pay are also likely dealing with a lack of paid family/medical leave, unaffordable childcare, an absence of earned sick days, barriers to high-quality education, and more.

All in one person. Sometimes all in one day.

In short, we have an entire system that hasn't caught up to our modern labor force and is failing women and our economy. You don't have to take my word for it. A 2014 *Washington Post* headline put it simply: "The U.S. ranks last in every measure when it comes to family policy."[2] Other countries have done better. We can, too.

Childcare Dominoes

The falling domino of childcare is often a big surprise. Many parents are completely shocked to discover that the cost of childcare in America will eat up a huge chunk of their paychecks. In fact, a *New York Times* article nearly went viral because it shared the calculation that if parents started saving for childcare the same way we save for college, parents would have to save for their future children's childcare at only seven years old.[3]

Every day, I hear a story about a parent struggling to get access to affordable, high-quality early learning opportunities like childcare, pre-K, day care, home visiting, early intervention services, and more. Jodi shared that her childcare expenses are more than her mortgage. She pays $1,355 per month for her nineteen-month-old and about $500 for her six-year-old. It's essential that her children are somewhere safe and enriching while she's at work. "It's incredible how our economy forces a dual income and then doesn't provide an affordable and accessible childcare infrastructure. And when it doesn't work, instead of looking at the system, it looks at the parents—as though we have done something wrong," said Jodi, who also shared that the high cost of childcare is also making it impossible to pay back the more than $100,000 in student loans that she and her husband owe. "We have good incomes and we live modestly, but we have been thrown into financial insecurity—first because there is no paid leave and second because childcare expenses are astronomical. The promise that if we work hard both in education and in the workforce, then we can make a better future for our children is broken."

Jodi isn't the only one caught in a childcare web. For a parent with two young children, the average cost of center-based childcare exceeds the average cost of rent in every state in the country.[4] In fact, over the past thirty years, childcare costs for working families have increased by 70 percent.[5] Seventy percent! No wonder women and families are feeling like they have it tougher than the last generation. We do. Adding further challenge is that the overall cost of raising children is higher than most people imagine. It now costs $200,000 to raise a child from birth to age eighteen, not including college.[6]

The sky-high costs for childcare are happening at a time when a quarter of young families in our nation are living in poverty. In fact, having a baby is one of the leading causes of poverty, and it's safe to say that the high cost of childcare is playing a role in driving women and families toward poverty. The price tag on childcare is even more troubling when you look at the impact on low-income families: On average, families making less than $1,500 a month with children under the age of five who paid for childcare spent more than half of their monthly income on childcare expenses (52.7 percent).[7]

Affordability isn't the only hurdle. Access is a hurdle, too. Sioban started looking for childcare seven months before her son was even born. She thought she was ahead of the game, but found two-year waiting lists at some places, with many people putting themselves on the wait list before they even got pregnant. "The only day care in my neighborhood always has a wait list of over three hundred families." Sioban eventually got a spot in an excellent day care but had to work a reduced schedule because there weren't any full-time slots open until the next year. She shares, "We are lucky to have a good day care, but day care in our city is very expensive (average $1,900/month). If we had two children, I would have to quit my job because my entire salary would go toward day care."

Adding to this crisis is the fact that many low-income families are more likely to live in a "childcare desert," an area where affordable, high-quality childcare is extremely difficult to find. In fact, a recent study found that 51 percent of women and families live in an area classified as a childcare desert, with children in Latino families and rural communities impacted the most.[8] Studies also show that living in a childcare desert can drive more women into poverty, because not having childcare makes it next to impossible for those women to work.[9]

There are three big falling dominoes that regularly hit each other when it comes to childcare: affordability, access, and quality. Quality is key. A growing body of research indicates that preschool programs need to have the right mix of high-quality educational ingredients to be truly effective. That includes a developmentally appropriate, evidence-based curriculum, as well as coaching for early learning teachers, adequate teacher pay, and engaging environments in order to best prepare every child to be ready and successful in school and life.[10]

Of course, in order to be a high-quality education program, all kids must be equitably educated. Done right, high-quality early learning environments decrease gaps and increase opportunity for all children. Dual language learning programs are one powerful way to help reach that goal.[11] Right now, there are 11.5 million children in the United States who are dual language learners and stand to benefit from dual language programs within our education system.[12] Study after study shows that dual language learning programs are one of the best ways to increase student achievement for language learners while also giving kids a big boost across the board regardless of language background.[13]

And, as all of this is happening, parents are struggling at home, too. Another key policy area to advance is home visiting after a new child arrives. A program that can link parents with trained home visitors (nurses, social workers, and educators), home visiting has been shown to help break cycles of poverty, increase self-sufficiency, get more kids into great educational situations, and save tax dollars. In fact, for every dollar invested in home visiting, as much as $5.70 is returned to the community.[14]

Between a Rock and a Hard Place

Since the vast majority of moms work outside of the home and more than 40 percent of mothers are now the primary breadwinners for their families,[15] it's clear we need childcare/early learning opportunities that are affordable, high quality, and accessible. Yet we have a broken system.

We can't talk about childcare without also talking about childcare workers. There are two sides to the same broken childcare coin: Parents and childcare workers are both struggling. Most parents can't afford to pay any more for childcare, and childcare workers are among the lowest-paid workers in our nation, earning an average of $21,170 per year.[16] A recent study found that nearly half of all childcare workers, many of whom are moms, have to rely on a government program (SNAP, welfare, Medicaid) just to make ends meet because their pay is too low.[17] This isn't good for anyone.

If you're a childcare worker who is also a parent, you get hit even harder. With 95 percent of the childcare workforce composed of women, it should come as no surprise that nearly two-thirds (63 percent) of childcare workers with children report that they have to depend on public support programs to get by and often struggle themselves to afford high-quality childcare for their own families.[18]

Sonia is a mother of three and an early childhood educator. She told me, "I've seen the power of high-quality early learning from both perspectives. At home, I've seen my oldest daughter struggle to catch up to her peers who benefited from early learning and pre-K in a way she didn't. I've seen my son, who had access to free public pre-K, enter kindergarten on a level playing field, and excel in school in a way I fear my oldest never will. I see my baby, my two-year-old, who spends his days in a high-quality early childhood education center and will soon transition into pre-K, and I know I'm already setting him up for success. Three children, three educational trajectories—and the differences are obvious."

Working in early childhood education opened Sonia's eyes, but it didn't open up her financial situation. She still doesn't make enough money to pay for high-quality early learning for her own children. She notes, "The childcare and early learning affordability crisis in our country cuts both ways—neither parents nor providers can afford the system we currently have, and sadly it is kids who suffer most when they lose out on high-quality early learning opportunities."

We Can Fix It!

Fortunately, solutions are possible. Increasing access to high-quality, affordable early learning opportunities (like universal pre-K and childcare)—particularly for vulnerable children—doesn't just help children and parents; it also helps our national economy. There is almost no better return on investment for taxpayers than investing in early learning. For example, for every $1 invested in early learning programs, like childcare and pre-K, the taxpayers get back $8 later due to fewer grade repetitions, fewer interactions with the criminal justice system, and more.[19] Further, high-quality programs can actually help narrow the opportunity gap that is most often experienced by children in low-income families and children of color.[20]

We have to advance education opportunities for all kids, and as we do that we can't leave education professionals, most of whom are women, behind. Teachers and the early learning workforce, including the childcare providers who are our children's first teachers, are key to achieving what offering a high-quality education to every child can offer our nation. Teachers and childcare workers should be paid fairly—and that means being paid enough to afford children of their own and to stay in their job so there isn't high turnover.[21]

Fair compensation and world-class training and education opportunities so teachers are best equipped to support our learners are critical. Creating a culture that places high value on the role and importance of those caring for and teaching our future leaders is critical, too. There are models for success for parents, kids, and teachers alike, including in the U.S. military. That's right. As I'm typing this, the Department of Defense has over 200,000 children in their incredibly successful and highly respected childcare system.[22]

Popping primary colors, adorably shaped rockets, and fluffy white and blue clouds. That's the image that comes to mind when Sarah, a military veteran, remembers going into the military childcare facility where her children went to preschool.

Her daughter loved it so much that she'd walk in, look at her mom, and abruptly say, "Okay bye, Mom." Sarah remembers her daughter leaving and having an ironic chuckle with these words on the tip of her tongue: "Hey, why'd you leave me so easily?" Her daughter left her side so easily because she loved the space for learning and early childhood development she was entering into.

Sarah and her husband both joined the military and then had kids. Both of their kids did the preschool program on the military base. Sarah recalls, "It was a great program. And the cost was one of the main things that was a benefit to us because my husband was a lower enlisted soldier at the time, so we were on WIC and didn't have a lot of available funds. The sliding scale of childcare payments based on income made it affordable."

One of her fondest memories is walking into the room to pick up her daughter and finding her covered in red, blue, purple, and green paint, as she happily learned how to craft images, letters, and numbers on paper. Key features of childcare programs provided by our nation's military that can and should be replicated for nonmilitary parents include sliding-scale costs to parents that make it affordable, high-quality care, fair compensation and training for providers, and services that are easily accessible to families.

Of the trinity of childcare needs—affordability, quality, and accessibility—the military hits the mark with all three. The Department of Defense has taken the added step of creating policies to ensure caregivers are paid similar wages to those who work for them in other jobs that require similar amounts of "training, experience, and seniority" and provide additional training opportunities.[23] The civilian childcare system, or lack thereof, on the other hand, is still behind in all three of these areas.

One of the reasons is that the military childcare system requires an investment of resources that the Department of Defense is more than happy to make because it later pays off. On the civilian side, we haven't fully made the penny-wise and pound-foolish connection that investing in early learning, universal pre-K, and childcare pays off later…yet. But we will!

Break the School-to-Prison Pipeline

We can't discuss early education—or education at all—without discussing the importance of stopping the school-to-prison pipeline, which is a disturbing national trend where children are funneled out of schools and into the juvenile and criminal justice systems. Here's one glimpse of the school-to-prison pipeline: Black girls are five times more likely to be suspended from school than white girls even though they don't have more discipline problems.[24] Analysis shows that part of what's happening here is a double whammy of discrimination that starts in early education. The National Women's Law Center reports that on top of experiencing racism, "Black girls are punished for challenging what society deems 'feminine' behavior, like being candid or talking back." This punishment doesn't just come in the form of suspensions; it also too often also means being excluded from STEM (science, technology, engineering, and math) programs and other education opportunities.[25]

What's going on? To start, the practice and use of exclusionary discipline policies has increased over the past several decades, with the suspension rates of students of color doubling since the 1970s. That's despite zero evidence to suggest that there are behavioral differences among all students or even that suspensions reduce student misbehavior or improve academic outcome. Rather, school suspension and expulsion result in a number of negative outcomes for both schools and students. Research shows a correlation between kids who are suspended and then later get trapped in the criminal justice system, are held back a grade, or don't complete high school.[26] You read that right: Suspensions hurt, not help, kids.

To be blunt, students aren't disciplined in equitable ways. A comprehensive analysis reported by the National Institutes of Health found that Black, Hispanic, and American Indian youth are slightly more likely than white and Asian American youth to be sent to the office and substantially (two to five times) more likely to be suspended or expelled.[27] This is unfair—and it's not the fault of the children who are being punished. Studies are showing that there is a disparity in how children of color are unfairly and wrongly judged and disciplined by adults starting as young as preschool.[28]

This is not okay.

It's time to challenge the practices and policies that push students out of schools and into the juvenile and criminal justice systems, to promote social emotional development and trauma-informed care in schools, and to dismantle the school-to-prison pipeline and instead advance the cradle-to-(affordable)-college pathway.

Reading what's happening with kids, teachers, educators, and parents will get you fired up to take action. Overzealous school discipline policies have negative impacts not only on our children but also on working parents. One mom anonymously shared that her daughter, who has always been an honor student, was suspended last year for five days: "For what you ask? For something her brother said to another student in the school. She didn't do a single thing, and the superintendent would not reconsider his decision."

Another mom, Abby, shared that her son was suspended in fourth grade because she accidentally left a very small, bright orange plastic water gun in his backpack. "It was so small that it would fit inside my hand and not be seen. But somehow, a teacher saw it and he was suspended for three days!" Abby recalled. This led to a hardship, because she didn't have any sick days available to be home with her son, so she had to take unpaid time off. As a widow and single mom, she had a hard time paying the bills that month. Many of the students who are pushed out of schools and into the criminal justice system could garner lifelong benefits from additional services instead of punishment.

Inequalities are clearly not yet a thing of the past in our K–12 education system and beyond when it comes to academic opportunities, either. How do we know? On the whole, while girls are doing better than boys in reading, boys are doing better than girls in the lucrative STEM studies[29] unless girls are in single-sex schools where gender stereotyping isn't as ubiquitous.[30] The STEM problem continues through college, where only 14 percent of young women are focusing on a lucrative STEM field versus the much higher number of 39 percent of young men.

We still have some significant work to do. It's clear that public investments in early learning programs like childcare and pre-K, as well as in the K–12 education system and college, are all key to improving education and economic security for women.

Make College Affordable

The cost of college has also skyrocketed. College is expensive, even though later earnings are significantly increased (and significantly means doubled)[31] when you have a college degree, which, in turn, significantly improves women's lifetime economic security.[32] Even so, the rising cost of college has far outpaced inflation over time: In 2015 the average cost at a private, nonprofit, four-year university was $31,231, compared to only $1,832 (in current dollars) in 1971.[33]

Everyone should be able to attend a college institution—a community college, technical institution, four-year college, or other—but the problem is that few can afford it. Right now women are getting more college degrees than men,[34] but they are also accumulating more debt and are graduating into a gender wage gap. They have so much more debt that *Consumer Reports* recently published an article about senior citizens who are "crushed" by student debt.[35] Incredibly, the article states, "114,000 Americans have had Social Security income seized, up 440 percent from 2002 and up 540 percent for people over 65."[36] In addition, about 7 million Americans over age fifty have student loan debt.[37]

We have to fix this.

Mary Kusler of the National Education Association notes: "We need to step up and address this issue of college affordability because it's not just impacting our finances as adults, it's impacting our kids for the rest of their lives. We're setting up the next generation to be one in debt."

I think we can all agree on the need to reduce the cost of college. It's time to explore new policies like free college and public service loan forgiveness when people go into fields like teaching, medicine, and more.

Superheroine Change Makers

Wins are happening that move the proverbial ball down the field bit by bit. While there hasn't been a big comprehensive package for making massive change, like building a national early learning system, including pre-K and childcare, that mirrors the best of the Department of Defense program, or making pre-K part of the public education system at the national level, or ensuring everyone has access to full-day kindergarten, or fully resourcing the K–12 education system, or demolishing the school-to-prison pipeline and advancing free college (a woman can dream!), we are making advancements.

There have even been a few touchdowns along the way. School districts, cities, and states across the nation are making changes backed up by people who are speaking out. For example, in 2016 and 2017 alone, MomsRising members played a role in increasing investments in pre-K in California, North Carolina, Pennsylvania, and Washington State. We also played a role in winning expansions of dual language learning, a ban on suspensions, and raise-the-age campaigns in New York, Washington State, Maryland, and North Carolina.

Access to high-quality education at all stages of life is a necessity to make our economy thrive and for young girls (and boys, too) to grow into the leaders we all need. Time and time again, the game changer in passing these policies has been legislators and leaders hearing from real people like you and me, including hearing specific stories from parents, students, and childcare providers about how these policies impact them.

Another game changer is when people step up to run for office (or to support someone running), win, and champion the policy. So share your voice in whatever way works best for you, and know you'll have an impact. Together, we are a powerful force.

When Women Lead, America Succeeds

A group of women were sitting around a large conference table, giant windows bringing the light, rooftops, and skyscrapers of New York City into the room. One woman's phone started getting texts. The first buzz of her phone on the tabletop was ignored, the second and third were ignored, too. But by the fourth text in what seemed like as many minutes, Pramila Jayapal started paying attention to her phone. She had traveled to New York City from Seattle for a Women's Economic and Social Political Action Network meeting, and it was clear that something was going on at home.

That something turned out to be that Congressman Jim McDermott had just announced he was retiring from a seat he'd held since 1989 in Washington's seventh congressional district. There was an open seat in Seattle, and all minds were on Pramila. Her phone started blowing up. The group had come together in New York City to strategize about how to build political power, and that power had come to them.

But Pramila didn't realize at first that big time political power was knocking at her door. In fact, Pramila, who was at that time serving as a Washington state senator, thought that most people had the wrong idea. Even though she'd lived and voted in the seventh congressional district for a couple of decades, recent redistricting had her situated twenty blocks outside of the new district line. But her phone didn't stop buzzing. And the texts started including more important info: Pramila didn't need to live inside the district to run or to win. "Dozens of people texted me, from the heads of organizations, to people who have known my work for years, people who lived in my neighborhood and who lived far away," Pramila recalled. "I wouldn't have run if people hadn't texted me. It wouldn't even have occurred to me to run," she continued, "because I was twenty blocks outside the district line. I wouldn't have even thought of it. But just to see the outpouring of people who have known me and my work for so long here in Seattle and across the country meant a lot to me."

Pramila started thinking about running.

The texts kept coming over the days she was in New York City, and the idea was planted. As she waited for the plane back home in the airport, she called her husband, Steve. "Honey, I have some news. I think we should think about me running for Congress." He was supportive.

She got home to Seattle and started the process of thinking about running in earnest. There was a lot to consider. "It's not just deciding if you can win," she recalled. "That's only part of the decision. It's also deciding what does running mean for your family, your kid, your parents." Pramila's parents live in India, so running (and winning) would mean she couldn't see them as often because she'd lose a lot of her personal freedom and flexibility. She also took time to look into herself and think about what she wants to do in her life and to separate that from the alluring title of congresswoman. Having been an organizer for a long time, she's seen more than one person say, "I want to be a congresswoman," without thinking much about what they want to do when they get there. Pramila wanted to make sure she was interested in running for the right reasons and to do the right things. She took time for introspection. Several weeks after texts started blowing up her phone, after thinking and talking strategy with friends and family members, Pramila decided to officially throw her hat in the ring—and she won!

How to Run for Office (or Encourage a Friend To)

Women hold less than 20 percent of all seats in our national legislature, and women of color hold a small percentage of those seats, which means we have some catching up to do in order to reach political parity and to build a reflective democracy. Not everyone is ready or willing to make the substantial sacrifices of running for office. But I firmly believe everyone knows someone who would be great at serving in office—and that everyone can help someone else run and win. Plus, importantly, all of the policies in this book need a team of legislative champions in order to move forward and pass. That's someone you know. That might be you. That's us together building that team. So let's roll up our sleeves and get more women running. Let's go there!

How to Get a Friend to Run and Win

Ask! This may sound overly simple, but it's not. When women run for office, studies show it's typically because they've been asked to throw their hats in the ring—usually many, many times. Men, on the other hand, are more likely to decide to run for office on their own.[38] To be blunt, more women need to be actively and aggressively recruited to run for public office, just like Pramila was urged to run with text after text blowing up her phone. And that's where you come in. Here's how:

- **Make a list.**

Take a moment to reflect on your friends and colleagues and think if any of them would be spectacular elected leaders at the city, county, state, or federal level. Think about women who step up to take the lead in your neighborhood, at your kids' school, or in your faith community, or in your community as a whole. I bet you know at least one, maybe more.

- **Have coffee.**

Now that you have that person in mind, invite her out to coffee, tea, lemonade, or another fun beverage of your choice, and ask, "Hey, have you ever thought about running for office?" Remind her that she doesn't have to run for office this very moment, but can start picking which office she wants to run for now and also making a plan to run in the next year or more. Also emphasize that she is qualified, right now as she is, to run for office. Women often think they need a PhD and a career as a lawyer or government official to run for office. That is not true at all.

- **Look for the sparkle.**

Is there a glimmer of excitement in her eye? If so, ask friends to ask her to run, too. If she seems at all interested, even a teeny bit, if a sparkle lights up in her eye as she sips her coffee while you share that you think she'd make a great elected leader, then it's time for you to get more people on your #TeamAskAWomanToRun. Find five or so other women and tell them that you're working on a small project to get someone to run for office and need their help. Ask your five friends to ask her to run, too. Sometimes it takes a lot of asking for someone to run. Some research has even found that women have to be asked seven times in order to really think about running for office.[39]

■ **Build support!**

Depending on the person and your relationship, if they really do seem interested in running, then you may want to consider posting a nudge for them to run on social media. It not only helps people decide to run; it can also build the group of people who will support her while she's running. A simple post like this can work: *It's clearly past time to get more spectacular women in elected office. I'm looking at you, [name]. You'd make an excellent elected leader! Hope you run for office one day.*

■ **Celebrate!**

Okay, after you stop celebrating that she said yes, now you can help grow the circle of people who are helping with the future campaign. You can start by helping her bring together a "kitchen cabinet" of other women who will support her by volunteering and offering advice while she's campaigning. It's never too early to do this, even if she's not running for a year or more. More on that below.

■ **Find a hot meal and a checkbook.**

That sounds silly, but it's true. Year after year we hear from women candidates that one of the best supports they received from family, friends, or supporters was a hot, pre-made meal for them and their families from time to time. If you recruit someone to run for office, help them get to the finish line by reaching out and asking how you can help with a meal train or childcare. Just as importantly, write a check. It's not just enough to vote for women candidates; we have to invest in them, too.

- **Set aside time to help great candidates.**

Know that supporting and recruiting women leaders is an important form of leadership. Not everyone is called to or needs to run for office. It takes an entire community to elect anyone. So find someone you support, get on their kitchen cabinet, and be the wind that helps put them in office. This is just as important, if not sometimes more important, than running yourself.

So *You* Want to Run!

Did the idea of helping someone else run spark your interest? Do you want to run for office? *Yes!* Here's how to start:

- **Have a party for one!**

Celebrate that you decided you're going to throw your hat in the ring to run for office by having a party...alone. Take a moment with a favorite beverage and snack (choco-late, anyone?), a pen, and a piece of paper. Write down the top three things you want to do when elected to office, or the top three reasons why you're running. Add how your life experience relates to each of those issues, and then after each one list what level of government would be able to get that item done. This list shows you what your goal is in terms of if you want to run for city, county, state, or federal elected office. It also points to what messages you'll want to talk about the most on the campaign trail. Frame it. Don't forget it. This is why you're running for office, and you should use it as a touchstone in the future.

■ **Start a kitchen cabinet.**

Now it's time to grow your party from one to tons. The best (really only) way to win is to have a group of people supporting you. Think for a moment about who you know and who knows you. Gather together a group of ten to twelve people with varied experiences, including your very best friends, who'll volunteer on your campaign and give advice like only someone who knows you well can. Think about inviting local business owners, regular contributors to other similar campaigns, people involved in your political party, community leaders, and people who hold elected office. Invite a mixture of those folks to be part of your kitchen cabinet team. You can start with a small group and grow it. You'll want to meet about once a month to begin.

■ **Find training.**

Organizations across the country offer affordable (often free) campaign training throughout the year, some exclusively for women or people of color. Training is a powerful way to learn what it means to run for office and connect with local organizations and leaders who can help you along the way.

- **Make a plan.**

Bring together your kitchen cabinet. To start, ask for feedback on if the office you've selected to run for is the right one for you. There are a lot of options for running for office. If this is your first race and you're new to politics, think about running for a local office to start. Just like when you're at work, it's critical to get experience before going for the top job. Next, discuss whether you need to hire a campaign staff or not (you probably do even if you think you don't). Then think about how you will raise the money to pay them. (Don't let your family volunteer to do it for free. Trust me, you will thank me come Thanksgiving!) Start brainstorming a list of possible contributors and endorsers, including elected leaders, and set up one-on-one coffees with each of these people. Most importantly, make a plan for how to do voter contact and fundraising so you can win your race. You will be asked about this plan at each campaign event you do—be ready to talk about your strategy to win. And ask for people's feedback and ideas to make the whole plan stronger.

- **Get your ducks in a row.**

Research what you need to do to file to run for office and when, how to report your campaign spending, and other structural items like getting a campaign treasurer, Facebook and other social media presence, and website set up to take online contributions. (If this seems overwhelming, invite a local elected leader out to lunch and ask for advice on how they did this.)

- **Do some fundraising.**

Brainstorm a list of at least fifty people who will likely contribute to your campaign. (You should put your family, friends, and kitchen cabinet on that list of people to ask.) An easy line to ask for funds is: *Hello, I'm running for [name the seat] because I want to help lift our community. But I can't win alone. Can you contribute [amount] to this effort? All amounts are appreciated but the limit is [limit]. Can I count on your support?* Set aside a certain number of hours each week for fundraising and then hold yourself to that goal. Set up one-on-one coffees with each of the people on your fundraising list.

- **Reach out to movers and shakers.**

Reach out to your local political party (Democrat, Republican, Green, or other) as well as to other local elected leaders to let them know you're running and ask for their advice, help, and endorsement. Also reach out to local organizations and unions that support and help candidates (including by providing training) with your profile, such as Emily's List, Emerge America, Collective PAC, VoteRunLead, National Women's Political Caucus, Higher Heights, Democracy for America, and more. Also ask the staff at your legislative district organization or state party office if they can give you a list of which organizations are typically involved in local races near you as well as contact information for who to connect with at each of those organizations. When you talk with any organization or leader, be sure to ask for their endorsement and then put those endorsements on your website.

- **Contact voters.**

Work with people who've run races in your area and have won them to make your voter contact plan. You may want to hire a consultant for this. In many areas creating a voter contact plan includes purchasing or getting the voter file so you can mail, doorbell, and otherwise reach the right voters to let them know you're running and that they should vote for you. Targeting is key. You're going to want to work on turning out people who don't normally vote and would very likely support you and also on convincing swing voters (who might be convinced to vote for either candidate) that they really want to cast a ballot for you. Get some folks involved who've done this before if you never have—and make sure they're on your kitchen cabinet, too.

- **Have fun!**

Getting to meet new people, learn about new policy issues, and march in new parades is actually super fun. Enjoy your time running for office! And remember, if you lose the first time, be sure to run again. You've made an investment in name recognition with voters in your area, and it's not uncommon to have to run more than once before being elected to an office.

- **Give back.**

This is about women helping other women. Support other women running for office. Try to avoid splitting the vote in ways that hurt women candidates. Once you have run for office or managed a campaign, you have an incredibly valuable perspective to share with other women candidates. Whether you win or lose, the tools, insights, and knowledge you gained on the campaign trail are powerful and they should be shared. Support other women leaders who are running for office.

Together, we can make a ladder of opportunity for every woman and girl. Our voices are powerful and so very needed. Use yours to build the team of leaders who fight for all of us!

12

An Unjust System

Charleena Lyles was pregnant. A mother of four, she called the police in June 2017 to report a robbery. Charleena needed support and help. Instead, she was killed by police in front of her young children.

There's no question that the Seattle Police Department could have and should have used de-escalation tactics instead of shooting first and asking questions later. Unfortunately, unacceptable tragedies have become almost routine in our country.

Pause, step back from the political rhetoric, close your eyes for a moment to clear your head of the clutter of grocery lists and the chaos of your own life, and then try to imagine what this situation means in your heart. Can you imagine for a moment just being in this situation? Calling the police, terrified that a robbery might be happening while your children are home, and then the police arrive and make your children orphans? Can you imagine being pulled over for a broken taillight and that being the last time you saw your loved ones? It's unimaginable for some. But racial profiling and police brutality is a reality for too many women in our communities. We absolutely need to address the crisis of our entire criminal justice system, in which racial profiling and police brutality are happening at the same time as women are now one of the fastest growing incarcerated populations.

This is a women's rights issue, and it must be front and center in our priorities. So while we touched on this topic in prior chapters, we're going to dive deeper now. Across the country, Black people are three times more likely than white people to be killed when they encounter police. And Black women are especially vulnerable—studies show that Black women are falsely viewed as more threatening and "masculine" by police than white women.[1] That means that not only are the police more likely to use deadly force against Black women, like they did to Charleena, but also that police are more likely to unjustly arrest and charge Black women.

Here are just a few cases that demonstrate this troubling truth: A Black woman was made to put her infant child on the sidewalk so police could search the stroller for drugs (nothing was found).[2] When Miriam Carey was killed in a hail of bullets, her one-year-old daughter was in the backseat.[3] And a New York police officer put a woman who was seven months pregnant in a chokehold after a dispute over illegal grilling.[4] Illegal. Grilling. As in illegally cooking food. *Are you kidding me?!* Sadly, this is not a joke. It's all too real.

The names of Black women lost to police violence can't be swept under the rug. Rekia Boyd, Miriam Carey, Tanisha Anderson, Charleena Lyles, and too many others must be remembered and honored. The list grows tragically longer every day.

Racial discrimination and gender bias are part of the entire criminal justice system and fabric of our nation.[5] For instance, people of color are disproportionately represented in the roughly 2 million people who are in prison or jails nationwide despite the fact that in some areas, like drug use, white people are more likely to offend.[6] Here are some specifics: Even though people of color represented roughly 38 percent of the overall American population in 2016, at least 59 percent of the people in state prisons at that time were people of color. In fact, Black people are incarcerated at five times the rate of white people in state prisons.[7] "Nationwide, the criminal justice system is failing communities, hurting the economy and destroying families—and putting women and mothers disproportionately behind bars for drug and property crimes," wrote Monifa Bandele, vice president of MomsRising, in an article for the ACLU.[8]

Bringing actual justice to our criminal justice system is a core part of the modern women's rights movement. It's on us to raise the alarm and fight for fixes. That includes advocating for police reform and accountability; reforms in sentencing, bail, and prosecution; ending mandatory minimums and the death penalty; as well as largely divesting from the prison industrial complex, including for-profit prisons, prison labor beneficiaries, and satellite industries—all of which profit from incarceration.

Enough Is Enough

Enough is enough. Women's lives are at stake. Black lives matter. It's time for each of us to stand up and demand an end to what we're all seeing and reading in the news and on social media.

This is a women's rights issue. This is a national issue. This needs to stop.

The truth of the matter is that structural racism permeates our society, including within the criminal justice system. From the moment police are called or an officer decides to investigate a car on the road or a person walking down the street, an unjust system is activated. This system disproportionately punishes communities of color, leading to arrests, incarceration, and lifelong stigma for those caught in its grasp. And women of color face the compounded impact of violence both in the criminal justice system and everyday life. The United States has the highest incarceration rate in the world, with women among the fastest growing incarcerated populations.[9]

How did we get here? The path starts early, before a person commits a crime or is incarcerated. The cradle-to-prison pipeline begins in preschool, when Black kids are suspended at higher rates than white kids for the same actions.[10] *In preschool!* As mentioned, the pipeline extends to schools, where there are now more police than counselors in the largest public school districts.[11] And it goes on in the daily racial profiling that happens on our streets, in stores, and in our communities, where who gets pulled over—and who gets shot—too often hinges primarily on skin color. Studies prove these points over and over again.[12] The pipeline affects who gets arrested, why certain charges are chosen, how bail levels are set, who is sitting in jail. Structural racism is woven into our entire system, not just the criminal justice system, from the moment a child is born. Sexism is often added to the toxic mix, and the impact is too often brutal.

Too Many Women Are Trapped in a For-Profit Prison System

To make matters worse, there's a monetary incentive to continue this crisis in our nation: Private correctional facilities were a $4.8 billion industry in 2015, with profits of $629 million.[13] The numbers are horrifying. We are allowing an entrenched for-profit prison industrial complex—where companies run jails for profit—to run amok. That's part of the reason why the incarcerated population in the United States grew sevenfold over the past forty years, even as crime is going down.[14] Between 1980 and 2014, the number of women in prison in the United States increased by more than 700 percent. Currently 54 percent of all inmates are parents with children under the age of eighteen.[15] And right now over 60 percent of incarcerated women have at least one child under the age of eighteen.[16]

This is horrible. It hurts families and our children, and the cost of incarceration is sky high for taxpayers. The *Federal Register* estimates that the average cost is $31,977.65 per year per incarcerated person,[17] and in some states, like California, where the cost is $75,560 per person per year,[18] the cost is much higher. Imagine if those funds were largely spent on education instead.

All of this adds up. It adds up to a lot. A regularly cited statistic puts the cost at $80 billion per year, and a new study from Washington University in St. Louis found the true cost, one that takes in the community and family impact, to be much higher: more than $1 trillion per year.[19] That's trillion with a *t*.

The costs aren't limited to dollars. With over 1 million women under the supervision of the criminal justice system in the United States,[20] it's easy to see that the economics of incarceration is costing our economy. But that's not all. Mass incarceration is costing women's families. "Imagine you're a seven-year-old girl, you come home from school, and your mom's not there," well-known advocate and attorney Amanda DuBois said. "The mom has been arrested for something, but the little girl has no way of knowing where her mother is or what's going on. The child doesn't get to say goodbye. Her mom doesn't have any time to make arrangements because if somebody gets arrested, they just get thrown in jail."

There are tens of thousands of women who haven't been convicted of any crime at all, but who are sitting in jail simply because they can't afford bail. This means that little girls or boys are without their moms due to minor crimes like having a suspended driver's license. Women, including moms, can be thrown in the county jail without the ability to make bail for weeks or months even though they haven't been convicted of a crime. When we have for-profit companies operating our prisons, these companies are more likely to push for laws and procedures that send people to jail and to prison for longer periods of time. We shouldn't live in a society where companies have an incentive to tear up families in order to improve their bottom line. As Amanda concludes, "We're traumatizing families over and over." This shouldn't be happening. As women and mothers, we must look out for these details, like the need for bail reform that are in emergency need of fixing, and look out for each other.

Mass Incarceration Harms Children

Carol is an elementary school teacher who has taught many students whose parents either are or were incarcerated. She's seen firsthand that incarceration has traumatic effects on families, particularly for children who grow up without a parent in the home. Carol notes, "Many people who are incarcerated have not committed violent crimes, or are not actually guilty of their crimes, and are disproportionately people of color. Our society requires radical justice and sentencing reform to humanize families and children who are victims of criminal injustice."

Carol's right. When it comes to children and trauma, psychologists have created a list of adverse childhood experiences (ACEs) to determine if a child needs support and intervention. Not surprisingly, having a parent in prison is an ACE. To figure out a child's overall ACE score, each type of trauma counts as one point. The points are added to tally a total score.[21]

Some ACEs relate to the child's own experience: physical

abuse, verbal abuse, sexual abuse, physical neglect, and emotional neglect. Others relate to the family environment: a parent who's an alcoholic, a mother who's a victim of domestic violence, a family member in jail, a family member diagnosed with a mental illness, and the disappearance of a parent through divorce, death, or abandonment.

While the ACE study measured only ten types of childhood trauma, Jane Stevens, founder and publisher of the ACEs Connection Network, also notes that recent ACE surveys are adding other evaluation experiences, including racism, bullying, witnessing violence outside the home, gender discrimination, witnessing a sibling being abused, experiencing war, involvement with the foster care system, involvement with the juvenile justice system, witnessing a father being abused, and poverty.[22]

We know that ACEs can have damaging effects on a child's development, and we also know that early learning is an important time to intervene and build resiliency in kids to stave off these damaging impacts. A lot of new research is showing that particular ACEs can have long-lasting negative impacts on children, but if early intervention and support are provided, then that negative impact can be diminished.[23]

"There is a huge ripple effect from the mass incarceration of women through families," notes Amanda DuBois. "Here's an example: You have trauma in your childhood. Then you got in a domestic violence situation as an adult. You became a drug addict. You ended up in prison. And the next thing you know your children are being taken away from you. So, instead of treating people who have addiction problems as a medical problem, which is what it is, they throw them in prison, and then they take away their children. And that carries the trauma on."

Nadia knows firsthand how harmful our country's harsh

sentencing policies can be for children and families. When her father was incarcerated for a nonviolent drug charge, it was devastating to their family. Though Nadia's father was a veteran with no prior criminal history, due to our country's harsh sentencing laws, he was locked away instead of getting the counseling and treatment that he needed.

Nadia told me, "My father's imprisonment was disastrous for us emotionally and economically. It forced us to move into public housing and to rely on food stamps, and led me to finance my own college education." Nadia isn't the only daughter or son negatively impacted by America's failed—and failing—system of mass incarceration. One in three Americans now has a criminal record, our prisons are overcrowded, and families are being torn apart.[24]

Solving the Crisis

Women are being impacted by incarceration in big ways. Two-thirds of the women in federal prisons are serving time for challenges related to nonviolent drug use.[25] Instead of increasing public safety, current sentencing laws have led to a massive sweeping of nonviolent offenders into prisons, harming women, costing at least a billion taxpayer dollars,[26] and fracturing families like Nadia's.[27]

It's important to take a look at who is incarcerated and why in order to figure out how we can begin to solve this crisis.[28] To start, mandatory minimums have been used against communities of color at a staggeringly disproportionate rate. According to the U.S. Sentencing Commission, approximately 70 percent of mandatory minimums are imposed on Black and Latino individuals.[29] Compounding these numbers are so-called three strikes penalties that mandate life sentences for certain individuals if they have three convictions in certain areas of the law. Additional studies show that Black women are eight times more likely than white women to be incarcerated, and Latina women are four times more likely to be incarcerated.[30] This isn't fair.

Women are among those who are hit hardest by the extreme unfairness in our criminal justice system. The trauma of the criminal justice system is all too often added on top of personal trauma in a vicious cycle that we must help break. For instance, the overwhelming majority of women in prison are survivors of domestic violence. Three-quarters have histories of severe physical abuse by an intimate partner during adulthood, and 82 percent suffered serious physical or sexual abuse as children.[31] This means that women who experience violence in their daily lives are also astronomically more likely to experience harm by our criminal justice system.

Compounded Harm

Too often incarceration compounds harm, not heals it. One heartbreaking fact is that girls and women who are victims of sex trafficking are regularly arrested on prostitution charges and incarcerated rather than being supported as survivors of violence, whereas the men who exploit them are rarely prosecuted or punished. The subsequent time in prison compounds the trauma these girls and women have already experienced.[32]

Another is the prevalence of prison rape. According to the Department of Justice, an estimated 4 percent of state and federal prison inmates and 3.2 percent of jail inmates report experiencing one or more incidents of sexual victimization by another inmate or facility staff.[33] But we know this number is a gross underestimate, given that these are only the instances of abuse in prison that are reported.

These are just two examples of compounding harm. But make no mistake, harsh sentencing practices, without any access to counseling and treatment, regularly do more harm than good.

Further, strict penalties designed to combat the distribution of illegal drugs have done little to stem the drug trade. Instead, the result has been a massive influx of incarcerating people experiencing challenges related to drug addiction into an ever-expanding criminal justice system that fractures families and wastes resources that would be infinitely better invested in community services, schools, rehabilitation services, and health care. For instance, in-prison vocational programs—which are largely lacking in today's for-profit system—produce a return of $12.62 for every dollar invested.[34]

But too often, instead of investing in people, incarcerated people are taken advantage of by the prison industrial complex. One example of this happened as the 2017 wildfires raged across the West, ripping through neighborhoods and forests, and raining ash and fire on cities: Women inmates in California were paid just $1 per hour, with a bonus of $2 per day, to work on the hazardous front lines of the fires. These imprisoned women earned only a fraction of the $40,000 per year that firefighters earn, despite performing the same job. The inmates were saving lives and land on the front lines without the pay but with all the hazards, including breathing toxic air that could leave lasting negative impacts on their lungs.[35]

Our Families

Our justice system is failing families, damaging women and children, and hurting our economy. We are living in a time when more than 2.7 million children in the United States have an incarcerated parent[36] (1 in 28 children[37])—and around 35 million children in the United States—nearly half of U.S. children—now have at least one parent with a criminal record.[38,39]

Jessica, who grew up with an incarcerated parent, highlights the importance of reconsidering how we value family in society. "Sentencing women of low-income families for harsh drug or minor offenses keeps mothers away for years," she suggests. She advises that instead of investing time trying to keep family apart from one another, we should try to do the best we can to keep families together.

Joana, at only one and a half years old, was still nursing when she was separated from her mother after they crossed the southern border into the United States, seeking safety. It was three very long months of separation until the toddler was finally reunited with her mother.[40] Joana and her mother were placed in detention centers, which is a form of incarceration. Most of these centers are for-profit, unsafe, unsanitary, and far away from where pro bono attorneys can easily come to help. This last fact is important, because studies show that the majority of women coming from the southern border would qualify for asylum if they had access to an attorney.[41] It should be noted that not only is it legal to seek asylum in our nation, it's also an international human right.[42]

Yet human rights abuses are happening in the name of immigration enforcement, including separations like baby Joana and her mom experienced. They also aren't happening by accident.[43] Shortly after taking office, Trump proposed that the Department of Homeland Security enact a policy of purposefully separating children and mothers who are seeking asylum at our southern border.[44]

This is damaging on a number of levels. Evidence shows that kids who are separated from their parents after dangerous journeys north are often retraumatized, and experts agree that "prolonged separations from parents have profound disruptive influence on children's development."[45]

Recent court cases give a glimpse into detention center conditions that are horrific.[46] Conditions in facilities show the use of *hieleras*, or iceboxes, to detain people, as well as forcing people to sleep on cold floors, amid trash, for days without soap, showers, hot water, or beds. Conditions like these are nothing short of human rights abuse in the name of immigration enforcement.

There's no question: Allowing human rights abuses in the name of immigration or law enforcement is wrong. Our current approach relating to prisons, jails, and immigration detention centers is nothing short of devastating. Excessive incarceration continues to do harm. The continued growth of incarceration in America perpetuates cycles of poverty for women and entrenches structural racism.[47]

Racial Profiling Must Stop

We need smart reform—yesterday—that will positively impact millions of families across the country, reduce the billions of taxpayer dollars we're spending on the federal justice system, and improve community safety. Sentencing, bail, and police reforms, along with strengthening treatment, rehabilitation, and counseling programs, are a necessity. One way to see who is valued and who isn't in our nation is to see who is disproportionately incarcerated in our prison system; another is to take a look at who is disproportionately harmed or killed by the police. Racial profiling and police brutality are major aspects of mass incarceration in our nation that can't be ignored. People are dying.

Diamond Reynolds and her four-year-old daughter were driving in the car with her fiancé, Philando Castile, a much-loved longtime local school worker in St. Anthony, Minnesota, when they were pulled over by police for a broken taillight on July 6, 2016.

Within one minute of being pulled over, Castile was killed by seven bullets from a police officer while still wearing his seatbelt as Diamond and her daughter sat just inches away.[48] Dashcam footage shows that Castile did nothing wrong. Yet the police officer who killed him was acquitted of all charges.[49]

Diamond livestreamed her horror, terror, and despair on Facebook in the immediate aftermath while still in the car, drawing the attention of tens of millions. Heartbreaking. Beyond tragic. Tears. Sitting in that seat next to her dying boyfriend while she and her daughter were in the firing line was a form of violence itself. Police brutality is a form of violence against women, as is racism. Diamond's four-year-old-daughter will never be the same.

The numbers are stark and should be a wake-up call for all women—no matter our race. Black people are three times more likely to be killed by police than whites[50]—and young Black men are twenty-one times more likely to be killed by police than young white men.[51]

Twenty-one times more likely to be killed by police.

This is not okay. This is why we must chant "Black Lives Matter" in the women's movement—and is also why the Black Lives Matter movement, co-founded by three women, Patrisse Khan-Cullors, Alicia Garza, and Opal Tometi, won a global peace prize from the Sydney Peace Foundation in 2017.[52]

No mother, father, son, daughter, friend, beloved, or family member should have to fear the loss of a loved one at the hands of police officers who are sworn to serve and protect us. But this type of violence happens all too often. Philando Castile was one of 963 people shot and killed by the police in 2016 alone.[53]

This has to stop. Together, we can build systems of policing and law enforcement that are accountable to the people they are charged to protect. Reforms should include training police to de-escalate violence, understand mental health emergencies, render first aid on the scene, and apply a good-faith standard for the use of deadly force, and the removal of the de facto immunity that police have today. Also, we must insist upon completely independent investigations of use of deadly force when there is injury or death, and bring diverse community stakeholders to the table for the development of standards and curriculum.

Violence against women, against communities, comes in many forms. Police brutality rooted in racial profiling or otherwise is one tragic form of violence against women. To be clear, it's not just men of color who are targeted and harmed; women of color are harmed by this violence, too—both directly and indirectly— and are all too often invisible and ignored. The statistics speak for themselves: In 2013, Black women accounted for 53 percent of all women stopped by police,[54] even though Black women only make up 13 percent of the female population in the United States,[55] and Black women account for 20 percent of unarmed people of color killed by the police between 1999 and 2014.[56]

TACKLING THE ELEPHANTS IN THE ROOM

———

Let's talk about some of the many elephants in the room. Often, I hear questions—mostly from people who look like me, who don't have to insist that their lives matter—after someone is killed or injured by an authority figure like, "Well, what did the victim do wrong?"

Before we go on, I hope we can all agree that even if someone did something wrong or was imperfect in some way (and we are all imperfect, by the way), the punishment should never be immediate death.

Because of this we must proactively stand up and say "Black Lives Matter." It's not because *anyone's* lives matter less; it's because structural racism permeates our culture, rendering Black people at far greater risk of violence, which necessitates that we have to specifically say Black. Lives. Matter.

Stand Up, Speak Out

Our country was built on the concept of innocent until proven guilty, in writing at least. But the statistics show that the rampant practice of racial profiling by law enforcement is conducted in a manner that too often presumes that people of color are considered guilty until proven innocent.

The high incarceration rate isn't the "fault" of people of color, as many have insinuated. Instead, racial profiling is alive and well, doing harm in America throughout every aspect of our criminal justice system. For example, the *St. Louis Post-Dispatch* editorial board found that racial profiling is all too common, and the stats are getting worse over time: "Black Missourians were 66 percent more likely in 2013 to be stopped by police, and Blacks and Hispanics were both more likely to be searched, even though the likelihood of finding contraband was higher among Whites."[57] Further, studies show that people of color have higher drug-related arrest rates even though they aren't more likely to use or sell illegal drugs than white people.[58] Racial profiling adds up in incredibly unfair and deadly ways.

Women Are Rising

Women are rising to make our country better. In 2016 in New York State, a group of twelve mothers who lost their children to police murders worked with an organization called the Justice Committee to design an executive order appointing a special prosecutor for instances where police killed civilians.[59]

Why is this important? There's inherent conflict of interest between prosecutors and police officers because they work together every day in their regular jobs.[60] These relationships factor in when local prosecutors have to decide whether to press charges against local police officers or not. Studies show the chances of prosecution are lower when the victim is Black or brown.[61] For instance, *in the last fifteen years, at least 179 people—86 percent whom were Black or brown—have been killed by on-duty NYPD officers. Only three of the tragic police killings led to an indictment, and only one of the officers has been convicted.*[62]

Due to the efforts of these twelve moms and the organizations that had their backs, the bill passed. New York State now has a special prosecutor for police killings. This victory led by women of color is a shining example of what other states and our federal government can and should do immediately.

Checking Implicit Bias

Why is this happening? Implicit bias adds up to violence. I went to high school in Maryland in the 1980s, when the murder rate in the District of Columbia and Baltimore was among the highest in the nation. I lived right between those two cities. On more than one occasion I found myself ducking and crawling beneath a car because a gun was pulled. On more than one occasion police came to break up the chaos.

Never did the police look twice at me, a blond white girl. They looked at my friends, though. I remember one moment when I was in high school like it was yesterday. The police came to break up a party where a gun had been pulled amid the dancing. A deep, unfriendly quiet had come over the darkened house. And as I stood near the side of the room and looked around, I saw that my friends who were Black, and who had done nothing wrong, were in handcuffs as I stood free from police scrutiny.

I'm a witness. The police, at least where I grew up, racially profiled in extremely unfair ways.

Unchecked implicit bias results in subconscious decisions made not just at the individual level but also at the institutional and societal levels on who to hire, fire, pay more or pay less, as well as who to suspect of criminality, and, as a result, impacts who is arrested and incarcerated and who gets killed when police respond. Study after study shows racial bias woven through our criminal justice system[63]—and there's no doubt that racial bias in our criminal justice system is doing harm to families, to our safety, to our freedoms, and to our democracy. It's on us to stop it.

The Impact of Our Generation

Our future grandchildren and great-grandchildren will likely read about our generation in history books. They will ask us what we were doing when these human rights abuses were happening, when the United States had the highest incarceration rate in the world.

People created this system, so we can fix it, too. Women are needed to fight for reforms in every aspect of our criminal justice system, from fair policing standards and better accountability to changes in sentencing, bail, and prosecution; ending mandatory minimums and the death penalty; and also largely divesting from the for-profit prison industrial complex and investing in our families and children. Part of fixing the system is also giving back the right to vote to the over 6 million people who have been stripped of that right because they've had a conviction.[64]

Our generation is facing a crisis in the criminal justice system. There is a severe lack of equity and equality in the entire system, and it's long past time for us all to stand up to fix it. We want to be able to say that we, as a community of women, did everything we could to lift women and children like Joana, Jessica, and Nadia, and to prevent women from experiencing tragedies like those that befell women like Rekia Boyd, Miriam Carey, Tanisha Anderson, Charleena Lyles, and Diamond Reynolds. As women we must stand together. The violence must stop.

How to Change Minds

Ever wanted to meet with a powerful decision maker or influencer?[65] Now's the time! Setting up a meeting with an influential decision maker or elected leader at any level of government (or their staff) is easier and less uncomfortable than many people think. In fact, these meetings can often be fun!

Even if you don't have a lot of common ground with an individual leader, for the most part these leaders are polite and considerate and will spend time absorbing and understanding the information that you bring to their attention in a meeting. That being said, persistence is often key here. I've seen many elected officials change their minds over time. Sometimes it takes a couple years of meetings and organizing, so don't give up if a particular leader doesn't agree with you the first time you meet.

In-person meetings also pack political power because they demonstrate that people are tracking and prioritizing an issue, which then helps a leader focus on that particular issue. In-person meetings also allow time for the legislator to hear what's happening with their constituents in a way that helps them champion solutions.

You don't have to fly to Washington, DC, to make this happen. Members of Congress have local offices, as do your state legislators, county council members, and city council members. Don't be worried if the meeting ends up being with a staff person. Members of Congress in particular deal with such a wide variety of issues that they often delegate specific staff to focus on different policy areas. Getting a key staffer involved can be critical to moving policy forward.

Here are some tips for setting up and attending a high-impact meeting with any influencer, local leader, or decision maker:

- **Look online to find the nearest office to your home.**
  Search online for the nearest office of the elected leader that
  you want to meet with in order to find their phone number
  and office location.

- **Figure out if you're meeting alone or bringing friends.**
  Bringing friends can be fun and maximize your impact.

- **Pick up the phone to schedule your meeting.** Let the
  person who answers the phone know that you're a constituent, share briefly the topic that you'd like to meet
  about, and let them know how many people will be coming and if any organizations will be represented. Then ask
  for your meeting. If they suggest you meet with a staff
  person, then be sure to ask to meet with the staff person
  who is assigned to cover the policy area that you're going
  in to discuss. Be aware that sometimes it takes weeks to
  get a meeting on the books. Don't be afraid to check back
  in with them if you don't get a date the first or even the
  second time you call. Also, feel free to leave a voicemail
  message that says something like: *Hi, my name is _____ and
  I'm a constituent. I have a quick question. Please call me back at
  this number _____.*

- **Research the elected leader's position on your policy
  area.** Before your meeting, take some time on the Internet
  to find out how your candidate has stood in the past on the
  issue area you're coming in to discuss, as well as to get their
  full name and title and some background from their biogra-
  phy on their website. See if you find any common interests
  that could help move your conversation forward.

- **Pick your top three talking points for the meeting.** What are the three points you want to get across about your issue? Write down your very short three main points and print them out before you go in for the meeting. Bring stories to share if you have them, and feel free to succinctly share your own experience, too. Don't forget to figure out your "ask." Do you want them to vote yes or no on a certain policy? If so, let them know!

- **Bring friends and/or colleagues!** Bringing a small group, no more than six people, with a variety of different perspectives but a shared goal on an issue can be highly effective.

- **Have a pre-meeting with your group.** Make time to meet with the people going with you, even if it's just a short time alone for fifteen minutes right before your meeting, to figure out who is saying what and how. (Feel free to make the pre-meeting fun— bring chocolates, cupcakes, or something yummy to share. Make it a meeting that people will want to do again.)

Here's a sample agenda for a pre-meeting:

- Make sure everyone agrees on the goal of the meeting. Is it to tell an elected leader to vote yes or no on a certain bill? Is it to start thinking about a new policy area? Make sure everyone in the room is looking for the same outcome so you don't accidentally contradict one another. Also, be sure that your group agrees to talk about the same policy area— and understands that focusing on only one policy area in your meeting will have the most impact.
- Do a very basic review of the legislation or topic you're going in to meet about so everyone is on the same page.

This review doesn't have to be a lengthy report; it can be a paragraph. Look up where it is in the legislative process (or ask the legislator's staff), as well as where the legislator stands so far on it, and share that info with the group.

- Figure out what each person will say in the meeting and the order in which you all will be speaking. Choose a person to lead your meeting—i.e., your lead communicator, who will get the meeting started and keep it going. Pick a note taker and determine who will make the "ask." (Example: *Can we count on your support to vote [YES/NO] on ___ bill?*) Make sure everyone knows the game plan.
- Be sure to provide a mixture of information: some facts, a story or two, and the "ask." Leave time to listen, too!

In your meeting, make sure to do the following:

- The lead communicator should tell the elected leader why you're there, what bill number or policy you care about, and how you hope they'll vote and then introduce the rest of the group.
- If you brought a small group, consider opening by going around a circle and each sharing why this matters to you very briefly. Make sure the top three points about the issue you're there to discuss are covered among everyone. Feel free to share a personal story. Just keep it brief. A two-minute story can pack tremendous power.
- Make sure someone makes the ask: *Can we count on your [YES/NO] vote for ___ bill or policy?*
- If they respond positively to your ask, then thank them and ask how you can help and if there are other leaders

you should reach out to in particular so you can build even more support for change.

■ If they are not supportive, don't argue. Try to politely find out why they don't support your position (Example: *I'm sad to hear that. Can you share why? I'd love to know more.*)—and if there is any information or resources that seem like it could help them change their mind, then offer to try to follow up with those.

■ Thank them for meeting with you.

■ In addition to getting support on your issue, in-person meetings are about building relationships with the decision maker. Write to say thank you after your meeting and be sure to provide any requested materials. If they commit to a specific action, also be sure to write to thank them if they do what you requested.

In your meeting, make sure *not* to do any of these things:

■ Don't feel intimidated! Lawmakers work for all of us, and are human just like us. It's their job to listen to constituents. That's you! Not only do you have a right to be there, this is how democracy is supposed to work.

■ Don't think you have to be an authority on every microscopic detail on the issue. Feel free to say, "I don't know." You are an expert on personal experiences, which happen to be what matters the most. Having a PhD in technical policy specifics isn't necessary.

■ Don't talk for too long at any one time. Your time there is limited so prioritize sharing your three key points and your "ask."

■ Enjoy! This is what democracy and fighting for change is all about. This is how things get done. You're changing the world for the better. Thank you!

Conclusion

You. Are. Needed. The earth moved with the power of our feet at the Women's March, but that was just the beginning. We got a glimpse of how very much power we have together during that march, just as this book gave you a glimpse of how much there is to fix and improve upon for each and every woman, child, and family in America.

Now it's up to you to help create the next chapter. Now more than ever you, the person reading this page, are needed. Now more than ever our earth-shaking, marching feet together are necessary to lift every single person in our nation. This book is both a love letter and a call to action to all the women who marched and who have been—and who are—standing up for justice in our nation and around the world. It's a valentine to the leaders who are stepping forward in big and small ways every day to support our democracy, women, families, communities, and future.

The book you're holding in your hands is titled *Keep Marching* for a reason. If you've already been doing the important work, please keep going. If you haven't jumped in yet, it's time to step up. As you step up, know that leadership doesn't have to look exactly like it has in the past. At this moment in our history, we don't need a single, charismatic leader; we need many leaders. We need to include more voices from every corner of our nation. We need more doers and more marchers at the local, state, and national levels. We need leaders who represent a broad American experience, who give voice to the hopes and dreams of all our communities and families. We need you.

It's time for us to open doors to new forms of leadership for each other. Leadership can be standing up to hate in an online post; sharing your experience with a member of Congress, a corporate leader, or the media; signing your name on a letter to elected leaders; stepping in when a child is getting bullied; making sure you always (always!) vote and reminding your friends to do the same; taking time to write a letter to the editor or to call elected leaders; attending local meetings with other people to push for a policy; visiting your city council, state legislature, or Congress; running for office or supporting someone else who does; advocating for policies to be updated in your state legislature or workplaces or Congress; organizing people in your local or regional community; starting a local #KeepMarching Circle; and so much more.

Keep in mind that you don't have to do everything to have an impact. I've shared a wide variety of different tactics and tips in this book. Do what feels right for you, and what's accessible. We will need to use a variety of different tactics and cover a wide spectrum of issues among all of us in order to make the big changes our nation needs. Every action that each of us takes has an impact; but no one person has to do it all.

We win when multiple voices, perspectives, and strategies, along with many layers of different tactics, are heard and happen at the same time. We win when many organizations and people are engaged across many different policy areas and approaches. And we win when leadership includes the most impacted people among us—as well as when we follow the vision and leadership of people who have firsthand experience with the issues we're hoping to change and the solutions we're working to move forward.

We also win by focusing on agreeing on big things and agreeing to disagree on little things (and to treat each other with grace as we do). To do this movement right, we have to embrace our imperfections, love the many ways that people are working to do and be better, treat each other with dignity and respect, and open as many avenues for voices to be heard in as many ways as possible.

What's needed right now is for every woman to step up. What's needed is you. We all can be leaders, defined in the way and in the time that works best for us.

But please—don't wait. As you've seen on the pages that you hold in your hands, your voice is urgently needed—and not just to help fight for equity and equality, but also to help protect our democracy. Together we truly can create a country where women, families, and businesses thrive. As we do that, always know, in the words of dream hampton, an award-winning filmmaker and author, that "Our solidarity doesn't have to be built on our suffering. It can also be built on resistance and our will to create a better world."

Dream big. Envision the nation we want for the future—a nation with gender justice, racial justice, and economic justice, not just what we need to resist now. We can build power together, knowing that the whole of all of us is greater than any one individual. And also knowing that every little and big thing you do counts.

Resist, Persist, Enlist, and Effect Change

The task of building women's power can be daunting. We will not always agree on everything. Know that our aim is to celebrate our differences as we unite together. Remember to breathe and to believe. Know that we together really do carry the impact and power to help build a better nation. And so do our votes. Vote in every election possible, both in the primary and the general elections—and remind everyone you know to register to vote and to vote, too. We have a case of voting anemia in America. The data shows that not everyone who is registered to vote is voting, and that not all eligible voters are even registered to vote in the first place. Case in point: Donald Trump was elected president of the United States of America with just 27 percent of eligible voters casting a ballot for him, due to low voter engagement.[1] In short, you know a ton of people who are eligible to vote but aren't voting. It's time to get those people involved and to the polls—because every vote at the city, county, state, and national levels does count.

U.S. Representative Rosa DeLauro recently shared an important reminder that we not only need to reach out to Congress about our policy priorities, we also need to remember our power at the ballot box: "People need to write, people need to call, and to use all of the tools at our disposal to let members of Congress know that they are at risk of not being reelected if they ignore us. If some members of Congress are willing to put millions of people in this country at risk, they need to know that they are at risk for not coming back to the U.S. House of Representatives because the voters will make another choice. They need to know that we will find candidates who in fact will champion the cause of working families in this nation if they won't step up."

Keep on Your Toes

Stay alert. There have been champions for women and families in both the Democratic and Republican parties in the past, so don't write people off blindly. If we ever write all the people in one party completely off, then we're closing the door on being able to maximize our power for change. For instance, in 2017, thirteen

Republican Washington State senators moved forward one of the most progressive and visionary paid family/medical leave policies in the country and worked with Democrats to help pass it. This was a huge win. This groundbreaking state legislation never would have happened without Republicans because Democrats, who championed and voted unanimously for the critically important bill, simply didn't have enough votes to pass the bill on their own.

In this instance and many others, the political calculus for winning should always be held close: Protect the base (the champions who we know are on our side), persuade the swing (people who can be convinced to be on our side, and this includes people of all parties), and forget about those in the absolute opposition that will never vote for the policy we seek. Which elected leaders are in the base for a policy, the swing, and the opposition will change from policy to policy, so it's important to keep on your toes. It's also important to hold all leaders accountable as we continue to persist, enlist, and insist on everyone having the opportunity to thrive. And we can never forget that when we march together, we are an incredibly powerful force.

START A #KEEPMARCHING CIRCLE

One way to make a difference is to join our #KeepMarching project. If you're fired up in defense of the rights of women, families, communities, and our country and are ready to gather your family, friends, and neighbors to stand strong against hate and for policies that lift us all, then consider signing up to be a #KeepMarching Circle leader.

Here's how it works: In the #KeepMarching Circles, women organize with their friends, family, and other personal networks for discussions and maybe even to take action together. Moms-Rising will provide discussion topics, advice, policy information, and legislative updates. We'll also give you resources to support and amplify your efforts, such as issue tool kits, training, and social media support. MomsRising also gives #KeepMarching members regular, specific, and timely actions they can take as individuals or as Circles that mirror the actions being coordinated by the campaign teams. As always, you participate as much as you'd like—there's no pressure. And, it's free, of course. Interested? Sign up at http://keepmarching.momsrising.org.

You Are Not Alone

The pages before this one included a lot of heavy data and sad truths. How much further we have to go to reach equity and equality can feel flat-out overwhelming at times. But don't wallow in that overwhelmed feeling. Instead, remember that you're not alone and use any "Oh $hit, it's worse than I thought" feelings to fuel your steps forward.

I know that simply hearing that you as an individual and we collectively as women have power often isn't enough. If you ever feel overwhelmed, just take a moment, take a deep breath or three, and imagine yourself in the middle of the Women's March of January 2017, which was the largest outpouring of people on a single day in the history of our nation.[2] Feel the rushing crowd that contained people of all ages, races and ethnicities, genders, sexualities, abilities, income levels, religions, shapes, and sizes from every state in the nation who spanned as far as the eye could see in many cities, with powerful, funny, outraged, fierce, and righteous signs raised high in the air.

The power of that roaring crowd is at your back. Resources like this book and many organizations are there for you. We're all in this together. Understand that we don't have to solve everything at the exact same time—and that every single step we each take makes a ripple of positive changes. Don't give up. You're not alone.

This Book Is Yours

It is my hope that readers use this book, the policies, the tips and tactics, and the resources on the pages to help lead the way forward, up, and out of our current crisis—and to continue on to help build a nation of opportunity that we all dream possible for ourselves, for our nation's children, and for future generations. It's time to resist destructive policy that's proposed, *and* to proactively insist on moving forward solutions-oriented policies like those detailed in this book. It's time to rise, to be advocates, to vote, to build an ever-stronger movement together.

So take out a pen and make this book your own: Underline what you like, write in new ideas, scratch out what you don't agree with, and write in the phone numbers of friends you want to march forward with in the days and months ahead.

It's also my hope that after you read these pages, you pass along this book or get a copy for a friend, so it can be picked up, like a baton, in homes across America. You see, to do this right, to win, we have to build what Detroit-based organizer Adrienne Maree Brown calls for: a strong "leaderful movement." We have to mesh our networks together as we also take action individually, and rise together as incredibly powerful, imperfect, beautiful hell-raisers for justice in order to win together.

That's what real democracy is about.

We have to imagine the better world and then reach for it. And we can make that reach knowing that we are stunningly powerful when we rise together. Now is our moment. Stand with the people you see lifting love. Invest in the positive. Find beauty in imperfection. Appreciate and lift one another. Be kind. Turn toward those who are different from you and listen closely. Look for opportunities to do good and step into those moments. Try to leave your community, state, nation, and world—not just ourselves—a little bit better than you found it (because you can't take it with you after all). We each have a limited time on this planet. Let's make the most of it.

We all have a stake in making sure everyone has a chance to thrive, and there is a tremendous amount on the line. It's time to stand, to march, to rise for each other—and, as we rise, we can never forget that gender justice is racial justice is economic justice. One won't happen without the others.

We rise knowing our movement isn't about one day, one election, one Oval Office, one woman, or one piece of legislation. Knowing that the arc of justice bends only when we act. Knowing that together we are the fierce, determined, and intersectional leaders our nation needs.

Generations of work brought us here today and future generations are counting on us to stand up now. We will not back down. I believe in us. I believe in our power and our voices. I know you do, too. Women have moved mountains in the past, we're doing it now, and we'll do so in the future, too.

So step into your leaderfulness.

And keep marching!

Acknowledgments

This book would quite literally not be possible without a whole team of brilliant people playing major roles in its creation. First and foremost, it owes its very existence to the superstars at Moms-Rising, including its members, volunteers, and team. This book comes directly out of our work together, our stories, and the expertise of every single person in our movement. This book is yours, and is the reason why 100 percent of the proceeds of this book go to MomsRising to help provide the fuel to keep us all marching.

Many leaders helped bring this book into the world, and some were there every step of the way. I'm looking at especially Donna Norton, Monifa Bandele, Ruth Martin, and dream hampton. Thank you. These women braved many versions of chapters at all times of the day. Thank you for fielding dozens of emails, phone calls, and texts with more questions than I can count, and for the massive amount of brilliance you shared. This book would not be in existence without you. And, the entire movement wouldn't be strong without you, either. Donna Norton, your leadership in founding and building MomsRising from the very start—over the past eleven years—has been absolutely essential to our success. We wouldn't be where we are today without you. Monifa Bandele, your vision has created an unstoppable movement and advanced an incredible number of wins, and your leadership has shaped and built our organization and nation. I'm in awe. Ruth Martin, you turn ideas into action, and while we are millions strong, your leadership leverages our power and makes our marches fruitful. dream hampton, your wisdom and insights always lead to the truth of these issues. I don't know how you do it, but I'm thankful you do! The words, ideas, and inspiration you all provide are woven into every sentence of this book. I wish there was a way to convey how grateful I am, but these are the best I can do here: *Thank you.*

To everyone who went above and beyond in contributing their ideas and policy expertise to this book project, I'm eternally grateful. Beth Messersmith offered invaluable help by leading the way on envisioning, outlining, and creating *The #KeepMarching Moms-Rising Advocacy and Organizing Tactics and Tips* guide, which laid the framework for many of the action plans in the book. I'm also thankful to Gloria Pan for her expertise on all things gun safety, #KeepMarching organizing, and wordsmithing; Sara Alcid, who shared expertise on workplace justice; Beatriz Beckford for her expertise on how to break the school-to-prison pipeline, social emotional development, trauma-informed care, and education; Nina Perez for her expertise in dual language learning, early learning, and more; Felicia Willems for her expertise on health care policy; Xochitl Oseguera, Khadija Gurnah, and Carolina Rubio for their brilliance in immigration policy; Nadia Hussain for her expertise in maternal justice; Elyssa Koidin Schmeir for her expertise in budget and tax policy; Lauren Hipp for expertise in early learning, dual language learning, pre-K, and childcare; Sili Recio for expertise in social media and content; Danielle Ness for graphics, images, and artistry; Nathan White for all things technology; Olivia Roskill for helping pull together the stories; Keisha Robinson for keeping everything on track; Lisa Lederer for rapid grammar fixes and wordsmithing brainstorming; Marc Boone for beautiful images; and Maggie Humphreys for her expertise on economic security policies and how to run for office—and win! The best of this book reflects the brilliance and passion you all bring to these issues.

A standing ovation to the MomsRising team, who provided information, expertise, ideas, inspiration, and brilliance, including Sara Alcid, Beatriz Beckford, Christina D' Allesandro, Diarra Diouf, Abbie Gately, Khadija Gurnah, Lauren Hipp, Donna Hoffman Cullinan, Sarah Howard, Maggie Humphreys, Nadia Hussain, Anita Jackson, Patrisse Khan-Cullors, Elyssa Koidin Schmeir, Ruth Martin, Rosie McLaughlin, Beth Messersmith, Susan Milotich, Danielle Ness, Casey Osborn-Hinman, Xochitl Oseguera, Gloria Pan, Nina Perez, Sili Recio, Migdalia Rivera, Keisha Robinson, Tina Sherman, Karen Showalter, Ruby Sinreich, Mason Trapp, Nathan White, Jennifer Whitley, and Felicia Willems. And a giant special thank-you to the one and only Joan Blades for being a founder of MomsRising in 2006 and helping to spark a movement that's now over a million women strong. I am humbled and honored every day to work with you all on the MomsRising team.

To the members of MomsRising: Thank you. Thank you for leading the way, sharing your stories, calling elected leaders, sending letters, signing petitions, attending meetings, organizing, and so much more. You inspired this book. Thank you.

Meghan Stevenson, word wrangler, your talents helping to take this to the finish line on a tight timeline are awe-inspiring. Thank you also to Robin Templeton for early and important edits, to Stacy Phillips Booth for making sure the endnotes were beautiful and perfect, and to Jill Marr for moving mountains for this book. Sarah Jane Glynn, data detective extraordinaire—I don't know how you do it, but every number and data source seems to be at your fingertips. Thank you, Sarah Jane, for making this book well researched and definitely not fake news. My dear friend and brilliant reality checker, Kirstin Larson, offered incisive edits and well-timed perspective for which I'm incredibly grateful. And a giant thank-you to Krishan Trotman for believing in this book and bringing it to life!

Thanks also go to Rinku Sen, Pramila Jayapal, Elisa Batista, Celinda Lake, Rebecca Cokley, Holly Finkbeiner, Kimberlé Crenshaw, Kim Gandy, Erin Villardi, Shireen Mitchell, Ai-jen Poo, Alicia Garza, Miriam Yeung, Lucy McBath, Cheryl Contee, Yiqing Dong, Carmen Perez, Linda Sarsour, Bob Bland, Janaye Ingram, Sarah Sophie Flicker, Paola Mendoza, Tamika Mallory, Mary Olivella, Ashley Boyd, Adam Bartz, asha bandele, Ann Crittenden, Mia Birdsong, Allison Branham, Scott Dudley, Katie Bethell, and Ilyse Hogue for inspiring me and sharing their brilliance for this book and over the years.

Thank you also to the women who have led the way and on whose shoulders we stand, including those in my own family who inspire me to this work: my great grandmother Elizabeth Brewster Wolcott, as well as Jane Wolcott Steinhausen, my grandmother, and, perhaps most importantly, Jane Steinhausen Semich, my departed and dearly missed mom.

A special thank-you to my daughter, Anna, for brilliant insights, for keeping me on my toes, for teaching me through her wise observations as she grows, and for inspiring me to keep typing, and for my son, Connor, who spent time editing these pages and has taught me so much as he's grown up that's reflected in this book. And, Bill, thank you for always believing I can do things that I'm not sure I can do, reading a thousand drafts, sharing important insights, and then bringing chocolate. I'm so very thankful for you.

Thank you also to my family: my dad, Stephen Rowe, who has

always had an eye to social justice and worked toward it; my sister and brothers; and also to my dear stepfather, Bebop (Chuck Semich). Thank you also to all my friends who gave advice and cheered along the way, including Julia Morse, Jen Stone, Kerry Miyashita, Amy Friedan, and Justina Chen. Thank you also to the Facebook community, who kept me on track reaching word count goals and shared important insights throughout this process. It would take an entire second book to thank everyone adequately whose support and inspiration made this possible—and one day I want to write that book.

Ultimately a book has no meaning without a reader. All the work and dedication from those listed here, and many more, made this book for you so that we together can do this work and make the changes we all need. To you, who holds this book in your hand, thank you. Thank you for caring, for sharing, and for marching.

Words to Inspire and Fire You Up!

The Co-chairs of the 2017 Women's March on Why It's Important to Keep Marching

"The Women's March has been successful in terms of getting people to continue to show up, be active and make their voices heard. But more importantly, we have put an intentional focus on educating people about issues they may not have been aware of in the past, because they aren't personally affected. We have been very intentional about raising the concern around race in America, issues within the African American community, within the immigrant community and within the Muslim community. For us, that has been the greatest contribution of the Women's March: unapologetically and blatantly speaking about issues that are difficult and uncomfortable, but that we really need to unite around in order to make change."

—TAMIKA MALLORY, CO-CHAIR, WOMEN'S MARCH

"When I decided to organize what later would become the largest mass mobilization in U.S. history, I didn't hesitate to take action. Some ideas can be so clear, and you can have such immediate passion, that you just can't say no. Before the Women's March one of my mantras was, it's either 'Hell, yes!' or 'Heck, no.' Don't do anything if it's a 'meh.' For me the Women's March was a big 'Hell, yes!' And it became such a huge momentous thing because it was a 'Hell, yes!' for millions of other women, too. People just hopped on planes and trains and went there. It was an unbelievable 'Hell, yes!' Amtrak was completely sold out the first day. It was the same with some plane routes. So many people were saying, 'Hell yes!,' with no excuses and no hesitation. Trust your gut, don't let anyone stop you from pursuing your vision, and keep saying 'Hell, yes!' to what moves you."

—BOB BLAND, CO-CHAIR, WOMEN'S MARCH

"If women decided on January twenty-first to say, 'You know what, they won't miss me at the Women's March, so I've decided not to attend,' we wouldn't have had anybody at the Women's March. It was the importance of every individual showing up that made it the largest single-day protest in U.S. history. So, keep showing up if you hear there's a local rally, if there's a rally in front of a member of Congress or U.S. Senate office, even if you can just show up for a little bit, even if you are on the way home from work and want to stop by just for a little bit, your body, your physical body, adds numbers and adds power. People need to understand that their showing up, their participation, their staying informed and aware is for the survival of some of our fellow Americans. Also, stay informed, don't help spread misinformation, and let's stay united because these folks want to divide us. One of the best ways to stand up to this type of hate and vitriol is to say, 'We will not allow you to divide our community.'"

—LINDA SARSOUR, CO-CHAIR, WOMEN'S MARCH

"Women should absolutely keep marching because it demonstrates to the world that women need to put their bodies on the line and show solidarity for each other's issues and to show what true resistance looks like—grounded in love. Oftentimes we say the future is female but we've always been resisting—we've been the backbone of every movement effecting change. It's our responsibility as women to show younger generations of girls that they too can lead."

—CARMEN PEREZ, CO-CHAIR, WOMEN'S MARCH

Policy Recommendations

It's time to roll up our sleeves. We need to keep resisting and fighting back against bad policy that gets thrown our way, like the attempts to roll back the much needed Affordable Care Act. We must also keep persisting in advocating for solutions-oriented policy that lifts everyone in our country, like advancing fair pay and paid family/medical leave for everyone. The following pages are your resource to do exactly that.

As we do this, we need to remember two things: First, that sometimes the best defense is a solid offense, which in this case is a great list of proactive policies and a movement behind them to make them viable. Second—and this is even more critical—it's important to always hold a long-term vision of proactive change that will allow us to adapt our public policies to best support our always-changing communities, economy, workforce, and lives.

If we're doing democracy right, we'll always be proactively updating our policies to match our constantly changing worlds. Democracy isn't a destination, it's a journey. Change in our communities, workforce, and economy happens no matter what happens in the halls of legislative power, so it's on us to use the levers of democracy to keep our public policies current with the world we all live in together. It's also on us to try to leave our world a little bit better than we found it.

Wondering what specific solutions-oriented policies would boost women, families, and our economy? Looking for a proactive list of good policies that will move our nation forward? Or need a menu of to-dos to choose from when you contact elected leaders? In this section, you'll find lists of specific solutions-oriented policies, grouped by each chapter, that you can use as a road map for your advocacy at the city, county, state, and federal levels.

This is by no means a comprehensive list. There could be an entire encyclopedia of solutions-oriented policies that will lift our country, and policy proposals constantly change in real time, but this list does reflect important priority policies at the time this book was written. So feel free to add to this list, scratch out the ones that don't work for you, and use it to help change our worlds for the better! Whatever you do, never forget that together we're an incredibly powerful force for good.

Chapter 2: The Benjamins

- **Support and pass the Paycheck Fairness Act.** The Paycheck Fairness Act would help to close the wage gap by eliminating loopholes in the Equal Pay Act of 1963, helping to break harmful patterns of pay discrimination and strengthening workplace protections for women.

- **Promote bans on salary history requirements.** The administration and Congress should also work to ensure that employers are barred from requiring job candidates to disclose previous salary histories, which contributes to the wage gap over time.

- **Raise the federal minimum wage and include tipped workers.** Raise the minimum wage to $15 per hour or higher for all minimum wage workers, including tipped workers, and index the minimum wage to inflation.

- **Audit salary reviews for gender bias.** The administration and Congress should conduct their own agency reviews and audits of salaries to ensure that gender bias is being rooted out and

eliminated and continue to highlight, as models, private companies that are doing the same.

- **Use multiple approaches to close the wage gap.** Closing the
  wage gap and ending discriminatory pay practices isn't as simple
  as passing one single piece of legislation. Studies show that passing family economic security policies—like paid family/medical
  leave, affordable childcare, sick days, and a living wage—all help
  lower the wage gap. In addition, pay transparency and nondiscrimination policies help close the wage gap, too.
- **Raise the overtime threshold.** Raising the overtime threshold so more people receive overtime pay for working extra
  hours, in addition to benefiting families, is likely to strengthen
  the economy overall. A higher overtime threshold could lead
  employers to hire more employees or increase the hours of
  part-time workers. To the extent that more workers receive
  overtime pay, these increased earnings could lead to increased
  consumer spending and stronger economic growth.

Chapter 3: The Invisible Glass Ceilings

- **Advocate for full enforcement of federal laws that protect
  people from harassment,** knowing that harassment (including from unwelcome sexual advances and verbal and physical
  harassment of a sexual nature) is a form of employment discrimination that violates several federal laws, including Title VII of
  the Civil Rights Act of 1964, the Age Discrimination in Employment Act of 1967, and the Americans with Disabilities Act of
  1990. In addition, state and federal enforcement programs need
  to be fully funded. More information on this area of the law,
  including how to file a discrimination claim, can be found at
  the website of the U.S. Equal Employment Opportunity Commission[1] and at LegalMomentum.com.

- **Check to see if your state has robust anti-harassment laws.** Some states do, but not all. Check in to see if your state needs one. There are sample policies at StopStreetHarassment.org.
- **Stand behind bills that combat sexual harassment at the state and federal levels,** like the Protecting Young Victims from Sexual Abuse and Safe Sport Authorization Act, and more.
- **Advance the policies listed under the "Women against Violence" chapter.**
- **Advance policies that help break the glass ceiling,** including pay transparency (Fair Pay Act) and family economic security policies (paid family/medical leave, sick days, and affordable childcare), and more.

Chapter 4: Sound the Alarm

- **Raise the wage.** Raise the minimum wage to $15 per hour or higher for all minimum wage workers, including tipped workers, and index the minimum wage to inflation.
- **Expand the Fair Labor Standards Act.** Cover all workers, including domestic workers and farm workers, under the Fair Labor Standards Act at the federal level and at the state level with a domestic workers bill of rights.
- **Protect the safety net.** Make investments to lift women, families, and the economy; protect the social safety net programs like Social Security, Medicaid, WIC, SNAP, TANF, Medicare, and childcare assistance that low- and moderate-income families are boosted by; raise revenue by requiring the richest Americans and big corporations to pay a fair share of taxes; and cut wasteful Pentagon spending.
- **Ensure the national budget boosts women, families, and our economy.** Any national budget and tax plan must protect key programs like Medicaid, Medicare, WIC, SNAP, child

nutrition, TANF, Head Start, childcare assistance, and housing assistance, which stimulate our national economy and that
women and their families depend on to improve their health,
obtain quality childcare and higher education, and help them
meet their basic needs during difficult times and as they age.
More than just ending the sequester and protecting these programs, we must also invest more in critical domestic appro-
priated programs. The budget must also adhere to the (at one
time) bipartisan principle that deficit reduction should not
increase poverty or income inequality.

- **Advance tax improvements.** Advance tax improvements
  that help boost working families and our economy. This
  includes increasing the Child Tax Credit (CTC) for families
  with younger children, as well as starting refundability with
  the first dollar of earnings and improving the credit for low-
  wage families with children. Positive improvements should
  be made to the Child and Dependent Care Tax Credit to make
  it refundable, increase the credit rate for low-income families, expand the sliding scale, increase the allowable expenses,
  and index the expense limits and income levels for inflation
  to help make childcare more affordable to more families.
  Additionally, the Earned Income Tax Credit (EITC) should
  be expanded to low-income workers not raising children
  in the home. The CTC and EITC are two of the best tools
  our government has to help reduce poverty. Childcare costs
  more than college tuition in most states, leading to financial
  restraints among many families with small children. Improvements can and should be made to our tax system to assist
  those families most in need, while at the same time boosting
  our economy and making sure wealthy corporations and individuals pay their fair share.

- **Ensure access to healthy food and nutrition for all kids in schools.** Ensure all kids and families have access to safe and accessible drinking water through investments in infrastructure, testing, and remediation efforts. Ensure parents and families can make healthy choices by limiting the presence of marketing in schools, child-directed advertising, and more. Promote a healthy school day through robust implementation and protection of achievements, including healthy school meals and snacks, and wellness policies.
- **Advance universal family-care policy.** Move forward one social insurance framework that creates a portable, flexible, and universal benefit allowing all working families to receive support for childcare, eldercare, and paid family/medical leave, including a benefit for family caregivers and stay-at-home moms as proposed by Caring Across Generations (a campaign led by Ai-jen Poo and Sarita Gupta).

Chapter 5: The Maternal Wall

- **Advocate for paid family/medical leave insurance.** Congress should prioritize the swift passage of a national paid leave insurance program that covers all people—employers and employees—attached to the workforce, including self-employed people, for at least twelve weeks of job-protected paid family/medical leave they can use when a new child is born, adopted, or placed through a foster care system; when a family member faces a serious health condition and needs care; when workers themselves face a serious health condition and need treatment or recovery time; or when a military family needs time to address the exigencies of deployment or to care for a wounded service member. This proposal must provide adequate wage replacement of at least two-thirds of workers' typical wages, preferably with higher levels of wage replacement for lower-wage workers, and should include a broad definition of the kinds of family relationships permitted for family caregiving. Most important, this system must include an adequate and sustainable revenue stream to ensure the strength and integrity of this program now and for generations to come, and to make paid family/medical leave available to employees of both smaller and larger businesses in affordable, sustainable ways. State paid family and medical leave programs provide a strong model, as does the Family and Medical Insurance Leave Act (known as the FAMILY Act) introduced in the 113th and 114th Congresses.

- **Expand the Family and Medical Leave Act of 1993.** The FMLA was an important start, but the law has significant gaps that leave 40 percent of all workers ineligible for FMLA leave, and it currently provides only unpaid leave. In addition, the law also fails to recognize that, in today's families, workers are caring for siblings, grandparents, and other close relatives—individuals who are not covered by the FMLA. Those workers left out include workers in businesses with fewer than fifty employees; part-time workers (an increasing portion of workers, as businesses reduce their hours); and workers who need time off to care for seriously ill domestic partners, children of domestic partners, or many types of seriously ill elderly relatives (especially problematic as the population ages). Parents also need to be able to attend meetings with their child's teachers and school administrators without risking their job or disciplinary action at work.

- **Modernize paid leave for the military.** Issue directives to the Department of Defense (DOD) and urge Congress to modernize paid leave for the military by equalizing the duration of leave for mothers, fathers, and adoptive parents and work with Congress to expand paid leave for DOD personnel to include family caregiving as well.

- **Urge Congress to prioritize passage of the Healthy Families Act.** The Healthy Families Act would allow workers in businesses with fifteen or more employees to earn up to seven job-protected paid sick days each year to be used to recover from their own illnesses, access preventive care, provide care to a sick family member, or attend school meetings related to a child's health condition or disability. Workers in businesses with fewer than fifteen employees would earn up to seven job-protected unpaid sick days each year to be used for the same reasons, unless their employers choose to offer paid sick days.

- **Protect and enforce previous executive actions.** The administration must also work to protect and enforce the executive actions and regulations put in place by the previous administration to expand coverage of earned paid sick days to federal workers and federal contractors as well as instruct agencies to study the impact of earned paid sick days to determine the impacts of cost savings to businesses and to our economy.

- **Support the Pregnant Workers Fairness Act.** Congress needs to pass and the president needs to sign into law the Pregnant Workers Fairness Act, which would require employers to make the same sorts of reasonable accommodations for pregnancy, childbirth, and related medical conditions that they already make for disabilities, ensuring pregnant women can continue to do their jobs and support their families. These accommodations are simple things like being able to sit down or having a water bottle on shift.

- **Support the Supporting Working Moms Act.** Federal law currently provides nonexempt employees (hourly wage-earning and some salaried employees exempt from overtime) reasonable break time to express milk in a private, non-bathroom location, for one year after the child's birth. While this provides protection and support for the most vulnerable workers, this distinction in the law was unintentional and is causing confusion about who is covered and how to implement it efficiently and fairly in all worksites. The Supporting Working Moms Act will ensure a fair and uniform national policy by extending the existing federal provision to cover approximately 12 million additional salaried employees, including elementary and secondary school teachers. Twenty-eight U.S. states, Puerto Rico, and the District of Columbia also have state legislation to support breastfeeding in the workplace.

- **Support the Friendly Airports for Mothers Act.** The FAM Act requires all large and medium hub airports to provide a private, non-bathroom space in each terminal for mothers to express breast milk. The space must be accessible to persons with disabilities, available in each terminal building after the security checkpoint, and include a place to sit, a table or other flat surface, and an electrical outlet.

- **Support the Fairness for Breastfeeding Mothers Act of 2017 (H.R. 1174).** Introduced in February 2017, this law would require that certain public buildings provide a lactation room, other than a bathroom, that is hygienic and available for use by members of the public to express milk. The lactation room must be shielded from public view, be free from intrusion, and contain a chair, a working surface, and (if the building is supplied with electricity) an electrical outlet.

- **Support the Schedules that Work Act.** Congress should curb abusive scheduling practices and give working people the right to request schedule predictability and flexibility by passing the Schedules that Work Act.

Chapter 6: Saving Lives

- **Ensure a strong Medicaid and Children's Health Insurance Program.** Medicaid and the Children's Health Insurance Program (CHIP) provide health care coverage for more than one half of our nation's children and are essential to our nation's health and well-being. Medicaid is the foundation of the expansion of health care coverage under the Affordable Care Act. Therefore, MomsRising opposes proposals that arbitrarily cut Medicaid, make structural changes to the program (for example, a cap or block grant), and shift a fiscal burden to the states. Ultimately, these proposals would transfer the burden to seniors who depend on the program for long-term care, people with disabilities, children, and families. We also oppose all harmful cost shifting such as converting the program to a block grant, imposing a per capita cap or any cap on Medicaid spending that inevitably would result in drastic cuts to patients and health care providers who rely on Medicaid, and any other proposal or waiver that would cut or otherwise undermine Medicaid and CHIP.

- **Protect the improvements and gains in coverage under the Affordable Care Act.** The passage and implementation of the ACA has brought the percentage of uninsured people in the United States to a record low. In addition to increasing the availability of coverage, the ACA drastically improved the coverage options available for families not offered health insurance through their employer, as well as eliminating many harmful practices by insurance companies like annual or life-time caps on coverage and discrimination based on preexisting conditions. The ACA requires that all new health insurance plans offer ten essential health benefits, including maternity care, prescription drugs, and mental health care. These new protections and improvements have ensured that families no longer have to claim bankruptcy due to a major medical illness and that they have the coverage they need, when they need it. Therefore, we oppose all efforts to roll back or cut these measures such as repealing and replacing the ACA with a less robust plan that would result in a larger number of uninsured people in the United States, or that allow states to opt out of provisions of the plans, or any other proposal that would otherwise diminish the expansion of and improvements to health care coverage.

- **Ensure that every woman and family has access to quality, affordable health care coverage.** Health care is a right—*not* a privilege. We support policies that will further the goal of reaching universal, quality health care coverage for every family.

Chapter 7: The Choice Is Ours!

- **Fight for quality, affordable reproductive health care.** Ensure that every woman and family has access to quality, affordable health care coverage that includes comprehensive reproductive health care coverage, including birth control.
- **Continue to fund Planned Parenthood.** Defunding Planned Parenthood would cut off health care—including birth control, cancer screenings, and other essential health services—for millions of low-income women, many of whom have no other health care provider. One in five women visits a Planned Parenthood clinic in her lifetime for health care.

Chapter 8: Women against Violence

- **Invest in ending domestic violence and sexual assault.** Provide sustained services such as shelter, crisis intervention, advocacy, legal services, children services, and specialized services for specific populations—so every survivor can access help and safety.

- **Prevent sexual abuse and assault.** Encourage investment in prevention efforts to disrupt harmful social norms and the acceptance of violence against women, intimate partner violence, and sexual assault, and to prevent teen dating violence. Similarly, invest in programs that address gender bias in institutions and systems such as law enforcement, legal and court settings, housing, health care, child welfare, workplaces, education, as well as culturally competent responses to violence against women.

- **Ensure economic justice for survivors.** Support equal pay, a living wage, and affordable childcare, as well as strengthen and expand social safety nets—TANF, SNAP, SSDI, unemployment insurance. Expand eligibility for EITC and CTC tax credits. Support paid sick and safe days, including for doctor/hospital treatment and for seeking a restraining order or testifying in court. Include domestic violence survivors in employment nondiscrimination protections, since many domestic violence victims have been fired because of their abuse. Support workplace assistance for survivors of domestic violence. Support unemployment insurance for domestic violence and sexual assault survivors who must leave a job due to the abuse and violence. Preserve access to health care, including comprehensive health and mental health plans.

- **Support immigrant survivors.** Strengthen existing protections for immigrant survivors. Strengthen the U visa program for immigrant victims of violence by increasing the number of available U visas. Support survivor self-sufficiency and remove vulnerabilities to further victimization (e.g., provide assistance to achieve legal status, work authorization, and protect and increase safety net benefits). Prohibit penalties for organizations helping to feed, house, and protect undocumented immigrants. Support protections for detainees who have applied for U, T, or VAWA self-petitions. Ensure no separation of survivors and children in immigration enforcement actions.

- **Support housing for survivors.** Support funding for safe, affordable housing and shelters. Support stronger protections against discrimination against domestic violence victims in public and private housing and prohibit harmful "nuisance ordinances" relating to victims of domestic violence.

- **Support students and youth in preventing dating violence and sexual assault.** Enforce Title IX. Support continued access to school disciplinary processes for survivors. Support robust prevention education and services for children, youth, and college students.

- **Support tribal survivors.** Support access to services and justice for Native American survivors by investing in those services and affirming tribal sovereignty to address crimes.

- **Protect women against online attacks.** Support robust protections against the use of spyware to abuse, as well as protection against the online posting of nonconsensual intimate images.

- **Protect our families and communities from gun violence.** Guns kill ninety Americans every day. Mass shootings like the ones at Sandy Hook Elementary School in Newtown, Connecticut; the Emanuel African Methodist Episcopal Church in Charleston, South Carolina; Pulse Nightclub in Orlando, Florida; and the Route 91 Harvest country music festival in Las Vegas, Nevada, are recurring reminders of our gun violence epidemic, which claims more than 33,000 lives a year. With around 90 percent of Americans in favor of stronger background checks on gun sales, we have virtually universal agreement that there should be some reasonable limits on gun ownership. The solution to America's gun violence epidemic is wholesale cultural and policy reform that prioritizes public safety, including:

- Universal background checks on firearms sales.
- Bans on military-grade assault rifles and on high-capacity magazines.
- A strong federal anti–gun trafficking law with stiff penalties to discourage straw purchasing.
- Investment in evidence-based community antiviolence programs that have proven to reduce the risk of gun violence in highly impacted communities.
- Rolling back Stand Your Ground laws, common in many states, which facilitate racial profiling and casual gun culture, and are a huge step backward for civil rights.
- Closing loopholes that allow stalkers and abusive dating partners to access firearms, requiring states to adopt effective firearm surrender and removal protocols for use in domestic violence cases, requiring the FBI/ATF to notify local law enforcement when a domestic violence offender attempts to acquire a firearm, and notifying the victim of the prohibited purchaser through the VINE system.
- Supporting gun violence restraining orders that allow family members and law enforcement, with a court order, to temporarily prohibit a person from possessing a firearm.
- Investing in the National Instant Criminal Background Check System for more streamlined and comprehensive record collection.

A big thanks to the National Network to End Domestic Violence for their help with this policy list.

Chapter 9: Maternal Mortality

- **Advance measures to improve maternal health.** The United States has the highest rate of maternal deaths during labor and delivery than any other nation in the developed world. Support the Maternal Health Accountability Act of 2017/Preventing Maternal Deaths Act of 2017. Support the improvement of hospital protocols relating to all aspects of pregnancy and childbirth.

- **Promote equitable access to health care services before, during, and after pregnancy.** Resist dismantling of ACA and Medicaid and expand access to health care. Promote the demand for transparency and data collection relating to pregnancy and childbirth.

- **Promote health equity and antiracism measures throughout the health care delivery system.** Black women suffer the most with a maternal mortality rate four times that of white women. Ensure equal access to best practices and shared plans for childbirth emergencies for all doctors and hospitals, along with training. Women shouldn't die in childbirth simply because they choose the wrong hospital.

Chapter 10: Lady Liberty

- **Reform immigration policy so there is fair treatment of women, children, and families.** Pass comprehensive immigration policy reform legislation to establish a road map to permanent legal status that recognizes the contributions of women's paid and unpaid work. Pass the Dream Act to provide a path to legal status to 1.8 million Dreamers, young people who were brought to the United States as children and have grown up in the United States. Ensure protection of family unity by creating pathways that would allow for mixed-status families to stay together legally in this country, without fear of separation.

- **Protect children.** Provide clear protections for children's basic rights, safety, and well-being, including access to government-funded legal counsel and advocates for children in immigration proceedings. End immediately the harmful practices of family detention, protect parental rights, ensure due process, and increase alternatives to detention. Advance policies and programs that keep families together, such as implementing administrative relief options to allow parents to live and work legally in the United States, halting deportations of parents, and reforming the family-based immigration systems to address the backlogs and reunite more families.

- **Offer equal opportunity to immigrant women.** Provide equal employment-based migration opportunities and workplace protections so that immigrant women may safely pursue economic opportunity. End programs that discourage reporting crimes to law enforcement. Advance protections and expand programs like the Violence Against Women Act and U visas, which are set aside for victims of crime, women fleeing state and interpersonal violence, and victims of trafficking or exploitation. Ensure that immigrants and their children have access to the services and supports all people need to thrive, including health care, nutrition, and other critical programs and income supports.

Chapter 11: The Domino Effect

- **Increase access to high-quality, affordable early childhood education (including pre-K and childcare).** High-quality early childhood education is one of the best investments we can make for the short- and long-term health of our children, our families, and the economy. Excellent birth-to-age-five programs more than pay for themselves by preventing achievement gaps and producing better outcomes in education (including home culture and language support), social emotional development, health, personal productivity, and economic vitality. Our young children don't have enough affordable, high-quality early learning opportunities. The investments outlined below will go a long way toward fixing that.

- **Support national high-quality, affordable, universal pre-K for all three- and four-year-olds** in a mixed delivery model, that focuses on whole-child development (including cognitive and social emotional development), offer bilingual classroom settings for all dual language learners, and practice alternatives to punitive and bias disciplinary practices like the use of suspensions and expulsions.

- **Provide childcare subsidies (on a sliding scale) for low- to middle-income families** so that the cost does not exceed 7 percent of a family's income.

- **Support increased investments in affordable, high-quality early learning opportunities** (including significant investments for Child Care Development Block Grants) to ensure all children are ready and successful for school and life. This includes investments in supporting childcare providers to provide high-quality early learning environments, including excellent preservice training, professional development, and coaching that incorporates anti-bias education and racial equity and social justice lenses.

- **Support a livable wage for childcare providers with opportunities for continued professional development.** Advocate for intentional investments in building and supporting the educator pipeline, and attracting and maintaining a diverse workforce that reflects the diversity of the children and families it serves. Encourage a specific focus on the bilingual educator pipeline (with supportive training) that follow two tracks: (1) designing alternate paths to licensure that are flexible about final credentials and recognize teacher candidates' cultural language abilities as strengths, and (2) identifying where multilingual teacher candidates get stuck on traditional paths to licensure and providing resources to help them overcome obstacles.

- **Insist on regular and reliable disaggregated data on the achievement, development, absenteeism, discipline, and dual language learning.** Data focused on dual language learners shows what early learners know and can do in both English and their home languages. Continue to collect data in this area to inform and strengthen policy and implementation.

- **Promote increased investments to continue robust funding for Head Start** programs (including Early Head Start), including expansion to meet full-day, full-year requirements and the expansion of Early Head Start for infants and toddlers.

- **Strengthen the Child and Dependent Care Tax Credit (CDCTC).** The CDCTC allows families to claim a credit if they paid expenses for the care of a qualifying individual that enabled parents to work, go to school, or actively look for work. To strengthen the CDCTC, Congress should make the credit fully refundable, increase allowable expenses, and increase the top credit rate, which is currently capped at 35 percent.

- **Advance the College for All Act at the federal level and push for affordable public college and university policies at the state level.** Public college institutions—including community colleges, technical institutions, and four-year colleges and universities—should be accessible and affordable. It's time to explore new policies like free public colleges and universities for students from households with family income under $125,000, tuition-free community colleges, major student loan rate cuts, increasing Federal Work-Study programs, public service loan forgiveness when people go into fields like teaching or medicine, and much more.

- **End the school-to-prison pipeline and advance model school codes.** Avoid out-of-school suspensions and promote restorative justice. Integrate social emotional learning. Adopt discipline policies aimed at dignity in schools with a focus on:
  - Understanding and addressing the causes of behavior.
  - Resolving conflicts and repairing the harm done.
  - Restoring relationships.
  - Reintegrating students into the school community.
- **End the regular presence of law enforcement inside schools and increase the number of counselors inside schools.**
- **Implement and reauthorize the Every Student Succeed Act (ESSA).** Recommendations for the reauthorization of the ESSA include:
  - Mandatory data collection on school discipline from all schools, Accountability mechanisms for addressing discipline and implementing best practices in the lowest-performing schools.
  - Funding for restorative justice practices and school-wide positive behavior supports.
  - Parental involvement in developing school discipline codes.
  - Requiring states to describe how they will reduce suspensions, expulsions, referrals to law enforcement, and other actions that remove students from instruction.
  - Funding competitive grants for school partnerships with community-based organizations.

- **Raise the age.** Move policies forward so that juveniles can't be charged as adults for certain crimes, including the age in all states to twenty-one.

Chapter 12: An Unjust System

- **End mass incarceration.** One million women, mostly mothers, are under criminal justice supervision in the United States, and hundreds of thousands of women are currently incarcerated. Two-thirds of the women in federal prisons are serving time for challenges related to nonviolent drug abuse. They need treatment and counseling, not incarceration. Our justice system is failing families, hurting our economy, and in need of some serious reforms. We have the highest incarceration rate in the world, which is nothing to brag about. In fact, we are living in a time when more than 2.7 million children in the United States have an incarcerated parent, and approximately 10 million children have experienced parental incarceration at some point in their lives. Harsh sentencing practices have done more harm than good. Strict penalties designed to combat the distribution of illegal drugs have done little to stem the drug trade; instead, the result has been a massive sweeping of people experiencing challenges related to drug addiction into an ever-expanding criminal justice system that directly fractures families and hurts our economy. We urge Congress and the next presidential administration to act on sentencing reform and to end mandatory minimums.

- **Support Federal Sentencing Reform.** Advance the Sentencing Reform and Correction Act.

- **Advance sentencing and bail reform work at the state and municipal level.** End the cash bail system.

- **Support the Dignity for Incarcerated Women Act.**
- **Pursue prosecutorial reform.**
- **End the death penalty.**
- **Advocate for police reform.** In 2014, MomsRising launched our national racial justice and police reform campaign to push forward demands to bring greater independent oversight, transparency, accountability, and justice for victims of police brutality and misconduct. No family should have to suffer from their loved ones being injured or killed by guns, especially at the hands of those charged to protect them. More than nine hundred people were killed by police in 2016. Studies show that, even though white Americans outnumber Black Americans fivefold, Black people are three times more likely than white people to be killed when they encounter the police in the United States, and Black teenagers are twenty-one times more likely to be killed by police than white teenagers. Our campaign strategies include:
  - A fully resourced and rigorous civil rights and criminal investigation by the DOJ into discriminatory policing, excessive force, and death or injury by police in every state in the country.
  - A comprehensive, streamlined, public national-level database of police shootings, excessive force, and misconduct complaints, traffic and pedestrian stops, and arrests, broken down by race and other demographic data, with key privacy protections, the exclusion of personally identifying factors and information, and deportation immunity for civilians.
  - Mandating of Peace Officer Standards and Training (POST) commissions in every state and interstate coordination among all POSTs.

- An executive order that creates a strong and enforceable prohibition on police brutality and discriminatory policing based on race, ethnicity, religion, national origin, age, gender, gender identity or expression, sexual orientation, immigration status, disability, and housing status.

- Limit federal funding for police departments that demonstrate abuse of power, and move forward massive reinvestment in community-controlled and -based safety practices.

- Support for the passage of the End Racial Profiling Act.

- Streamlined national use of the force matrix and mandating that state and local police have clear and streamlined matrices.

- Limits on asset seizure without due process and the transfer of any military equipment to local law enforcement under the 1033 program, guidelines that ensure that the equipment is not used on nonviolent protesters, and an end to the requirement that such military weaponry is used within a year.

- **Advocate for special prosecutors for police misconduct in states.**

- **End the use of military-grade combat equipment in local communities targeting civilians.** Support the passage of the Right to Know Act in New York City and similar local legislation in other jurisdictions.

Organizations That Support Change

Chapter 2: The Benjamins

Here are some of the many organizations that MomsRising loves working with on fair pay policies:

1,000 Days
9to5
American Association of University Women
AFL-CIO
American Sustainable Business Council
A Better Balance
Black Mothers' Breastfeeding Association
Black Women's Roundtable
Caring Across Generations
Casa Ruby
Center for American Progress
Center for Law and Social Policy
Center for Popular Democracy
Economic Opportunity Institute
Equal Pay Today!
Family Equality Council
Family Values @ Work
Forward Together

Gender Justice League
Human Rights Campaign
Institute for Women's Policy Research
Main Street Alliance
Make It Work Campaign
Movement Advancement Project
Ms. Foundation for Women
National Employment Law Project
National LGBTQ Task Force
National Partnership for Women and Families
National Women's Law Center
PL+US
Service Employees International Union
Southerners on New Ground
United Food and Commercial Workers International Union
United States Breastfeeding Committee

Chapter 3: The Invisible Glass Ceilings

Here are some of the many organizations that MomsRising loves working with on stopping harassment and busting open glass ceilings:

The Advocates for Human Rights
American Association of University Women
Annie's List
The Audre Lorde Project
Catalysts
Center for American Women in Politics
Collective Action for Safe Spaces
The Collective PAC
Democracy for America
Emerge America
Emily's List
Higher Heights
Hollaback!
Just Be, Inc.—MeTooMvmt.org
Men Can Stop Rape
National Girls Collaborative Project
National Women's Political Caucus
Race Forward
RAINN (Rape, Abuse and Incest National Network)
She Should Run
SheSource
Stop Street Harassment
Stop Violence Against Women
VoteRunLead
Women Also Know Stuff
Women Who Code
Women's Media Center
Workplaces Respond to Domestic and Sexual Violence

Chapter 4: Sound the Alarm

Here are some of the many organizations that MomsRising loves working with on workers' rights and safety net policies:

Workers' Rights

Asian Pacific American Labor Alliance, AFL-CIO
Caring Across Generations
Desis Rising Up and Moving
Hand in Hand
Mujeres Unidas y Activas
National Domestic Workers Alliance

SAFETY NET AND FOOD JUSTICE

Allies Reaching for Community Health Equity

American Heart Association

Berkeley Media Studies Group

Center for Science in the Public Interest

Cooperation Jackson

Feeding America

Food Research and Action Center

Food Trust

Funders' Collaborative on Youth Organizing

HEAL Food Alliance

Interfaith Council on Corporate Responsibility

MAZON: A Jewish Response to Hunger

National Black Food and Justice Alliance

National Drinking Water Alliance

National WIC Association

The Praxis Project

Rooted in Community

Salud America!

UConn Rudd Center for Food Policy and Obesity

Voices for Healthy Kids

BUDGET/TAX/ECONOMIC ISSUES

Americans for Tax Fairness

Center for American Progress

Center for Tax Justice

Center on Budget and Policy Priorities

The Century Foundation

Coalition on Human Needs

Economic Policy Institute

First Focus

National Priorities Project

National Women's Law Center

Chapter 5: The Maternal Wall

Here are some of the many organizations that MomsRising loves working with on workplace justice policies:

9to5

1,000 Days

AFL-CIO

American Association of University Women

American Sustainable Business Council

A Better Balance

Black Mothers' Breastfeeding Association

Black Women's Roundtable

Caring Across Generations

Center for American Progress

Center for Law and Social Policy

Center for Popular Democracy
Economic Opportunity Institute
Equal Pay Today! Campaign
Family Values @ Work
Institute for Women's Policy
    Research
Main Street Alliance
Make It Work Campaign
National Employment Law
    Project
National Partnership for
    Women and Families

National Women's Law
    Center
PL+US
Service Employees International
    Union
United Food and Commercial
    Workers International
    Union
United States Breastfeeding
    Committee

Chapter 6: Saving Lives

Here are some of the many organizations MomsRising loves working with on health care:

American Muslim Health
    Professionals
Black Women's
    Roundtable/#NotAPrivilege
    Campaign
Center for American Progress
Center for Children and Families,
    Georgetown University
Center for Public Representation
Center on Budget and Policy
    Priorities

Community Catalyst
Families USA
First Focus
GirlTrek
Health Care for America Now
National Council of La Raza
National Health Law Program
National Partnership for Women
    and Families
UltraViolet
Women's March

Chapter 7: The Choice Is Ours!

Here are some of the many organizations MomsRising loves working with on reproductive health care policies:

Center for Reproductive
    Rights

Forward Together
NARAL Pro-Choice America

National Asian Pacific American
   Women's Forum
National Latina Institute for
   Reproductive Health
Planned Parenthood

Prison Birth Project
Showing Up for Racial Justice
SisterSong
Unite for Gender and
   Reproductive Equity

Chapter 8: Women against Violence

Here are some of the many organizations MomsRising loves working with on ending domestic violence and sexual assault, as well as gun safety:

ENDING DOMESTIC VIOLENCE AND SEXUAL ASSAULT

Collective Action for Safe Spaces
End Rape on Campus
Futures Without Violence
Know Your IX
Love Is Respect
National Coalition Against
   Domestic Violence

The National Domestic Violence
   Hotline
National Network to End
   Domestic Violence
RAINN (Rape, Abuse and Incest
   National Network)

GUN SAFETY

Brady Campaign to Prevent Gun
   Violence
Campaign to Keep Guns Off
   Campus
Center for American Progress
The Coalition to Stop Gun
   Violence
Community Justice Reform
   Coalition
CREDO Action
Giffords: Courage to Fight Gun
   Violence

Million Hoodies Movement
   for Justice
Moms Demand Action/
   Everytown for Gun Safety
MoveOn
OnePULSE
PICO National Network
States United to Prevent Gun
   Violence
Violence Policy Center

Chapter 9: Maternal Mortality

Here are some of the many organizations MomsRising loves working with on improving maternal mortality:

American Congress of Obstetricians and Gynecologists
Ancient Song Doula Services
Association of Women's Health, Obstetric and Neonatal Nurses
Black Mamas Matter Alliance
Black Women for Wellness
Black Women's Health Imperative
Center for Reproductive Rights
Every Mother Counts
Forward Together
HealthConnect One
March of Dimes
National Advocates for Pregnant Women
National Perinatal Task Force
Planned Parenthood
Preeclampsia Foundation
SisterSong

Chapter 10: Lady Liberty

Here are some of the many organizations MomsRising loves working with on supporting the civil rights of religious and minority communities, as well as supporting immigrant communities:

CIVIL RIGHTS

Advancement Project
American-Arab Anti-Discrimination Committee
American Civil Liberties Union
Asian Americans Advancing Justice
Black Lives Matter
Black Women's Roundtable
Center for Constitutional Rights
Color of Change
Faith in Public Life
Institute for Social Policy and Understanding
Islamic Networks Group
Lawyers' Committee for Civil Rights Under Law
The Leadership Conference for Civil and Human Rights
The Movement for Black Lives
MPower
Muslim Advocates
NAACP
NAACP Legal Defense Fund
Repairers of the Breach
ReThink Media
Revolutionary Love Project

Sikh American Legal Defense
and Education Fund
Sikh Coalition

Southern Poverty Law Center
Transformative Justice
Coalition

FAIR TREATMENT OF ALL IMMIGRANTS

American-Arab Anti-
Discrimination Committee
American Immigration Council
American Immigration Lawyers
Association
AppleSeed Network
Asian Americans Advancing
Justice
Black Alliance for Just
Immigration
Border Kids Relief Project
Center for American Progress
Center for Law and Social Policy
Define American
Dreamer Moms
Emerging America
FWD.us
iAmerica
Immigration Hub
Kids in Need of Defense
League of United Latin American
Citizens
Make the Road New York
National Asian Pacific American
Women's Forum

National Association of Elected
Latino Elected and Appointed
Officials
National Immigration Law Center
National Immigration Project of
the National Lawyers Guild
OneAmerica
Presente.org
Reform Immigration for America
Sikh American Legal Defense and
Education Fund
Sikh Coalition
South Asian Americans Leading
Together
South Asian Network
Southeast Asia Resource Action
Center
Tennessee Immigrant and Refugee
Rights Coalition
Transformative Justice
Coalition
UnidosUS
United We Dream
We Belong Together
Welcoming America
Women's Refugee Commission

FAITH IN PUBLIC LIFE

Alliance of South Asians Taking
Action (ASATA)

American-Arab Anti-
Discrimination Committee

Arab American Association of
    New York
Council on American-Islamic
    Relations
Desis Rising Up and Moving
Faith in Public Life
Islamic Networks Group

MPower Change
Muslim Advocates
Repairers of the Breach
South Asian Americans Leading
    Together
South Asian Network

Chapter 11: The Domino Effect

Here are some of the many organizations MomsRising loves working with on early learning, including pre-K and childcare policies, as well as on opening opportunities for healthy kids:

EARLY LEARNING, INCLUDING CHILDCARE AND PRE-K

Alliance for Early Success
American Federation of Teachers
Center for American Progress
Center for Law and Social Policy
Child Care Aware
Children's Alliance
The Collaborative for Academic,
    Social, and Emotional
    Learning
Early Edge CA
Early Learning Action Alliance
First Five Years Fund

Make It Work Campaign
National Association for the
    Education of Young Children
National League of Cities
National Women's Law Center
New America
OneAmerica
School Readiness Consulting
Stop Parenting Alone
Washington State Association of
    Head Start and ECEAP
Zero to Three

OPENING OPPORTUNITIES FOR HEALTHY KIDS

Advancement Project
Afterschool Alliance
Alliance for a Healthier
    Generation
Alliance for Educational Justice
American Academy of Pediatrics

American Heart Association
Berkeley Media Studies Group
Campaign for Youth Justice
Center for Science in the Public
    Interest
Dignity in Schools Campaign

Food Research and Action Center
The Food Trust
GirlTrek
Interfaith Center on Corporate
    Responsibility
Journey for Justice Alliance
Rooted in Community

Safe Routes to School National
    Partnership
Salud America!
UConn Rudd Center for Food
    Policy and Obesity
Urban Youth Collaborative
Youth First

Chapter 12: An Unjust System

Here are some of the many organizations MomsRising loves working on police brutality, mass incarceration, and state sanctioned violence:

POLICE BRUTALITY

Black Lives Matter
Black Youth Project 100
Center for Constitutional Rights
Color of Change
Communities United for Police
    Reform
Dream Defenders
Ella Baker Center for Human
    Rights

Justice Committee
Justice League NYC
Million Hoodies Movement
    for Justice
NAACP Legal Defense and
    Educational Fund
PICO National Network

ENDING MASS INCARCERATION

American Civil Liberties Union
Brennan Center for Justice
Color of Change
Essie Justice Group
The Innocence Project
Leadership Conference on Civil
    and Human Rights

NAACP
NAACP Legal Defense and
    Educational Fund
The Sentencing Project

Notes

Introduction

1. Charlotte Alter, "How the Women's March Has United Progressives of All Stripes," *Time*, January 20, 2017, http://time.com/4641575/womens -march-washington-coalition.
2. Erica Chenoweth and Jeremy Pressman, "This Is What We Learned by Counting the Women's Marches," *Washington Post*, February 7, 2017, https://www.washingtonpost.com/news/monkey-cage/wp/2017/02/07/ this-is-what-we-learned-by-counting-the-womens-marches.
3. "Exit Polls 2016," CNN, updated November 23, 2016, http://www.cnn .com/election/results/exit-polls.
4. "Quick Facts," U.S. Census Bureau, https://www.census.gov/quickfacts/ table/PST045216/00. According to the U.S. Census, which doesn't have perfect data, but does track the most data: 62 percent of us are white non-Hispanic, 17 percent of us are Hispanic, 13 percent of us are Black, 5 percent of us are Asian, 0.8 percent of us are American Indian/Native Alaskan, 0.17 percent of us are Native Hawaiian/Pacific Islander, 5 percent of us are some other race, 2 percent of us are two or more races. U.S. Census Bureau, compiled by Sarah Jane Glynn, April 27, 2017, http://factfinder2.census.gov.
5. *Economist,* "Women in the Workforce: Female Power," December 30, 2009, http://www.economist.com/node/15174418?story_id=15174418.

    "Women in the Labor Force: A Databook," Bureau of Labor Statistics, United States Department of Labor, updated October 15, 2009, http://www .bls.gov/cps/wlf-databook2009.htm.
6. Bridget Brennan, "Top 10 Things Everyone Should Know about Women Consumers," *Forbes,* January 21, 2015, https://www.forbes.com/sites/bridget brennan/2015/01/21/top-10-things-everyone-should-know-about-women -consumers.
7. *The Human Development Report* (prepared by United Nations Development Programme and published by Oxford University Press, 1995), 97.
8. National Center for Education Statistics, "Digest of Education Statistics," table 318.10, https://nces.ed.gov/programs/digest/d15/tables/dt15_318.10.asp.

9. National Association of REALTORS, *2016 Profile of Home Buyers and Sellers, 35th Anniversary Edition*, October 13, 2016, https://www.nar.realtor/sites/default/files/reports/2016/2016-profile-of-home-buyers-and-sellers-10-31-2016.pdf.

10. "#KeepMarching MomsRising Advocacy and Organizing Tactics and Tips." https://s3.amazonaws.com/s3.momsrising.org/images/Keep_Marching _Toolkit_2_1.pdf.

Chapter 1: Waking Up

1. U.S. Census Bureau, "Facts for Features: Mother's Day: May 13, 2012," news release, March 19, 2012, https://www.census.gov/newsroom/releases/archives/facts_for_features_special_editions/cb12-ff08.html.

2. National Women's Law Center, *National Snapshot: Poverty Among Women and Families, 2014*, September 17, 2015, https://nwlc.org/resources/national -snapshot-poverty-among-women-families-2014. Jodi Grant et al., "Expecting Better: A State-by-State Analysis of Parental Leave Programs" (Washington, DC: National Partnership for Women and Families, 2005).

3. Claire Cain Miller, "The Gender Pay Gap Is Largely Because of Mother-hood," *New York Times*, May 13, 2017, https://www.nytimes.com/2017/05/13/upshot/the-gender-pay-gap-is-largely-because-of-motherhood.html.

4. Kathy Iandoli, "Gloria Steinem and Chelsea Handler Said the One Thing Most White Feminists Are Reluctant to Hear," *Bust*, April 5, 2017, http://bust.com/feminism/19481-gloria-steinem-chelsea-handler.html.

5. Kathy Iandoli, "Gloria Steinem and Chelsea Handler Said the One Thing Most White Feminists Are Reluctant to Hear," *Bust*, April 5, 2017, http://bust.com/feminism/19481-gloria-steinem-chelsea-handler.html.

6. Lauren Camera, "Black Girls Are Twice as Likely to Be Suspended, in Every State," *U.S. News and World Report*, May 9, 2017, https://www.usnews.com/news/education-news/articles/2017-05-09/black-girls-are-twice-as-likely -to-be-suspended-in-every-state.

7. Naa Oyo A. Kwate and Shatema Threadcraft, "Perceiving the Black Female Body: Race and Gender in Police Constructions of Body Weight," *Race and Social Problems* 7, no. 3 (2015): 213–226, http://doi.org/10.1007/s12552-015-9152-7.

8. Tanzina Vega, "Wage Gap between Blacks and Whites Is Worst in Nearly 40 Years," CNN Money, September 20, 2016, http://money.cnn.com/2016/09/20/news/economy/black-white-wage-gap/index.html.

9. Max Ehrenfreund, "Trying to Talk a Bus Driver into Giving You a Free Ride? Make Sure You're White, or Else Wear a Suit," *Washington Post*, February 25, 2015, http://www.washingtonpost.com/blogs/wonkblog/wp/2015/02/25/riding-buses-while-white-drivers-are-more-likely-to-let -white-passengers-skip-fares.

10. Michael A. Fletcher, "Whites Think Discrimination against Whites Is a Bigger Problem than Bias against Blacks," *Washington Post*, October 8, 2014, https://www.washingtonpost.com/news/wonk/wp/2014/10/08/white -people-think-racial-discrimination-in-america-is-basically-over.

11. Max Ehrenfreund, "There's a Disturbing Truth to John Legend's Oscar Statement about Prisons and Slavery," *Washington Post*, February 23, 2015, https://www.washingtonpost.com/news/wonk/wp/2015/02/23/theres -a-disturbing-truth-to-john-legends-oscar-statement-about-prisons-and -slavery.

12. Brian H. Levin, *Hate Crimes Rise in Major American Localities in 2016*, United States Department of Justice Hate Crime Summit, 2017, https://csbs.csusb .edu/sites/csusb_csbs/files/Levin%20DOJ%20Summit%202.pdf.

13. David Rock and Heidi Grant, "Why Diverse Teams Are Smarter," *Harvard Business Review*, November 4, 2016, https://hbr.org/2016/11/why-diverse -teams-are-smarter.

Chapter 2: The Benjamins

1. Nicole Goodkind, "Female Hedge Fund Managers Ruled the Markets in 2012," Yahoo! Finance, January 17, 2013, http://finance.yahoo.com/blogs/daily -ticker/female-hedge-fund-managers-ruled-markets-2012-135223093.html.

2. Claire Shipman, "What Is Womenomics?," ABC News, June 1, 2009, http:// abcnews.go.com/GMA/story?id=7721081.

3. National Partnership for Women and Families, *America's Women and the Wage Gap*, April 2017, http://www.nationalpartnership.org/research-library/ workplace-fairness/fair-pay/americas-women-and-the-wage-gap.pdf.

4. National Women's Law Center, *The Wage Gap by State for White, Non-Hispanic Women*, April 11, 2016, https://nwlc.org/resources/the-wage-gap-by-state -for-white-non-hispanic-women.

5. National Women's Law Center, *FAQ About the Wage Gap*, September 19, 2017, https://nwlc.org/resources/faq-about-the-wage-gap/.

6. National Asian Pacific American Women's Forum, *Fighting Invisibility Closing the Wage Gap: An Equal Pay Agenda for Asian Americans & Pacific Islanders*, March 2017, https://napawf.org/wp-content/uploads/2017/03/FIGHTING -INVISIBILITY_FINAL-4.03.17.pdf.

7. Crosby Burns, "The Gay and Transgender Wage Gap," *Center for American Progress*, April 16, 2012, https://www.americanprogress.org/issues/lgbt/ news/2012/04/16/11494/the-gay-and-transgender-wage-gap.

8. Catherine Rampell, "Before That Sex Change, Think about Your Next Paycheck," *New York Times*, September 25, 2008, https://economix.blogs .nytimes.com/2008/09/25/before-that-sex-change-think-about-your-next -paycheck.

9. National Asian Pacific American Women's Forum, *Achieving Pay Equity for Asian Americans and Pacific Islanders*, March 2017, https://napawf.org/wp-content/uploads/2009/10/EPD_Fact-Sheet_FINAL.pdf.

10. National Women's Law Center, *Equal Pay for Mothers Is Critical for Families*, May 22, 2017, https://nwlc.org/resources/equal-pay-for-mothers-is-critical-for-families.

11. National Women's Law Center, *Equal Pay for Mothers Is Critical for Families*, May 22, 2017, https://nwlc.org/resources/equal-pay-for-mothers-is-critical-for-families.

12. National Women's Law Center, *Equal Pay for Mothers Is Critical for Families*, May 22, 2017, https://nwlc.org/resources/equal-pay-for-mothers-is-critical-for-families.

13. National Women's Law Center, *Equal Pay for Mothers Is Critical for Families*, May 22, 2017, https://nwlc.org/resources/equal-pay-for-mothers-is-critical-for-families.

14. National Women's Law Center, *Equal Pay for Mothers Is Critical for Families*, May 22, 2017, https://nwlc.org/resources/equal-pay-for-mothers-is-critical-for-families.

15. Andrew J. Cherlin, Elizabeth Talbert, and Suzumi Yasutake, "Changing Fertility Regimes and the Transition to Adulthood: Evidence from a Recent Cohort," Johns Hopkins University, (2012), http://krieger.jhu.edu/sociology/wp-content/uploads/sites/28/2012/02/Read-Online.pdf.

16. U.S. Census Bureau, "The Majority of Children Live with Two Parents," news release, November 17, 2016, https://www.census.gov/newsroom/press-releases/2016/cb16-192.html.

17. R. Kelly Raley, Megan M. Sweeney, and Danielle Wondra, "The Growing Racial and Ethnic Divide in U.S. Marriage Patterns," *The Future of Children/Center for the Future of Children, the David and Lucile Packard Foundation* 25 no. 2 (2015): 89–109, https://www.ncbi.nlm.nih.gov/pmc/articles/PMC4850739/.

18. Jo Jones and William D. Mosher, "Fathers Involvement with Their Children: United States 2006–2010," *National Health Statistics Reports*, December 20, 2013, https://www.cdc.gov/nchs/data/nhsr/nhsr071.pdf.

19. Ginia Bellafante, "Two Fathers, with One Happy to Stay Home," *New York Times*, January 12, 2004, http://www.nytimes.com/2004/01/12/us/two-fathers-with-one-happy-to-stay-at-home.html.

20. Williams Institute UCLA School of Law, *Census and LGBT Demographic Studies*, 2017, https://williamsinstitute.law.ucla.edu/category/research/census-lgbt-demographics-studies.

21. Nolan Feeney, "Women Are Now More Likely to Have College Degree than Men," *Time*, October 7, 2015, http://time.com/4064665/women-college-degree.

22. Catherine Hill and Christianne Corbett, "Graduating to a Pay Gap: The Earnings of Women and Men One Year after College Graduation," American Association of University Women, http://www.aauw.org/research/graduating-to-a-pay-gap.

23. Claire Cain Miller, "Pay Gap Is Because of Gender, Not Jobs," *New York Times*, April 23, 2014, https://www.nytimes.com/2014/04/24/upshot/the-pay-gap-is-because-of-gender-not-jobs.html.

24. Francine D. Blau and Lawrence M. Kahn, "The Gender Wage Gap: Extent, Trends, and Explanations," Working Paper 9656, Institute for the Study of Labor (IZA), 2016.

25. "The Gender Shift," *DVM360 Magazine*, March 1, 2011, http://veterinarynews.dvm360.com/gender-shift-0.

26. Sarah Jane Glynn, "Explaining the Gender Wage Gap," Center for American Progress, May 19, 2014, https://cdn.americanprogress.org/wp-content/uploads/2014/05/WageGapBrief1.pdf.

27. Sarah Jane Glynn, "Explaining the Gender Wage Gap," Center for American Progress, May 19, 2014, https://cdn.americanprogress.org/wp-content/uploads/2014/05/WageGapBrief1.pdf.

28. Sarah Jane Glynn, Heather Boushey, and Peter Berg, "Who Gets Time Off? Predicting Access to Paid Leave and Workplace Flexibility," Center for American Progress, April 2016, https://cdn.americanprogress.org/wp-content/uploads/2016/04/20131209/WhoGetsTimeOff-report-04.20.16.pdf.

29. Laura Cohn, "Women Ask for Raises as Much as Men Do—But Get Them Less Often," *Fortune*, September 6, 2016, http://fortune.com/2016/09/06/women-men-salary-negotiations.

30. Katty Kay and Claire Shipman, "The Confidence Gap," *The Atlantic*, May 2014, https://www.theatlantic.com/magazine/archive/2014/05/the-confidence-gap/359815.

31. Nancy F. Clark, "Act Now to Shrink the Confidence Gap," *Forbes*, April 28, 2014, https://www.forbes.com/sites/womensmedia/2014/04/28/act-now-to-shrink-the-confidence-gap.

32. Kristin Rowe-Finkbeiner, "The Motherhood Penalty," *Politico Magazine*, April 30, 2014, http://www.politico.com/magazine/story/2014/04/the-motherhood-penalty-106173#.U5ooKHbLNUN.

33. John Bonazzo, "All-Male PR Panel Tells Women They Can Fix Sexism by 'Speaking Up More Loudly,'" *Observer*, June 9, 2017, http://observer.com/2017/06/sexism-at-work-mansplaining-public-relations.

34. Shadee Ashtari, "GOP Lawmaker Says Women Don't Deserve Equal Pay Because They're Lazier," *Huffington Post*, April 25, 2014, http://www.huffingtonpost.com/2014/04/24/will-infantine-paycheck-fairness-bill_n_5206350.html.

35. Francine D. Blau and Lawrence M. Kahn, "The Gender Wage Gap: Extent, Trends, and Explanations," Working Paper 9656, Institute for the Study of Labor (IZA), 2016.

36. Shelley J. Correll, Stephen Benard, and In Paik, "Getting a Job: Is There a Motherhood Penalty?" *American Journal of Sociology* 112, no. 5 (2007): 1297–1338, http://www.jstor.org/stable/10.1086/511799.

37. Heather Boushey, "The New Breadwinners," Shriver Report, September 10, 2009, http://shriverreport.org/the-new-breadwinners.

38. Michelle J. Budig, "The Fatherhood Bonus and the Motherhood Penalty: Parenthood and the Gender Gap in Pay," *Third Way*, September 2, 2014, http://www.thirdway.org/report/the-fatherhood-bonus-and-the-motherhood -penalty-parenthood-and-the-gender-gap-in-pay.

39. "Selected Characteristics of People 15 Years and Over, by Total Money Income, Work Experience, Race, Hispanic Origin, and Sex," U.S. Census Bureau, compiled by Sarah Jane Glynn, updated August 9, 2017, https:// www.census.gov/data/tables/time-series/demo/income-poverty/cps -pinc/pinc-01.html.

40. "The Economic Impact of Equal Pay by State," Institute for Policy Research, https://statusofwomendata.org/featured/the-economic-impact-of -equal-pay-by-state.

41. Heidi Hartmann, Jeff Hayes, and Jennifer Clark, "How Equal Pay for Working Women Would Reduce Poverty and Grow American Economy," Institute for Women's Policy Research, January 13, 2004, http:// www.iwpr.org/publications/pubs/how-equal-pay-for-working-women -would-reduce-poverty-and-grow-the-american-economy.

Chapter 3: The Invisible Glass Ceilings

1. "Selected Characteristics of People 15 Years and Over, by Total Money Income, Work Experience, Race, Hispanic Origin, and Sex," U.S. Census Bureau, compiled by Sarah Jane Glynn, updated August 9, 2017, https:// www.census.gov/data/tables/time-series/demo/income-poverty/cps -pinc/pinc-01.html.

2. "Street Harassment Statistics," ILR School Cornell University, April 17, 2015, https://www.ilr.cornell.edu/news/street-harassment-statistics.

3. "Street Harassment Statistics," ILR School Cornell University, April 17, 2015, https://www.ilr.cornell.edu/news/street-harassment-statistics.

4. ABC News, "One in Four U.S. Women Reports Workplace Harassment," news release, November 16, 2011, http://www.langerresearch.com/wp -content/uploads/1130a2WorkplaceHarassment.pdf.

5. "The Woman Who Created #MeToo Long Before Hashtags," *New York Times,* October 20, 2017, https://www.nytimes.com/2017/10/20/us/me-too -movement-tarana-burke.html.

6. "Women Earn More Degrees than Men; Gap Keeps Increasing," *The College Puzzle* (blog), Stanford University, May 28, 2013, https://collegepuzzle.stanford.edu/?tag=women-exceed-men-in-college-graduation.

7. "These Are the Women CEOs Leading Fortune 500 Companies," *Fortune*, June 7, 2017, http://fortune.com/2017/06/07/fortune-500-women-ceos.

8. "Women of Color in Elective Office 2017," Center for American Women and Politics, http://www.cawp.rutgers.edu/women-color-elective-office-2017.

9. Robert Sege, Linley Nykiel-Bub, and Sabrina Selk, "Sex Differences in Institutional Support for Junior Biomedical Researchers," *Journal of the American Medical Association* 314, no. 11 (2015): 1175–1177, https://doi.org/10.1001/jama.2015.8517.

10. Women's Media Center, *The Women's Media Center: The Status of Women in the U.S. Media 2014*, February 18, 2014, http://www.womensmediacenter.com/reports/2014-statistics.

11. Women's Media Center, *The Women's Media Center: The Status of Women in the U.S. Media 2014*, February 18, 2014, http://www.womensmediacenter.com/reports/2014-statistics.

12. Women's Media Center, *The Women's Media Center: The Status of Women in the U.S. Media 2014*, February 18, 2014, http://www.womensmediacenter.com/reports/2014-statistics.

13. Liam Stack, "Trump, in France, Tells Brigitte Macron, 'You're in Such Good Shape,'" *New York Times*, July 13, 2017, https://www.nytimes.com/2017/07/13/world/europe/trump-france-brigitte-macron.html.

14. Malin Malmstrom, Jeaneth Johansson, and Joakim Wincent, "We Recorded VCs' Conversations and Analyzed How Differently They Talk about Female Entrepreneurs," *Harvard Business Review*, May 17, 2017, https://hbr.org/2017/05/we-recorded-vcs-conversations-and-analyzed-how-differently-they-talk-about-female-entrepreneurs.

15. Malin Malmstrom, Jeaneth Johansson, and Joakim Wincent, "We Recorded VCs' Conversations and Analyzed How Differently They Talk about Female Entrepreneurs," *Harvard Business Review*, May 17, 2017, https://hbr.org/2017/05/we-recorded-vcs-conversations-and-analyzed-how-differently-they-talk-about-female-entrepreneurs.

16. Malin Malmstrom, Jeaneth Johansson, and Joakim Wincent, "We Recorded VCs' Conversations and Analyzed How Differently They Talk about Female Entrepreneurs," *Harvard Business Review*, May 17, 2017, https://hbr.org/2017/05/we-recorded-vcs-conversations-and-analyzed-how-differently-they-talk-about-female-entrepreneurs.

17. Anita Woolley and Thomas W. Malone, "Defend Your Research: What Makes a Team Smarter? More Women," *Harvard Business Review*, June 2011, https://hbr.org/2011/06/defend-your-research-what-makes-a-team-smarter-more-women.

18. Claire Shipman, "What Is Womenomics?" ABC News, June 1, 2009, http://abcnews.go.com/GMA/story?id=7721081.

19. Joe Pinsker, "Hedge Funds Run by Women Outperform Those Run by Men," *The Atlantic*, August 4, 2014, https://www.theatlantic.com/business/archive/2014/08/hedge-funds-run-by-women-outperform-other-hedge-funds/375542.

20. AAUW, *Barriers and Bias: The Status of Women in Leadership*, March 2016, http://www.aauw.org/aauw_check/pdf_download/show_pdf.php?file=barriers-and-bias.

21. AAUW, *Barriers and Bias: The Status of Women in Leadership*, March 2016, http://www.aauw.org/aauw_check/pdf_download/show_pdf.php?file=barriers-and-bias.

22. AAUW, *Barriers and Bias: The Status of Women in Leadership*, March 2016, http://www.aauw.org/aauw_check/pdf_download/show_pdf.php?file=barriers-and-bias.

23. Valentina Zarya, "Why There Are No Black Women Running Fortune 500 Companies," *Fortune*, January 16, 2017, http://fortune.com/2017/01/16/black-women-fortune-500.

24. AAUW, *Barriers and Bias: The Status of Women in Leadership*, March 2016, http://www.aauw.org/aauw_check/pdf_download/show_pdf.php?file=barriers-and-bias.

Chapter 4: Sound the Alarm

1. National Women's Law Center, *Minimum Wage*, http://www.nwlc.org/our-issues/poverty-%2526-income-support/minimum-wage.

2. "The 10 Fastest Growing Jobs," *U.S. Department of Labor Blog*, March 15, 2015, https://blog.dol.gov/2015/03/15/the-10-fastest-growing-jobs. "Occupations with the Most Job Growth," Bureau of Labor Statistics, United States Department of Labor, updated October 24, 2017, https://www.bls.gov/emp/ep_table_104.htm.

3. "The 10 Fastest Growing Jobs," *U.S. Department of Labor Blog*, March 15, 2015, https://blog.dol.gov/2015/03/15/the-10-fastest-growing-jobs. "Occupations with the Most Job Growth," Bureau of Labor Statistics, United States Department of Labor, updated October 24, 2017, https://www.bls.gov/emp/ep_table_104.htm.

4. Heidi Shierholz, "Low Wages and Scant Benefits Leave Many In-Home Workers Unable to Make Ends Meet," Briefing Paper 369, Economic Policy Institute, November 26, 2013, http://www.epi.org/publication/in-home-workers.

5. "What Home Health Aides Do," *Occupational Outlook Handbook, 2016–2017 edition*, Bureau of Labor Statistics, U.S. Department of Labor, December 17,

2015, https://www.bls.gov/ooh/healthcare/home-health-aides.htm#tab-2. "What Personal Care Aides Do," *Occupational Outlook Handbook, 2016–2017 edition,* Bureau of Labor Statistics, U.S. Department of Labor, December 17, 2015, https://www.bls.gov/ooh/personal-care-and-service/personal-care-aides.htm#tab-2.

6. Heidi Shierholz, "Low Wages and Scant Benefits Leave Many In-Home Workers Unable to Make Ends Meet," Briefing Paper 369, Economic Policy Institute, November 26, 2013, http://www.epi.org/publication/in-home-workers.

7. "2014 National Population Projections Tables," U.S. Census Bureau, updated May 9, 2017, https://www.census.gov/data/tables/2014/demo/popproj/2014-summary.

8. "Household Final Consumption Expenditure, etc. (% of GDP)," World Bank, accessed July 24, 2017, http://data.worldbank.org/indicator/NE.CON.PETC.ZS.

9. U.S. Census Bureau, *American Community Survey and Puerto Rico Community Survey 2015 Subject Definitions,* https://www2.census.gov/programs-surveys/acs/tech_docs/subject_definitions/2015_ACSSubjectDefinitions.pdf.

10. U.S. Census Bureau, *American Community Survey and Puerto Rico Community Survey 2015 Subject Definitions,* compiled by Sarah Jane Glynn, February 12, 2012, https://www2.census.gov/programs-surveys/acs/tech_docs/subject_definitions/2015_ACSSubjectDefinitions.pdf.

11. Jessica L. Semega, Kayla R. Fontenot, and Melissa A. Kollar, *Income and Poverty in the United States: 2016,* Poverty Table 3, September 12, 2017, https://www.census.gov/library/publications/2017/demo/p60-259.html.

12. Jessica L. Semega, Kayla R. Fontenot, and Melissa A. Kollar, *Income and Poverty in the United States: 2016,* Poverty Table 3, September 12, 2017, https://www.census.gov/library/publications/2017/demo/p60-259.html.

13. David Cooper and Dan Essrow, "Low-Wage Workers Are Older than You Think," Economic Policy Institute, August 28, 2013, http://www.epi.org/publication/wage-workers-older-88-percent-workers-benefit.

14. Bryce Covert, "Women Need a Raise in the Minimum Wage," *Forbes,* July 24, 2012, https://www.forbes.com/forbes/welcome/?toURL=https://www.forbes.com/sites/brycecovert/2012/07/24/women-need-a-raise-in-the-minimum-wage.

15. David Cooper and Dan Essrow, "Low-Wage Workers Are Older than You Think," Economic Policy Institute, August 28, 2013, http://www.epi.org/publication/wage-workers-older-88-percent-workers-benefit.

16. Catalyst, "Catalyst Quick Take: Buying Power," 2013.

17. "Minimum Wage," U.S. Department of Labor, 2017, https://www.dol.gov/general/topic/wages/minimumwage.

18. "Characteristics of Minimum Wage Workers, 2016," BLS Reports, Bureau of Labor Statistics, U.S. Department of Labor, updated April 2017, https://www.bls.gov/opub/reports/minimum-wage/2016/home.htm.

19. "May 2016 National Occupational Employment and Wage Estimates United States," Bureau of Labor Statistics, U.S. Department of Labor, updated March 31, 2017, https://www.bls.gov/oes/current/oes_nat.htm#00-0000.

20. Wendy Wang, Kim Parker, and Paul Taylor, "Breadwinner Moms: Mothers Are the Sole or Primary Provider in Four-in-Ten Households with Children; Public Conflicted about the Growing Trend," Pew Research Center, May 29, 2013, http://www.pewsocialtrends.org/2013/05/29/breadwinner -moms. Sarah Jane Glynn, "Breadwinning Mothers Are Increasingly the U.S. Norm," Center for American Progress, December 19, 2016, https://www.americanprogress.org/issues/women/reports/2016/12/19/295203/breadwinning-mothers-are-increasingly-the-u-s-norm.

21. "Characteristics of Minimum Wage Workers, 2016," BLS Reports, Bureau of Labor Statistics, U.S. Department of Labor, April 2017, https://www.bls .gov/opub/reports/minimum-wage/2016/home.htm.

22. "On 25th Anniversary of Last Tipped Minimum Wage Increase, Prominent National Advocacy and Research Groups Call for Nation to Adopt One Fair Wage for All Workers," ROC United, March 31, 2016, http://rocunited .org/25th-anniversary-2-13.

23. "The Glass Floor: Sexual Harassment in the Restaurant Industry," ROC United, October 7, 2014, http://rocunited.org/2014/10/new-report-the-glass -floor-sexual-harassment-in-the-restaurant-industry.

24. "Minimum Wages for Tipped Employees," Wage and Hour Division, U.S. Department of Labor, January 1, 2003, https://www.dol.gov/whd/state/ tipped2003.htm.

25. "A $15 Minimum Wage for New York's Fast Food Workers," National Employment Law Project, July 22, 2015, http://www.nelp.org/publication/ a-15-minimum-wage-for-new-yorks-fast-food-workers.

26. "On 25th Anniversary of Last Tipped Minimum Wage Increase, Prominent National Advocacy and Research Groups Call for Nation to Adopt One Fair Wage for All Workers," ROC United, March 31, 2016, http://rocunited .org/25th-anniversary-2-13.

27. "Labor Force Projections to 2024: The Labor Force is Growing, But Slowly," *Monthly Labor Review*, Bureau of Labor Statistics, U.S. Department of Labor, December 2015, https://www.bls.gov/opub/mlr/2015/article/labor-force -projections-to-2024.htm.

28. David Cooper, "Raising the Minimum Wage to $15 By 2024 Would Lift Wages for 41 Million American Workers," Economic Policy Institute, April 26, 2017, http://www.epi.org/publication/15-by-2024-would-lift-wages-for-41-million.

29. Economic Policy Institute, "It's Time to Raise the Wage," April 23, 2015, http://www.epi.org/publication/its-time-to-raise-the-minimum-wage.

30. David Cooper, "Raising the Minimum Wage to $15 By 2024 Would Lift Wages for 41 Million American Workers," Economic Policy Institute, April 26, 2017, http://www.epi.org/publication/15-by-2024-would-lift-wages-for-41 -million.

31. Ken Jacobs, Ian Perry, and Jenifer MacGillvary, "The High Public Cost of Low Wages," UC Berkeley Center for Labor Research and Education, April 2015, http://laborcenter.berkeley.edu/pdf/2015/the-high-public-cost-of-low -wages.pdf.

32. David Cooper and Douglas Hall, "Raising the Federal Minimum Wage to $10.10 Would Give Working Families, and the Overall Economy, a Much-Needed Boost," Economic Policy Institute, March 13, 2013, http://www .epi.org/publication/bp357-federal-minimum-wage-increase.

33. Cameron Davis, "Study: A Minimum Wage Hike Would Stimulate the Economy," Think Progress, July 8, 2013, https://thinkprogress.org/study -a-minimum-wage-hike-would-stimulate-the-economy-f02ca75732fc.

34. Chris Weller, "Obama Just Warned Congress about Robots Taking Over Jobs That Pay Less than $20 an Hour," *Business Insider,* March 10, 2016, http://www.businessinsider.com/obama-warns-congress-about-robot-job -takeover-2016-3.

35. Dottie Rosenbaum, "SNAP Is Effective and Efficient," Center on Budget and Policy Priorities, March 11, 2013, https://www.cbpp.org/research/ snap-is-effective-and-efficient.

36. Josh Bivens, "Don't Buy the Trickle-Down Myth Peddled by GOP Tax Plan," *The Hill,* November 7, 2017, http://thehill.com/opinion/finance/ 359080-dont-buy-the-trickle-down-myth-peddled-by-gop-tax-plan.

37. John D. Sutter, "What Is Income Inequality, Anyway?" CNN, October 29, 2013, http://edition.cnn.com/2013/10/29/opinion/sutter-explainer-income -inequality/index.html. "Income Inequality in the United States," Inequality .org, accessed July 24, 2017, https://inequality.org/facts/income-inequality.

38. Drew Desilver, "U.S. Income Inequality, on Rise for Decades, Is Now Highest since 1928," Pew Research Center, December 5, 2013, http://www.pewresearch .org/fact-tank/2013/12/05/u-s-income-inequality-on-rise-for-decades-is-now -highest-since-1928.

39. Drew Desilver, "U.S. Income Inequality, on Rise for Decades, Is Now Highest Since 1928," Pew Research Center, December 5, 2013, http://www.pewresearch .org/fact-tank/2013/12/05/u-s-income-inequality-on-rise-for-decades-is-now -highest-since-1928.

40. "Income Inequality in the United States," Inequality.org, https://inequality .org/facts/income-inequality.

41. Emmanuel Saez and Gabriel Zucman, "Wealth Inequality in the United States since 1913: Evidence from Capitalized Income Tax Data," National Bureau of Economic Research Working Paper Series, Working Paper 20625, October 2014, https://doi.org/10.3386/w20625.

42. "Americas Families and Living Arrangements: 2016," U.S. Census Bureau, last revised April 6, 2017, https://www.census.gov/data/tables/2016/demo/families/cps-2016.html.

43. Scott Stanley, "What Is the Divorce Rate Anyway? Around 42 Percent, One Scholar Believes," Institute for Family Studies, January 22, 2015, https://ifstudies.org/blog/what-is-the-divorce-rate-anyway-around-42-percent-one-scholar-believes.

44. Christian E. Weller and Michele E. Tolson, "Women's Economic Risk Exposure and Savings," Center for American Progress, April 27, 2017, https://www.americanprogress.org/issues/economy/reports/2017/04/27/431228/womens-economic-risk-exposure-savings.

45. Dedrick Asante-Muhammad, Chuck Collins, Josh Hoxie, and Emanuel Nieves, "The Road to Zero Wealth: How the Racial Wealth Divide Is Hollowing Out America's Middle Class," Prosperity Now, Institute for Policy Studies, September 2017, https://prosperitynow.org/files/PDFs/road_to_zero_wealth.pdf.

46. Elise Gould, "Racial Gaps in Wages, Wealth and More: A Quick Recap," Working Economics Blog, Economic Policy Institute, January 26, 2017, http://www.epi.org/blog/racial-gaps-in-wages-wealth-and-more-a-quick-recap.

47. Christopher Ingraham, "If You Thought Income Inequality Was Bad, Get a Load of Wealth Inequality," Washington Post, May 21, 2015, https://www.washingtonpost.com/news/wonk/wp/2015/05/21/the-top-10-of-americans-own-76-of-the-stuff-and-its-dragging-our-economy-down.

48. Board of Governors of the Federal Reserve System, "Financial Accounts of the United States: Flow of Funds, Balance Sheets, and Integrated Macroeconomics Accounts," news release, September 21, 2017, https://www.federalreserve.gov/releases/z1/current/z1.pdf.

49. Board of Governors of the Federal Reserve System, Report of the Economic Well-Being of U.S. Households in 2016, May 2017, https://www.federalreserve.gov/publications/files/2016-report-economic-well-being-us-households-201705.pdf.

50. "Moving On Up: Why Do Some Americans Leave the Bottom of the Economic Ladder, but Not Others?" Pew Charitable Trusts, brief, November 2013, http://www.pewtrusts.org/~/media/assets/2013/11/01/movingonuppdf.pdf.

51. Andrew Fieldhouse, "How Much Can Tax Policy Curb Income Inequality Growth? Maybe a Lot," Working Economics Blog, Economic Policy Institute, June 14, 2013, http://www.epi.org/blog/tax-policy-curb-income-inequality-growth.

52. "Income Inequality Remains High in the Face of Weak Recovery," Organisation for Economic Co-operation and Development, November 2016, http://www.oecd.org/social/OECD2016-Income-Inequality-Update.pdf.

53. Chloe Farand, "U.S. Has Regressed to Developing Nation Status, MIT Economist Warns," *Independent*, April 21, 2017, http://www.independent.co.uk/news/world/americas/us-developing-nation-regressing-economy-poverty-donald-trump-mit-economist-peter-temin-a7694726.html.

Chapter 5: The Maternal Wall

1. U.S. Department of Labor, Bureau of Labor Statistics, *National Compensation Survey: Employee Benefits in the United States, March 2016*, tables 16 and 32, accessed September 23, 2016, http://www.bls.gov/ncs/ebs/benefits/2016/ebbl0059.pdf.

2. U.S. Department of Labor, Bureau of Labor Statistics, *National Compensation Survey: Employee Benefits in the United States, March 2016*, tables 16 and 32, accessed September 23, 2016, http://www.bls.gov/ncs/ebs/benefits/2016/ebbl0059.pdf.

3. Gretchen Livingston, "Among 41 Nations, U.S. Is the Outlier When It Comes to Paid Parental Leave," Pew Research Center, September 26, 2016, http://www.pewresearch.org/fact-tank/2016/09/26/u-s-lacks-mandated-paid-parental-leave.

4. Sharon Lerner, "The Real War on Families: Why the U.S. Needs Paid Leave Now," *In These Times*, August 18, 2015, http://inthesetimes.com/article/18151/the-real-war-on-families.

5. Valentina Zarya, "The Percentage of Female CEOs in the Fortune 500 Drops to 4%," *Fortune*, June 6, 2016, http://fortune.com/2016/06/06/women-ceos-fortune-500-2016.

6. "Impact of Hunger," Feeding America, 2017, http://www.feedingamerica.org/hunger-in-america/impact-of-hunger.

7. National Women's Law Center, *National Shapshot: Poverty Among Women and Families, 2014*, September 17, 2015, https://nwlc.org/resources/national-snapshot-poverty-among-women-families-2014.

8. World Economic Forum, *The Global Gender Gap Report*, 2015, http://www3.weforum.org/docs/GGGR2015/cover.pdf.

9. Catherine Rampell, "Women Now a Majority in American Workplaces," *New York Times*, February 5, 2010, http://www.nytimes.com/2010/02/06/business/economy/06women.html.

10. Wendy Wang, Kim Parker, and Paul Taylor, "Breadwinner Moms: Mothers Are the Sole or Primary Provider in Four-in-Ten Households with Children; Public Conflicted about the Growing Trend," Pew Research Center, May 29, 2013, http://www.pewsocialtrends.org/2013/05/29/breadwinner-moms.

11. "CCW's Study Finds Paid Family Leave Leads to Positive Economic Out-comes," Rutgers School of Management and Labor Relations, January 19, 2012, https://smlr.rutgers.edu/news/cwws-study-finds-paid-family-leave-leads -positive-economic-outcomes.

12. "The Benefits of Paternity Leave," *The Economist*, May 15, 2015, http:// www.economist.com/blogs/economist-explains/2015/05/economist -explains-18.

13. "The Benefits of Paternity Leave," *The Economist*, May 15, 2015, http:// www.economist.com/blogs/economist-explains/2015/05/economist -explains-18.

14. Lisa Wade, "The Invisible Workload That Drags Women Down," *Money*, December 29, 2016, http://time.com/money/4561314/women-work-home -gender-gap.

15. Brigid Schulte, "Once the Baby Comes, Moms Do More, Dads Do Less around the House," *Washington Post*, May 7, 2015, https://www.washingtonpost .com/news/parenting/wp/2015/05/07/once-the-baby-comes-moms -do-more-dads-do-less-around-the-house.

16. United Nations Development Programme, *The Human Development Report* (Oxford University Press, 1995), 97.

17. United Nations Development Programme, *The Human Development Report* (Oxford University Press, 1995), 97.

18. Sakiko Tanaka, "Parental Leave and Child Health across OECD Coun-tries," *Economic Journal* 115, no. 501 (2005): 7–28. There is a strong correla-tion between parental leave entitlements and thriving children—one study (Christopher J. Ruhm, "Parental Leave and Child Health," working paper, National Bureau of Economic Research, Cambridge, MA, May 1998, www .nber.org/papers/w6554) found that a year of job-protected *paid* leave is tied to 25 percent fewer post-neonatal deaths and that those benefits continued forward in the child's life with 11 percent fewer deaths of children between one and five years old. Twenty-five percent fewer deaths is a pretty strong argument.

19. Nicholas Bakalar, "Breast-Feeding May Have Benefits Decades Later," *New York Times*, March 17, 2015, https://well.blogs.nytimes.com/2015/03/17/ breast-feeding-may-have-benefits-decades-later.

20. Nicholas Bakalar, "Breast-Feeding May Have Benefits Decades Later," *New York Times*, March 17, 2015, https://well.blogs.nytimes.com/2015/03/17/ breast-feeding-may-have-benefits-decades-later.

21. Eileen Appelbaum and Ruth Milkman, "Leaves That Pay: Employer and Worker Experiences with Paid Family Leave in California," 2011, http://cepr .net/documents/publications/paid-family-leave-1-2011.pdf. Heather Boushey and Sarah Gynn, "There Are Significant Business Costs to Replacing

Employees," *Center for American Progress*, November 16, 2012, https://cdn
.americanprogress.org/wp-content/uploads/2012/11/CostofTurnover.pdf.

22. Deepa Purushothaman, "Parental Leave Survey: Less than Half of People
Surveyed Feel Their Organization Helps Men Feel Comfortable Taking Parental Leave," Deloitte, news release, June 15, 2016, https://www2
.deloitte.com/us/en/pages/about-deloitte/articles/press-releases/deloitte
-survey-parental-leave.html.

23. Claire Cain Miller, "In Google's Inner Circle, a Falling Number of Women,"
New York Times, August 22, 2012, http://www.nytimes.com/2012/08/23/
technology/in-googles-inner-circle-a-falling-number-of-women.html.

24. Rutgers School of Management and Labor Relations, "CCW's Study Finds
Paid Family Leave Leads to Positive Economic Outcomes," January 19, 2012,
https://smlr.rutgers.edu/news/cwws-study-finds-paid-family-leave-leads
-positive-economic-outcomes.

25. Barbara Gault, Heidi Hartmann, Ariane Hegewisch, Jessica Milli, and Lind-
sey Reichlin, "Paid Parental Leave in the U.S.: What the Data Tells Us about
Access, Usage, Economic, and Health Benefits," Institute for Women's
Policy Research, March 2014, https://www.dol.gov/wb/resources/paid
_parental_leave_in_the_united_states.pdf.

26. Jane Waldfogel and Sara McLanahan, "Work and Family: Introducing the
Issue," *The Future of Children* 21, no. 2 (2011): 3–14. http://www.jstor.org/
stable/41289627.

27. Brigid Schulte, "Voters Want Paid Leave, Paid Sick Days, Poll Shows. Obama,
Too. Will Congress Oblige?" *Washington Post*, January 21, 2015, https://www
.washingtonpost.com/news/local/wp/2015/01/21/voters-want-paid-leave
-paid-sick-days-poll-shows-obama-too-will-congress-oblige.

28. National Partnership for Women and Families, *Paid Family/Parental Leave
Policies for Municipal Employees (Not Exhaustive): February 2017–April 2017*,
April 2017, http://www.nationalpartnership.org/research-library/work-family/
psd/paid-family-leave-policies-for-municipal-employees.pdf.

29. National Partnership for Women and Families, *Working Women Need Paid
Sick Days*, April 2013, http://www.nationalpartnership.org/research-library/
work-family/psd/working-women-need-paid-sick-days.pdf.

30. Bureau of Labor Statistics, U.S. Department of Labor, "Employee Benefits
in the United States—March 2017," news release, July 21, 2017, http://www
.bls.gov/news.release/pdf/ebs2.pdf. National Partnership for Women and
Families, *Paid Sick Days Improve Our Public Health*, April 2013, http://paidsick
days.nationalpartnership.org/site/DocServer/Fact_sheet_Paid_Sick
_Days_Improve_Public_Health.pdf?docID=4185.

31. Andrew Green, Kai Filion, and Elise Gould, "The Need for Paid Sick Days:
The Lack of a Federal Policy Further Erodes Family Economic Security,"

Economic Policy Institute, June 29, 2011, http://www.epi.org/publication/the_need_for_paid_sick_days.

32. National Partnership for Women and Families, *Paid Sick Days: Good for Business, Good for Workers*, August 2012, http://www.nationalpartnership.org/research-library/work-family/psd/paid-sick-days-good-for-business-and-workers.pdf.

33. Bryce Covert, "The U.S. Is the Only Developed Country without Paid Sick Days. Obama Is Calling for That to Change," Think Progress, January 14, 2015, https://thinkprogress.org/the-u-s-is-the-only-developed-country-without-paid-sick-days-obama-is-calling-for-that-to-change-21af09694174.

34. "About Us," Support Paid Sick Days (website), accessed July 10, 2017, http://www.paidsickdays.org/about-us.

35. "Paid Sick Days Campaigns," Support Paid Sick Days, accessed July 10, 2017, http://www.paidsickdays.org/campaigns.

36. Bureau of Labor Statistics, U.S. Department of Labor, "Employee Benefits in the United States—March 2017," news release, July 21, 2017, http://www.bls.gov/news.release/pdf/ebs2.pdf.

37. Andrew Green, Kai Filion, and Elise Gould, "The Need for Paid Sick Days: The Lack of a Federal Policy Further Erodes Family Economic Security," Economic Policy Institute, June 29, 2011, http://www.epi.org/publication/the_need_for_paid_sick_days.

38. Oxfam America, *Hard Work, Hard Lives*, 2013, https://www.oxfamamerica.org/static/media/files/low-wage-worker-report-oxfam-america.pdf.

39. Adapted from "#KeepMarching: MomsRising Advocacy and Organizing Tactics and Tips," https://s3.amazonaws.com/s3.momsrising.org/images/Keep_Marching_Toolkit_2_1. pdf and https://www.momsrising.org/blog/updated-keepmarching-meeting-guides-and-recordings. Beth Messersmith, MomsRising senior campaign director, led the creation of this guide along with the MomsRising team.

Chapter 6: Saving Lives

1. National Partnership for Women and Families, "Women: Health Care Decision Makers," September 2013, http://www.nationalpartnership.org/research-library/health-care/aca-enrollment-event-toolkit.pdf.

2. "Fact Sheet: The Affordable Care Act and the Disability Community," Advocacy Monitor, January 6, 2017, http://www.advocacymonitor.com/fact-sheet-the-affordable-care-act-and-the-disability-community.

3. "Health Insurance and Mental Health Services," U.S. Department of Health and Human Services, accessed July 7, 2017, https://www.mentalhealth.gov/get-help/health-insurance/index.html.

4. Danielle Kurtzleben, "Here's What the GOP Bill Would (and Wouldn't) Change for Women's Health Care," NPR, March 10, 2017, http://www.npr

.org/2017/03/10/519461271/heres-what-the-gop-bill-would-and-wouldnt
-change-for-womens-healthcare.

5. Josh Hoxie, "Join the Civilized World: America Is Ready for Sanders-Style Universal Health Coverage," *U.S. News and World Report*, September 15, 2017, https://www.usnews.com/opinion/policy-dose/articles/2017-09-15/bernie-sanders-medicare-for-all-would-give-us-civilized-health-care.

6. Zac Auter, "U.S. Uninsured Rate Edges up Slightly," *Gallup News*, April 10, 2017, http://www.gallup.com/poll/208196/uninsured-rate-edges-slightly.aspx.

7. Samantha Artiga, Petry Ubri, Julia Foutz, and Anthony Damico, "Health Coverage by Race and Ethnicity: Examining Changes under the ACA and the Remaining Uninsured," Kaiser Commission on Medicaid and the Uninsured, Henry J. Kaiser Family Foundation, November 2016, http://files.kff.org/attachment/Issue-Brief-Health-Coverage-by-Race-and-Ethnicity-Examining-Changes-Under-the-ACA-and-the-Remaining-Uninsured.

8. Michael Karpman, Laura Skopec, and Sharon K. Long, "QuickTake: Uninsurance Rate Nearly Halved for Lesbian, Gay and Bisexual Adults since Mid-2013," Health Reform Monitoring Survey, Urban Institute Health Policy Center, April 16, 2015, http://hrms.urban.org/quicktakes/Uninsurance-Rate-Nearly-Halved-for-Lesbian-Gay-and-Bisexual-Adults-since-Mid-2013.html.

9. Kenneth D. Kochanek, Sherry L. Murphy, Jiaquan Xu, and Betzaida Tejada-Vera, "Deaths: Final Data for 2014," *National Vital Statistics Reports* 65 no. 4 (June 30, 2016), https://www.cdc.gov/nchs/data/nvsr/nvsr65/nvsr65_04.pdf. "Life Expectancy at Birth (in Years), by Race/Ethnicity," State Health Facts, Henry J. Kaiser Family Foundation, accessed July 7, 2017, http://www.kff.org/other/state-indicator/life-expectancy-by-re.

10. Kenneth D. Kochanek, Sherry L. Murphy, Jiaquan Xu, and Betzaida Tejada-Vera, "Deaths: Final Data for 2014," *National Vital Statistics Reports* 65 no. 4 (June 30, 2016), https://www.cdc.gov/nchs/data/nvsr/nvsr65/nvsr65_04.pdf.

11. M. R. Benjamins, J. L. Herschtick, B. R. Hunt, M. M. Hughes, and B. Hunter, "Racial Disparities in Heart Disease Mortality in the 50 Largest U.S. Cities," *Journal of Racial and Ethnic Health Disparities*, (December 6, 2016), https://www.ncbi.nlm.nih.gov/m/pubmed/27924619/?i=9&from=racial%20disparities%20life%20expectancies.

12. Kenneth D. Kochanek, Sherry L. Murphy, Jiaquan Xu, and Betzaida Tejada-Vera, "Deaths: Final Data for 2014," *National Vital Statistics Reports* 65 no. 4 (June 30, 2016), https://www.cdc.gov/nchs/data/nvsr/nvsr65/nvsr65_04.pdf.

13. Alexandra Samuels, "U.Va. Report: Med Students Believe Black People Feel Less Pain than Whites," *USA Today College*, April 5, 2016, http://college.usatoday.com/2016/04/05/uva-report-med-students-black-people-feel-less-pain.

14. "Health Insurance Coverage of Children 0–18," State Health Facts, Henry J. Kaiser Family Foundation, accessed July 6, 2017, http://www.kff.org/other/state-indicator/children-0-18.

15. Medicaid and CHIP Payment and Access Commission, "People with Disabilities," 2017, https://www.macpac.gov/subtopic/people-with-disabilities.

16. Julia Paradise, "Medicaid Moving Forward," Henry J. Kaiser Family Foundation, March 9, 2015, https://www.kff.org/health-reform/issue-brief/medicaid-moving-forward.

17. Anne Rossier Markus, Ellie Andres, Kristina D. West, Nicole Garro, and Cynthia Pellegrini, "Medicaid Covered Births, 2008 through 2010, in the Context of the Implementation of Health Reform," *Women's Health Issues* 23, no. 5 (2013), http://dx.doi.org/10.1016/j.whi.2013.06.006.

18. Jesse Cross-Call, Tara Straw, Arloc Sherman, and Matt Broaddus, "House-Passed Bill Would Devastate Health Care in Rural America," Center on Budget and Policy Priorities, May 16, 2017, https://www.cbpp.org/research/health/house-passed-bill-would-devastate-health-care-in-rural-america.

19. Christopher Warshaw and David Broockman, "G.O.P. Senators Might Not Realize It, but Not One State Supports the Republican Health Care Bill," *New York Times*, June 14, 2017, https://www.nytimes.com/2017/06/14/upshot/gop-senators-might-not-realize-it-but-not-one-state-supports-the-ahca.html.

20. "Distribution of the Nonelderly with Medicaid by Race/Ethnicity," State Health Facts, Henry J. Kaiser Family Foundation, accessed July 6, 2017, http://www.kff.org/medicaid/state-indicator/distribution-by-raceethnicity-4.

21. Adapted from "#KeepMarching: MomsRising Advocacy and Organizing Tactics and Tips," https://s3.amazonaws.com/s3.momsrising.org/images/Keep_Marching_Toolkit_2_1.pdf and https://www.momsrising.org/blog/updated-keepmarching-meeting-guides-and-recordings. Beth Messersmith, MomsRising senior campaign director, led the creation of this guide along with the MomsRising team.

Chapter 7: The Choice Is Ours!

1. Rachael Combe, "The Head of NARAL on Why It's Not Strange That She's Pregnant," *Elle*, September 24, 2015, http://www.elle.com/culture/career-politics/a30204/illyse-hogue-profile.

2. Pew Research Center, *Public Opinion on Abortion*, June 2017, http://www.pewforum.org/fact-sheet/public-opinion-on-abortion.

3. Patrick Caldwell, "NARAL President Talks about Her Abortion in DNC Speech," *Mother Jones*, July 28, 2016, http://www.motherjones.com/politics/2016/07/naral-ilyse-hogue-dnc-abortion.

4. Guttmacher Institute, *Induced Abortion in the United States*, October 2017, https://www.guttmacher.org/fact-sheet/induced-abortion-united -states#2a.

5. Melanie Hicken, "Average Cost of Raising a Child Hits $245,000," CNN Money, August 18, 2014, http://money.cnn.com/2014/08/18/pf/child-cost/ index.html.

6. Genevieve Field, "Planned Parenthood's Cecile Richards: 'I Will Fight for Women's Rights Every Day,'" *Glamour*, October 29, 2015, https://www.glam our.com/story/cecile-richards.

7. "The Impact of Defunding Planned Parenthood," I Stand with Planned Parenthood, accessed August 6, 2017, https://www.istandwithpp.org/ defund-defined/impact-defunding-planned-parenthood.

8. Todd Ackerman, "Texas Pregnancy-Related Deaths Double," *Houston Chronicle*, August 18, 2016, http://www.houstonchronicle.com/news/houston-texas/ houston/article/Texas-pregnancy-related-deaths-double-9172022.php.

9. Guttmacher Institute, *Induced Abortion in the United States*, October 2017, https://www.guttmacher.org/fact-sheet/induced-abortion-united -states#2a.

10. Guttmacher Institute, *Induced Abortion in the United States*, October 2017, https://www.guttmacher.org/fact-sheet/induced-abortion-united-states#2a.

11. Joerg Dreweke, "U.S. Abortion Rate Reaches Record Low Amidst Looming Onslaught against Reproductive Health and Rights," *Guttmacher Policy Review* 20 (January 17, 2017), https://www.guttmacher.org/gpr/2017/01/ us-abortion-rate-reaches-record-low-amidst-looming-onslaught-against -reproductive-health.

12. Sean Illing, "Persuasive Proof That America Is Full of Racist and Selfish People," Vox, October 9, 2017, https://www.vox.com/conversations/ 2017/6/13/15768622/facebook-social-media-seth-stephens-davidowitz -everybody-lies.

13. Beth Skwarecki, "Which Policies Lead to Less Abortion? The ACA, State Law, and the Supreme Court," Public Health Perspectives, *PLOS Blog*, February 6, 2017, http://blogs.plos.org/publichealth/2017/02/06/which-policies-lead -to-less-abortion-the-aca-state-law-the-supreme-court.

14. Guttmacher Institute, *Induced Abortion in the United States*, October 2017, https://www.guttmacher.org/fact-sheet/induced-abortion-united-states#2a.

15. Jenna Jerman, Rachel K. Jones, and Tsuyoshi Onda, "Characteristics of U.S. Abortion Patients in 2014 and Changes since 2008," Guttmacher Institute, May 2016, https://www.guttmacher.org/report/characteristics-us-abortion -patients-2014.

16. Jessica Dickler, "The Rising Cost of Raising a Child," CNN Money, September 21, 2011, http://money.cnn.com/2011/09/21/pf/cost_raising_child/index.htm.

17. Kathrin F. Stanger-Hall and David W. Hall, "Abstinence-Only Education and Teen Pregnancy Rates: Why We Need Comprehensive Sex Education in the U.S.," *PLoS One* 6, no. 10 (2011), https://www.ncbi.nlm.nih.gov/pmc/articles/PMC3194801.

18. Guttmacher Institute, *Contraceptive Use in the United States*, September 2016, https://www.guttmacher.org/fact-sheet/contraceptive-use-united-states.

19. Guttmacher Institute, *Induced Abortion in the United States*, October 2017, https://www.guttmacher.org/fact-sheet/induced-abortion-united-states#2a.

20. Kathryn Kost and Isaac Maddow-Zimet, "U.S. Teenage Pregnancies, Births and Abortions, 2011: State Trends by Age, Race and Ethnicity," Guttmacher Institute, April 2016, https://www.guttmacher.org/report/us-teen-pregnancy-state-trends-2011.

21. "United States Abortion," Guttmacher Institute, accessed August 7, 2017, https://www.guttmacher.org/united-states/abortion.

22. Guttmacher Institute, *Induced Abortion in the United States*, October 2017, https://www.guttmacher.org/fact-sheet/induced-abortion-united-states#2a.

23. Martha J. Bailey, Brad Hershbein, and Amalia R. Miller, "The Opt-In Revolution? Contraception and the Gender Gap in Wages," *American Economic Journal: Applied Economics* 4, no. 3 (2012): 225–254.

24. "United States Abortion," Guttmacher Institute, accessed August 7, 2017, https://www.guttmacher.org/united-states/abortion. Guttmacher Institute, *Induced Abortion in the United States*, October 2017, https://www.guttmacher.org/fact-sheet/induced-abortion-united-states#2a. "Last Five Years Account for More than One-Quarter of All Abortion Restrictions Enacted since Roe," Guttmacher Institute, January 13, 2016, https://www.guttmacher.org/article/2016/01/last-five-years-account-more-one-quarter-all-abortion-restrictions-enacted-roe.

25. Beth Skwarecki, "Which Policies Lead to Less Abortion? The ACA, State Law, and the Supreme Court," Public Health Perspectives, *PLOS Blog*, February 6, 2017, http://blogs.plos.org/publichealth/2017/02/06/which-policies-lead-to-less-abortion-the-aca-state-law-the-supreme-court.

26. Jennifer J. Frost, Lori F. Frohwirth, and Mia R. Zolna, "Contraceptive Needs and Services, 2014 Update," Guttmacher Institute, September 2016, https://www.guttmacher.org/report/contraceptive-needs-and-services-2014-update.

27. Adapted from "#KeepMarching: MomsRising Advocacy and Organizing Tactics and Tips," https://s3.amazonaws.com/s3.momsrising.org/images/Keep_Marching_Toolkit_2_1.pdf and https://www.momsrising.org/blog/updated-keepmarching-meeting-guides-and-recordings. Beth Messersmith, MomsRising senior campaign director, led the creation of this guide along with the MomsRising team.

Chapter 8: Women against Violence

1. Soo Na Pak, "9 Stupid Things That Cops, Nurses, Lawyers and Friends Should Never Say to Rape Survivors—But, Alas, Have," Alternet, February 12, 2014, http://www.alternet.org/culture/9-stupid-things-cops-nurses-lawyers-and-friends-should-never-say-survivors.

2. National Center for Injury Prevention and Control, *Findings from the National Intimate Partner and Sexual Violence Survey 2010-2012 State Report*, accessed July 10, 2017 https://www.cdc.gov/violenceprevention/pdf/NISVS-StateReportFactsheet.pdf.

3. Legal Momentum, *Domestic and Sexual Violence and the Workplace*, accessed July 7, 2017, http://www.legalmomentum.org/sites/default/files/reports/DV%20SA%20and%20Workplace%202-2014-final.pdf.

4. Mary Emily O'Hara, "Domestic Violence: Nearly Three U.S. Women Killed Every Day by Intimate Partners," NBC News, April 11, 2017, https://www.nbcnews.com/news/us-news/domestic-violence-nearly-three-u-s-women-killed-every-day-n745166.

5. Camila Domonoske, "CDC: Half of All Female Homicide Victims Are Killed by Intimate Partners," NPR, July 21, 2017, http://www.npr.org/sections/thetwo-way/2017/07/21/538518569/cdc-half-of-all-female-murder-victims-are-killed-by-intimate-partners.

6. Malika Saada Saar, Rebecca Epstein, Lindsay Rosenthal, and Yasmin Vafa, "The Sexual Abuse to Prison Pipeline: The Girls' Story," Center on Poverty and Inequality, Georgetown University Law Center, 2015, http://rights4girls.org/wp-content/uploads/r4g/2015/02/2015_COP_sexual-abuse_report_final.pdf.

7. Service Women's Action Network, *Rape, Sexual Assault and Sexual Harassment in the Military: The Quick Facts*, April 2012, http://www.ncdsv.org/images/SWAN_Rape-SA-and-Sexual-Harassment-in-the-Military-the-Quick-Facts_4-2012.pdf. Jennifer Medina, "Too Scared to Report Sexual Abuse. The Fear: Deportation," *New York Times*, April 30, 2017, https://www.nytimes.com/2017/04/30/us/immigrants-deportation-sexual-abuse.html. Associated Press, "LAPD: Fear of Deportation Keeping Latinos From Reporting Sex Crimes," CBS Los Angeles, March 22, 2017, http://losangeles.cbslocal.com/2017/03/22/lapd-fear-of-deportation-keeping-latinos-from-reporting-sex-crimes. Migration Policy Institute, *Children in U.S. Immigrant Families*, https://www.migrationpolicy.org/programs/data-hub/charts/children-immigrant-families. U.S. Department of Health and Human Services, *Child Health USA 2014*, 2014, https://mchb.hrsa.gov/chusa14/population-characteristics/children-immigrant-parents.html.

8. Jennifer Medina, "Too Scared to Report Sexual Abuse. The Fear: Deportation," *New York Times*, April 30, 2017, https://www.nytimes.com/2017/04/30/

us/immigrants-deportation-sexual-abuse.html. Associated Press, "LAPD: Fear of Deportation Keeping Latinos From Reporting Sex Crimes," *CBS Los Angeles*, March 22, 2017, http://losangeles.cbslocal.com/2017/03/22/lapd-fear-of-deportation-keeping-latinos-from-reporting-sex-crimes.

9. Migration Policy Institute, *Children in U.S. Immigrant Families*, https://www.migrationpolicy.org/programs/data-hub/charts/children-immigrant-families. U.S. Department of Health and Human Services, *Child Health USA 2014*, 2014, https://mchb.hrsa.gov/chusa14/population-characteristics/children-immigrant-parents.html.

10. Devlin Barrett, "DHS: Immigration Agents May Arrest Crime Victims, Witnesses at Courthouses," *Washington Post*, April 4, 2017, https://www.washingtonpost.com/world/national-security/dhs-immigration-agents-may-arrest-crime-victims-witnesses-at-courthouses/2017/04/04/3956e6d8-196d-11e7-9887-1a5314b56a08_story.html.

11. Raquel Kennedy Bergen, "Marital Rape," Applied Research Forum, National Electronic Network on Violence Against Women, March 1999, https://web.archive.org/web/20111006080602/http://www.taasa.org/library/pdfs/TAASALibrary104.pdf.

12. Katherine S. Spaht and Cynthia Samuel, "Equal Management Revisited: 1979 Legislative Modifications of the 1978 Matrimonial Regimes Law," *Louisiana Law Review* 40, no. 1 (1979), http://digitalcommons.law.lsu.edu/cgi/viewcontent.cgi?article=4457&context=lalrev.

13. National Network to End Domestic Violence (website), 2017, https://nnedv.org.

14. Lindsay Peoples, "Marissa Alexander Fired a Warning Shot at Her Abusive Husband and Was Sentenced to 20 Years. Now She's Free," The Cut, March 29, 2017, https://www.thecut.com/2017/03/marissa-alexander-case-stand-your-ground-florida.html.

15. Christine Hauser, "Florida Woman Whose 'Stand Your Ground' Defense Was Rejected Is Released," *New York Times*, February 7, 2017, https://www.nytimes.com/2017/02/07/us/marissa-alexander-released-stand-your-ground.html.

16. "Survivors of Abuse and Incarceration," Correctional Association of New York (website), updated October 18, 2017, http://www.correctionalassociation.org/issue/domestic-violence.

17. Christine Hauser, "Florida Woman Whose 'Stand Your Ground' Defense Was Rejected Is Released," *New York Times*, February 7, 2017, https://www.nytimes.com/2017/02/07/us/marissa-alexander-released-stand-your-ground.html.

18. Free Marissa Now (website), updated January 27, 2017, http://www.freemarissanow.org.

19. Hayley Tsukayama, "George Zimmerman Raised Just over $200K Online, Lawyer Says," *Washington Post*, April 27, 2012, https://www.washington

post.com/business/technology/george-zimmerman-raised-200k-online -lawyer-says/2012/04/27/gIQApX4hlT_story.html.

20. Center for Gun Policy and Research, Johns Hopkins Bloomberg School of Public Health, *Intimate Partner Violence and Firearms*, accessed July 9, 2017, http://www.jhsph.edu/research/centers-and-institutes/johns-hopkins -center-for-gun-policy-and-research/publications/IPV_Guns.pdf.

21. Christopher Ingraham, "There Are Now More Guns than People in the United States," *Washington Post*, October 5, 2015, https://www.washington post.com/news/wonk/wp/2015/10/05/guns-in-the-united-states-one-for -every-man-woman-and-child-and-then-some.

22. *Small Arms Survey*, Annexe 4, "The Largest Civilian Firearms Arsenals for 178 Countries," 2007, http://www.smallarmssurvey.org/fileadmin/docs/A-Year book/2007/en/Small-Arms-Survey-2007-Chapter-02-annexe-4-EN.pdf.

23. *Small Arms Survey 2015*, Graduate Institute of International and Develop- ment Studies, Geneva, 2015, http://www.smallarmssurvey.org/fileadmin/ docs/A-Yearbook/2015/eng/Small-Arms-Survey-2015-Highlights-EN.pdf.

24. Center for American Progress, "Gun Owners Overwhelmingly Support Background Checks, See NRA as Out of Touch, New Poll Finds," news release, November 17, 2015, https://www.americanprogress.org/press/ release/2015/11/17/125618/release-gun-owners-overwhelmingly-support -background-checks-see-nra-as-out-of-touch-new-poll-finds.

25. Arkadi Gerney and Chelsea Parsons, "Women under the Gun: How Gun Violence Affects Women and 4 Policy Solutions to Better Protect Them," Center for American Progress, June 2014, https://cdn.americanprogress .org/wp-content/uploads/2014/06/GunsDomesticViolencereport -summary.pdf.

26. Kerry Shaw, "12 Facts That Show How Guns Make Domestic Violence Even Deadlier," The Trace, August 22, 2016, https://www.thetrace.org/2016/08/15 -facts-that-show-how-guns-make-domestic-violence-even-deadlier.

27. Louis Jacobson, "Hillary Clinton Says 33,000 Americans Die Each Year from Guns," *Politifact*, October 19, 2016, http://www.politifact.com/truth -o-meter/statements/2016/oct/19/hillary-clinton/hillary-clinton-says -33000-americans-die-each-year. Kenneth D. Kochanek, Sherry L. Mur- phy, Jiaquan Xu, and Betzaida Tejada-Vera, "Deaths: Final Data for 2014," *National Vital Statistics Reports* 65, no. 4 (June 30, 2016), https://www.cdc .gov/nchs/data/nvsr/nvsr65/nvsr65_04.pdf.

28. Erin Schumaker, "Guns Are Now the Third-Leading Cause of Death among Children," *Huffington Post*, updated June 30, 2017, http://www.huffingtonpost .com/entry/childhood-firearms-homicide_us_5947ddbbe4b0f15cd5bce3e6.

29. "Seattle Shootings: Day of Horror, Grief in a Shaken City," *Seattle Times*, updated May 31, 2012, http://www.seattletimes.com/seattle-news/seattle -shootings-day-of-horror-grief-in-a-shaken-city.

30. "The Assault Weapon: An Instant Guide," *The Week*, February 10, 2013, http://theweek.com/articles/467914/assault-weapon-instant-guide.

31. Lee Drutman, "Explaining the Power of the National Rifle Association, in One Graph," Sunlight Foundation, December 17, 2012, https://sunlight foundation.com/2012/12/17/gun-spending.

32. "Gun Rights," Center for Responsive Politics, updated March 2016, https://www.opensecrets.org/industries/indus.php?ind=Q13.

33. "Gun Violence Protective Orders," Giffords Law Center to Prevent Gun Violence, access July 9, 2017, http://lawcenter.giffords.org/gun-laws/policy-areas/who-can-have-a-gun/gun-violence-protective-orders.

34. U.S. Census Bureau, "Facts for Features: Mother's Day: May 13, 2012," news release, March 19, 2012, https://www.census.gov/newsroom/releases/archives/facts_for_features_special_editions/cb12-ff08.html.

35. Jennifer L. Truman and Rachel E. Morgan, *Nonfatal Domestic Violence, 2003–2012*, U.S. Department of Justice, April 2014, https://www.bjs.gov/content/pub/pdf/ndv0312.pdf.

36. E. Petrosky, J. M. Blair, C. J. Betz, K. A. Fowler, S. P. Jack, and B. H. Lyons, "Racial and Ethnic Differences in Homicides of Adult Women and the Role of Intimate Partner Violence—United States, 2003–2014," *Morbidity Mortality Weekly Report* 66 (2017): 741–746, http://dx.doi.org/10.15585/mmwr.mm628a1.

37. Adapted from "#KeepMarching: MomsRising Advocacy and Organizing Tactics and Tips," https://s3.amazonaws.com/s3.momsrising.org/images/Keep_Marching_Toolkit_2_1.pdf and https://www.momsrising.org/blog/updated-keepmarching-meeting-guides-and-recordings. Beth Messersmith, MomsRising senior campaign director, led the creation of this guide along with the MomsRising team.

Chapter 9: Maternal Mortality

1. "Pregnancy Mortality Surveillance System," Centers for Disease Control and Prevention (website), updated June 29, 2017, https://www.cdc.gov/reproductivehealth/maternalinfanthealth/pmss.html.

2. Priya Agrawal, "Maternal Mortality and Morbidity in the United States of America," *Bulletin of the World Health Organization* 93 (March 2015): 135, http://dx.doi.org/10.2471/BLT.14.148627.

3. Molly Redden, "Texas Has Highest Maternal Mortality Rate in Developed World, Study Finds," *The Guardian*, August 20, 2016, https://www.theguardian.com/us-news/2016/aug/20/texas-maternal-mortality-rate-health-clinics-funding.

4. "Preterm Birth," Centers for Disease Control and Prevention, updated October 25, 2017, https://www.cdc.gov/reproductivehealth/maternalinfanthealth/pretermbirth.htm.

5. "Maternal Morbidity and Mortality," AWHONN Postpartum Hemorrhage Project (website), http://www.pphproject.org/maternal-morbidity-mortality.asp.

6. Priya Agrawal, "Maternal Mortality and Morbidity in the United States of America," *Bulletin of the World Health Organization* 93 (March 2015): 135, http://dx.doi.org/10.2471/BLT.14.148627.

7. UNICEF Data: Monitoring the Situation of Children and Women, *Maternal Mortality Fell by Almost Half between 1990 and 2015*, updated February 2017, http://data.unicef.org/topic/maternal-health/maternal-mortality.

8. Sabrina Tavernise, "Maternal Mortality Rate in U.S. Rises, Defying Global Trend, Study Finds," *New York Times*, September 21, 2016, https://www.nytimes.com/2016/09/22/health/maternal-mortality.html.

9. "Building U.S. Capacity to Review and Prevent Maternal Deaths," CDC Foundation, https://www.cdcfoundation.org/building-us-capacity-review-and-prevent-maternal-deaths.

10. Rebecca Grant, "Pregnant Women's Medical Care Too Often Affected by Race," *Newsweek*, July 3, 2016, http://www.newsweek.com/2016/07/15/pregnant-womens-care-affected-race-477087.html.

11. Myra J. Tucker, Cynthia J. Berg, William M. Callaghan, and Jason Hsia, "The Black-White Disparity in Pregnancy-Related Mortality from 5 Conditions: Differences in Prevalence and Case-Fatality Rates," *American Journal of Public Health* 97, no. 2 (February 2007): 247-251, http://dx.doi.org/10.2105/AJPH.2005.072975.

12. "Pregnancy Mortality Surveillance System," Centers for Disease Control and Prevention, updated June 29, 2017, https://www.cdc.gov/reproductivehealth/maternalinfanthealth/pmss.html.

13. Priya Agrawal, "Maternal Mortality and Morbidity in the United States of America," *Bulletin of the World Health Organization* 93 (March 2015): 135, http://dx.doi.org/10.2471/BLT.14.148627.

14. "Preterm Birth," Centers for Disease Control and Prevention, updated October 25, 2017, https://www.cdc.gov/reproductivehealth/maternalinfanthealth/pretermbirth.htm.

15. Richard E. Anderson, "Ob-Gyn Shortage Is Going to Get Worse," Live Science, June 27, 2013, https://www.livescience.com/37824-obgyn-shortage-looming.html. Michael Ollove, "America's OBGYN Shortage Is Extremely Dangerous for Pregnant Women," *Huffington Post*, August 15, 2016, http://www.huffingtonpost.com/entry/americas-obgyn-shortage-is-extremely-dangerous-for-pregnant-women_us_57b1ec06e4b007c36e4f6df5.

16. Michael Ollove, "A Shortage in the Nation's Maternal Health Care," *Stateline* (blog), Pew Charitable Trusts, August 15, 2016, http://www.pewtrusts.org/en/research-and-analysis/blogs/stateline/2016/08/15/a-shortage-in-the-nations-maternal-health-care.

17. Priya Agrawal, "Maternal Mortality and Morbidity in the United States of America," *Bulletin of the World Health Organization* 93 (March 2015): 135, http://dx.doi.org/10.2471/BLT.14.148627.

18. California Department of Public Health, California Birth and Death Statistical Master Files, 1999–2013.

19. Priya Agrawal, "Maternal Mortality and Morbidity in the United States of America," *Bulletin of the World Health Organization* 93 (March 2015): 135, http://dx.doi.org/10.2471/BLT.14.148627.

20. Priya Agrawal, "Maternal Mortality and Morbidity in the United States of America," *Bulletin of the World Health Organization* 93 (March 2015): 135, http://dx.doi.org/10.2471/BLT.14.148627.

21. Priya Agrawal, "Maternal Mortality and Morbidity in the United States of America," *Bulletin of the World Health Organization* 93 (March 2015): 135, http://dx.doi.org/10.2471/BLT.14.148627.

22. Michael Ollove, "A Shortage in the Nation's Maternal Health Care," *Stateline* (blog), Pew Charitable Trusts, August 15, 2016, http://www.pewtrusts.org/en/research-and-analysis/blogs/stateline/2016/08/15/a-shortage-in-the-nations-maternal-health-care.

23. Victoria Law, "Pregnant and Behind Bars: How the US Prison System Abuses Mothers-to-Be," *The Guardian*, October 20, 2015, https://www.theguardian.com/us-news/2015/oct/20/pregnant-women-prison-system-abuse-medical-neglect.

24. Shelby Lin Erdman and Carma Hassan, "Texas Woman Claims She Gave Birth Alone in Jail, Baby Died," CNN, May 24, 2014, http://www.cnn.com/2014/05/23/us/texas-jail-baby-death.

25. "Pregnant in a Texas County Jail?" Texas Jail Project, January 1, 2013, http://texasjailproject.org/2017/09/pregnant-in-a-texas-jail.

26. "Shackling of Pregnant Prisoners in the United States," International Human Rights Clinic, University of Chicago, accessed July 5, 2017, https://ihrclinic.uchicago.edu/page/shackling-pregnant-prisoners-united-states.

27. Adapted from "#KeepMarching: MomsRising Advocacy and Organizing Tactics and Tips," https://s3.amazonaws.com/s3.momsrising.org/images/Keep_Marching_Toolkit_2_1. pdf and https://www.momsrising.org/blog/updated-keepmarching-meeting-guides-and-recordings. Beth Messersmith, MomsRising senior campaign director, led the creation of this guide along with the MomsRising team.

Chapter 10: Lady Liberty

1. Jose Antonio Vargas, "Immigration Debate: The Problem with the Word *Illegal*," *Time*, September 21, 2012, http://ideas.time.com/2012/09/21/immigration-debate-the-problem-with-the-word-illegal.

2. Brian H. Levin, "Hate Crimes Rise in Major American Localities in 2016," United States Department of Justice Hate Crime Summit, June 29, 2017, https://csbs.csusb.edu/sites/csusb_csbs/files/Levin%20DOJ%20Summit%202.pdf.

3. Chelsea Parsons, Eugenio Weigend Vargas, and Jordan Jones, "Hate and Guns: A Terrifying Combination," Center for American Progress, February 24, 2016, https://www.americanprogress.org/issues/guns-crime/reports/2016/02/24/131670/hate-and-guns-a-terrifying-combination.

4. Maureen B. Costello, "The Trump Effect: The Impact of the 2016 Presidential Election on Our Nation's Schools," Southern Poverty Law Center, November 28, 2016, https://www.splcenter.org/20161128/trump-effect-impact-2016-presidential-election-our-nations-schools.

5. Institute for Social Policy and Understanding, *American Muslim Poll 2017*, 2017, https://www.ispu.org/public-policy/american-muslim-poll.

6. Institute for Social Policy and Understanding, *American Muslim Poll 2017*, 2017, https://www.ispu.org/public-policy/american-muslim-poll.

7. Dalia Mogahed and Youssef Chouhoud, "American Muslim Poll 2017: Muslims at the Crossroads," Institute for Social Policy and Understanding, 2017, https://www.ispu.org/wp-content/uploads/2017/06/AMP-2017_Full-Report.pdf. Michael Lipka, "Muslims and Islam: Key Findings in the U.S. and Around the World," Pew Research Center, August 9, 2017, http://www.pewresearch.org/fact-tank/2017/05/26/muslims-and-islam-key-findings-in-the-u-s-and-around-the-world.

8. Dalia Mogahed and Youssef Chouhoud, "American Muslim Poll 2017: Muslims at the Crossroads," Institute for Social Policy and Understanding, 2017, https://www.ispu.org/wp-content/uploads/2017/06/AMP-2017_Full-Report.pdf.

9. Daniel Cox and Robert P. Jones, "Nearly Half of Americans Worried That They or Their Family Will Be a Victim of Terrorism," PRRI, December 10, 2015, https://www.prri.org/research/survey-nearly-half-of-americans-worried-that-they-or-their-family-will-be-a-victim-of-terrorism.

10. "2015 Hate Crime Statistics," Federal Bureau of Investigation, Criminal Justice Information Services Division, table 1, 2015, https://ucr.fbi.gov/hate-crime/2015/tables-and-data-declarations/1tabledatadecpdf.

11. Colleen Shalby, "Parents Ask: What Happens to My Child If I'm Deported?" *Los Angeles Times*, March 22, 2017, http://www.latimes.com/politics/la-na-questions-trump-immigration-20170322-htmlstory.html.

12. Melissa Gonzalo, "Mother Arrested In Front of Children," 12 News, February 5, 2009, http://www.azcentral.com/12news/news/articles/2009/02/05/20090205motherarrested02052009-CR.html.

13. Melissa Gonzalo, "Mother Arrested in Front of Children," 12 News, February 5, 2009, http://www.azcentral.com/12news/news/articles/2009/02/05/20090205motherarrested02052009-CR.html.

14. Mahwish Khan, "Sherriff Arpaio Comes out as Birther, Assigned 'Cold Case Posse' to Obama Birth Certificate Case," America's Voice, September 20, 2011, http://www.americasvoiceonline.org/page/content/sheriff.

15. Bill Chappell, "Maricopa Sheriff Joe Arpaio Loses Re-Election Fight," NPR, November 9, 2016, http://www.npr.org/sections/thetwo-way/2016/11/09/501388042/maricopa-sheriff-joe-arpaio-loses-reelection-fight.

16. American Immigration Council, *The Facts about the Individual Tax Identification Number (ITIN)*, April 5, 2016, https://www.americanimmigrationcouncil.org/research/facts-about-individual-tax-identification-number-itin.

17. Maria Santana, "5 Immigration Myths Debunked," CNN Money, November 20, 2014, http://money.cnn.com/2014/11/20/news/economy/immigration-myths.

18. "Crime in the United States 2011," Federal Bureau of Investigation, Criminal Justice Information Services Division, table 43A, 2011, https://ucr.fbi.gov/crime-in-the.u.s/2011/crime-in-the-u.s.-2011/tables/table-43.

19. "Crime in the United States 2011," Federal Bureau of Investigation, Criminal Justice Information Services Division, table 43A, 2011, https://ucr.fbi.gov/crime-in-the.u.s/2011/crime-in-the-u.s.-2011/tables/table-43.

20. Ana Gonzalez-Barrera, "More Mexicans Leaving than Coming to the U.S.," Pew Research Center, November 19, 2015, http://www.pewhispanic.org/2015/11/19/more-mexicans-leaving-than-coming-to-the-u-s.

21. Gustavo Lopez, Neil G. Ruiz, and Eileen Patten, "Key Facts about Asian Americans, a Diverse and Growing Population," Pew Research Center, September 8, 2017, http://www.pewresearch.org/fact-tank/2017/09/08/key-facts-about-asian-americans.

22. Dan Restrepo and Ana Garcia, "The Surge of Unaccompanied Children from Central America: Root Causes and Policy Solutions," Center for American Progress, July 24, 2014, https://www.americanprogress.org/issues/immigration/reports/2014/07/24/94396/the-surge-of-unaccompanied-children-from-central-america-root-causes-and-policy-solutions.

23. Julia Edwards Ainsley, "Trump Administration Drafts Plan to Raise Asylum Bar, Speed Deportations," Reuters, February 18, 2017, https://www.reuters.com/article/us-usa-immigration-asylum/trump-administration-drafts-plan-to-raise-asylum-bar-speed-deportations-idUSKBN15Y04A.

24. Suzanne Gamboa, "DHS Announces Arrests, Deportations as Groups Scramble to Warn Immigrants," NBC News, January 4, 2016, https://www.nbcnews.com/news/latino/dhs-announces-arrests-deportations-groups-scramble-warn-immigrants-n490011.

25. Elizabeth Llorente, "Despite White House Claims, up to 80% of Migrant Children Can Legally Stay in Country," Fox News, June 27, 2014, http://www.foxnews.com/politics/2014/06/26/despite-white-house-claims-up-to-80-migrant-children-can-stay-as-refugees-or.html.

26. Randy Capps, Michael Fix, and Jie Zong, *A Profile of U.S. Children with Unau-thorized Immigrant Parents*, Migration Policy Institute, January 2016, http://www.migrationpolicy.org/research/profile-us-children-unauthorized-immigrant-parents.

27. Quote courtesy of Carolina Rubio MacWright, immigration attorney and activist.

28. German Lopez, "Research Says There Are Ways to Reduce Racial Bias. Call-ing People Racist Isn't One of Them," *Vox*, August 14, 2017, https://www.vox.com/identities/2016/11/15/13595508/racism-trump-research-study.

29. Showing Up for Racial Justice (website), updated September 1, 2017, http://www.showingupforracialjustice.org.

30. Ryan Struyk, "Blacks and Whites See Racism in the United States Very, Very Differently," CNN, August 18, 2017, http://www.cnn.com/2017/08/16/politics/blacks-white-racism-united-states-polls/index.html.

31. Don Gonyea, "Majority of White Americans Say They Believe Whites Face Discrimination," NPR, October 24, 2017, http://www.npr.org/2017/10/24/559604836/majority-of-white-americans-think-theyre-discriminated-against.

32. National Partnership for Women and Families, *America's Women and the Wage Gap*, April 2017, http://www.nationalpartnership.org/research-library/workplace-fairness/fair-pay/americas-women-and-the-wage-gap.pdf.

33. National Women's Law Center, *The Wage Gap for White, Non-Hispanic Women*, April 11, 2016, https://nwlc.org/resources/the-wage-gap-by-state-for-white-non-hispanic-women.

34. National Asian Pacific American Women's Forum, *Achieving Pay Equity for Asian Americans and Pacific Islanders*, March 2017, https://napawf.org/wp-content/uploads/2009/10/EPD_Fact-Sheet_FINAL.pdf. National Asian Pacific American Women's Forum, *Fighting Invisibility Closing the Wage Gap: An Equal Pay Agenda for Asian Americans and Pacific Islanders*, March 2017, https://napawf.org/wp-content/uploads/2017/03/FIGHTING-INVISIBILITY_FINAL-4.03.17.pdf.

35. National Women's Law Center, *FAQ about the Wage Gap*, September 19, 2017, https://nwlc.org/resources/faq-about-the-wage-gap.

36. Allie Bidwell, "Report: Higher Education Creates 'White Racial Privi-lege,'" *U.S. News and World Report*, July 31, 2013, http://www.usnews.com/news/articles/2013/07/31/report-higher-education-creates-white-racial-privilege?s_cid=rss:report-higher-education-creates-white-racial-privilege.

37. Allie Bidwell, "Report: Higher Education Creates 'White Racial Privilege,'" *U.S. News and World Report*, July 31, 2013, http://www.usnews.com/news/articles/2013/07/31/report-higher-education-creates-white-racial-privilege.

38. Ian Ayres, "When Whites Get a Free Pass," *New York Times*, February 24, 2015, http://www.nytimes.com/2015/02/24/opinion/research-shows-white-privilege-is-real.html.

39. Max Ehrenfreund, "Trying to Talk a Bus Driver into Giving You a Free Ride? Make Sure You're White, or Else Wear a Suit," *Washington Post*, February 25, 2015, http://www.washingtonpost.com/blogs/wonkblog/wp/2015/02/25/riding-buses-while-white-drivers-are-more-likely-to-let-white-passengers-skip-fares.

40. Michelle Bernard, "Despite the Tremendous Risk, African American Women Marched for Sufferage, Too," *Washington Post*, March 3, 2013, https://www.washingtonpost.com/blogs/she-the-people/wp/2013/03/03/despite-the-tremendous-risk-african-american-women-marched-for-suffrage-too.

Chapter 11: The Domino Effect

1. Centers for Disease Control and Prevention, *Percentage of Births to Unmarried Mothers by State*, January 5, 2017, https://www.cdc.gov/nchs/pressroom/sosmap/unmarried/unmarried.htm.

2. Brigid Schulte, "The U.S. Ranks Last in Every Measure When It Comes to Family Policy, in 10 Charts," *Washington Post*, June 23, 2014, https://www.washingtonpost.com/blogs/she-the-people/wp/2014/06/23/global-view-how-u-s-policies-to-help-working-families-rank-in-the-world.

3. Christopher Ingraham, "Start Saving Now: Day Care Costs More than College in 31 States," *Washington Post*, April 9, 2014, https://www.washingtonpost.com/news/wonk/wp/2014/04/09/start-saving-now-day-care-costs-more-than-college-in-31-states.

4. Elise Gould and Tanyell Cooke, "High Quality Child Care Is out of Reach for Working Families," Economic Policy Institute, October 6, 2015, http://www.epi.org/publication/child-care-affordability.

5. Danielle Paquette and Peyton M. Craighill, "The Surprising Number of Parents Scaling Back at Work to Care for Kids," *Washington Post*, August 6, 2015, https://www.washingtonpost.com/business/economy/the-surprising-number-of-moms-and-dads-scaling-back-at-work-to-care-for-their-kids/2015/08/06/c7134c50-3ab7-11e5-b3ac-8a79bc44e5e2_story.html.

6. Jessica Dickler, "The Rising Cost of Raising a Child," CNN Money, September 21, 2011, http://money.cnn.com/2011/09/21/pf/cost_raising_child/index.htm.

7. Sarah Jane Glynn, *Child Care: Families Need More Help to Care for Their Children*, Center for American Progress, August 16, 2012, https://cdn.americanprogress.org/wp-content/uploads/2012/10/ChildCareFactsheet.pdf.

8. Rasheed Malik and Katie Hamm, *Mapping America's Child Care Deserts*, Center for American Progress, August 30, 2017, https://www.americanprogress.org/issues/early-childhood/reports/2017/08/30/437988/mapping-americas-child-care-deserts.

9. Rasheed Malik and Katie Hamm, *Mapping America's Child Care Deserts*, Center for American Progress, August 30, 2017, https://www.american

progress.org/issues/early-childhood/reports/2017/08/30/437988/
mapping-americas-child-care-deserts.

10. Brookings and Duke University Center for Child and Family Policy, *The
Current State of Scientific Knowledge on Pre-Kindergarten Effects*, 2017, https://
www.brookings.edu/wp-content/uploads/2017/04/duke_prekstudy
_final_4-4-17_hires.pdf.

11. Ashely Simpson Baird, "Dual Language Learners Reader Post #5: Models of Language Instruction," New America, June 8, 2015, https://www
.newamerica.org/education-policy/edcentral/dllreader5.

12. Maki Park, Anna O'Toole, and Caitlin Katsiaficas, *Dual Language Learners: A National Demographic and Policy Profile*, Migration Policy Institute,
October 2017, https://www.migrationpolicy.org/research/dual-language
-learners-national-demographic-and-policy-profile.

13. Melinda D. Anderson, "The Economic Imperative of Bilingual Education,"
The Atlantic, November 10, 2015, https://www.theatlantic.com/education/
archive/2015/11/bilingual-education-movement-mainstream/414912.

14. Pew Center on the States, *Policy Framework to Strengthen Home Visiting
Programs*, November 2011, http://www.pewtrusts.org/~/media/legacy/
uploadedfiles/pcs_assets/2011/homevisitingmodelpolicyframework
pdf.pdf.

15. Mark Memmott, "Moms Are Now Primary Breadwinner in 40 Percent of
Homes," NPR, May 29, 2013, http://www.npr.org/sections/thetwo-way/
2013/05/29/187019187/moms-are-now-primary-breadwinners-in-40-percent
-of-homes.

16. Bureau of Labor Statistics, U.S. Department of Labor, "Childcare Workers," *Occupational Outlook Handbook, 2016–17 Edition*, December 17, 2015,
https://www.bls.gov/ooh/personal-care-and-service/childcare-workers
.htm. Danielle Paquette, "Half of America's Childcare Workers Need Food
Stamps, Welfare Payments or Medicaid," *Washington Post*, July 11, 2016,
https://www.washingtonpost.com/news/wonk/wp/2016/07/11/the
-people-taking-care-of-our-kids-live-in-poverty.

17. Danielle Paquette, "Half of America's Childcare Workers Need Food
Stamps, Welfare Payments or Medicaid," *Washington Post*, July 11, 2016,
https://www.washingtonpost.com/news/wonk/wp/2016/07/11/
the-people-taking-care-of-our-kids-live-in-poverty.

18. National Women's Law Center, *Child Care Is Fundamental to America's Children, Families and Economy*, January 4, 2017, https://nwlc.org/resources/
child-care-is-fundamental-to-americas-children-families-and-economy.

19. Anna Bahney, "Child Care Is Biggest Expense for a Growing Number of Families," *Forbes*, June 29, 2015, https://www.forbes.com/sites/
annabahney/2015/06/29/child-care-is-biggest-expense-for-a-growing
-number-of-families/#75dea28fe8ad.

20. Anna Bahney, "Child Care Is Biggest Expense for a Growing Number of Families," *Forbes*, June 29, 2015, https://www.forbes.com/sites/annabahney/2015/06/29/child-care-is-biggest-expense-for-a-growing-number-of-families/#75dea28fe8ad.

21. Rebecca Ullrich, Katie Hamm, and Leila Schochet, *6 Policies to Support the Early Childhood Workforce*, Center for American Progress, February 6, 2017, https://www.americanprogress.org/issues/early-childhood/reports/2017/02/06/298085/6-policies-to-support-the-early-childhood-workforce.

22. Terri Moon Crook, "DoD Launches Childcare Website to Ease Moving Transitions," U.S. Department of Defense, January 28, 2015, https://www.defense.gov/News/Article/Article/604010/.

23. Kathleen Maclay, "Childcare Workers' Pay Remains Stagnant, Study Shows," Berkeley Research, January 21, 2015, https://vcresearch.berkeley.edu/news/childcare-workers-pay-remains-stagnant-study-shows.

24. Michael Harriot, "Report: Black Girls 5 Times More Likely to Be Suspended from School than White Girls," *The Root*, May 11, 2017, http://www.theroot.com/report-black-girls-5-times-more-likely-to-be-suspended-1795125619.

25. Michael Harriot, "Report: Black Girls 5 Times More Likely to Be Suspended from School than White Girls," *The Root*, May 11, 2017, http://www.theroot.com/report-black-girls-5-times-more-likely-to-be-suspended-1795125619.

26. Libby Nelson and Dara Lind, "The School to Prison Pipeline, Explained," Justice Policy Institute, February 24, 2015, http://www.justicepolicy.org/news/8775.

27. J. M. Wallace, S. Goodkind, C. M. Wallace, and J. G. Bachman, "Racial, Ethnic, and Gender Differences in School Discipline among U.S. High School Students: 1991–2005," *Negro Educational Review* 59, no. 1–2 (2008): 47–62, https://www.ncbi.nlm.nih.gov/pmc/articles/PMC2678799.

28. Adrienne Green, "How Black Girls Aren't Presumed to Be Innocent," *The Atlantic*, June 29, 2017, https://www.theatlantic.com/politics/archive/2017/06/black-girls-innocence-georgetown/532050.

29. Eduardo Porter, "Gender Gap in Education Cuts Both Ways," *New York Times*, March 10, 2015, https://www.nytimes.com/2015/03/11/business/gender-gap-in-education-cuts-both-ways.html.

30. Loren Bridge, "More Girls Study Science, Technology, Engineering and Mathematics in Single-Sex Learning Environments," *Daily Telegraph*, October 1, 2017, http://www.dailytelegraph.com.au/newslocal/wentworth-courier/more-girls-study-science-technology-engineering-and-mathematics-in-singlesex-learning-environments/news-story/dc0bd3b4bdd1d12138b13942a51c3055.

31. Tami Luhby, Tal Yellin, and Caroline Matthews, "Just How Much Better Off Are College Grads Anyway?" CNN Money, April 5, 2016, http://money.cnn.com/infographic/economy/college-degree-earnings/index.html.

32. Tami Luhby, Tal Yellin, and Caroline Matthews, "Just How Much Better Off Are College Grads Anyway?" CNN Money, April 5, 2016, http://money .cnn.com/infographic/economy/college-degree-earnings/index.html.

33. John W. Schoen, "Why Does a College Degree Cost So Much?" CNBC, June 16, 2015, https://www.cnbc.com/2015/06/16/why-college-costs-are-so -high-and-rising.html.

34. Matt Rocheleau, "On Campus, Women Outnumber Men More than Ever," *Boston Globe*, March 28, 2016, https://www.bostonglobe.com/metro/2016/03/28/ look-how-women-outnumber-men-college-campuses-nationwide/YROqwf CPSlKPtSMAzpWloK/story.html.

35. Donna Rosato, "How Seniors Crushed by Old Student Loans Can Get Relief," *Consumer Reports*, December 21, 2016, https://www.consumerreports.org/ student-debt/solutions-for-seniors-who-are-in-default-on-student-loans.

36. Donna Rosato, "How Seniors Crushed by Old Student Loans Can Get Relief," *Consumer Reports*, December 21, 2016, https://www.consumerreports.org/ student-debt/solutions-for-seniors-who-are-in-default-on-student-loans.

37. Donna Rosato, "How Seniors Crushed by Old Student Loans Can Get Relief," *Consumer Reports*, December 21, 2016, https://www.consumerreports.org/ student-debt/solutions-for-seniors-who-are-in-default-on-student-loans.

38. Kira Sanbonmatsu, Susan J. Carroll, and Debbie Walsh, *Poised to Run: Women's Pathways to State Legislatures*, Center for American Women and Politics, Rutgers Eagleton Institute of Politics, 2009, http://www.cawp.rutgers.edu/ sites/default/files/resources/poisedtorun_0.pdf.

39. Pamela O'Leary and Shauna Shames, "Shattering the Glass Ceiling for Women in Politics," *Scholars Strategy Network,* November 2013, http://www .scholarsstrategynetwork.org/brief/shattering-glass-ceiling-women -politics.

Chapter 12: An Unjust System

1. Naa Oyo A. Kwate and Shatema Threadcraft, "Perceiving the Black Female Body: Race and Gender in Police Constructions of Body Weight," *Race and Social Problems* 7, no. 3 (2015): 213–226, http://doi.org/10.1007/ s12552-015-9152-7.

2. Alex Ronan, "It's Time to Talk about the Female Victims of Police Brutality," The Cut, April 29, 2015, https://www.thecut.com/2015/04/black-women -and-girls-face-police-brutality-too.html.

3. Alex Ronan, "It's Time to Talk about the Female Victims of Police Brutality," The Cut, April 29, 2015, https://www.thecut.com/2015/04/black-women -and-girls-face-police-brutality-too.html.

4. Alex Ronan, "It's Time to Talk about the Female Victims of Police Brutality," The Cut, April 29, 2015, https://www.thecut.com/2015/04/black-women -and-girls-face-police-brutality-too.html.

5. The Sentencing Project, *Criminal Justice Facts*, accessed July 27, 2017, http://www.sentencingproject.org/criminal-justice-facts. Sophia Kerby, "The Top 10 Most Startling Facts about People of Color and Criminal Justice in the United States," Center for American Progress, March 13, 2012, https://www.american progress.org/issues/race/news/2012/03/13/11351/the-top-10-most-startling -facts-about-people-of-color-and-criminal-justice-in-the-united-states.

6. NAACP, *Criminal Justice Fact Sheet*, accessed July 26, 2017, http://www .naacp.org/criminal-justice-fact-sheet.

7. Ashley Nellis, *The Color of Justice: Racial and Ethnic Disparity in State Prisons*, The Sentencing Project, June 2016, http://www.sentencingproject .org/wp-content/uploads/2016/06/The-Color-of-Justice-Racial-and-Ethnic -Disparity-in-State-Prisons.pdf.

8. Monifa Bandele, "Here's How Prison and Jail Systems Brutalize Women, Especially Mothers," ACLU, October 23, 2017, https://www.aclu.org/blog/ womens-rights/women-and-criminal-justice/heres-how-prison-and-jail -systems-brutalize-women.

9. The Pew Charitable Trusts, *Collateral Costs: Incarceration's Effect on Economic Mobility*, 2010, http://www.pewtrusts.org/~/media/legacy/uploadedfiles/ pcs_assets/2010/collateralcosts1pdf.pdf.

10. NPR, "Black Preschoolers Far More Likely to Be Suspended," March 21, 2014, http://www.npr.org/sections/codeswitch/2014/03/21/292456211/black -preschoolers-far-more-likely-to-be-suspended.

11. Carimah Townes, "There Are More Officers than Counselors in the Largest Public School Districts," Think Progress, March 28, 2016, https:// thinkprogress.org/there-are-more-officers-than-counselors-in-the-largest -public-school-districts-57af05880c25.

12. Kia Makarechi, "What the Data Really Says about Police and Racial Bias," *Vanity Fair*, July 14, 2016, https://www.vanityfair.com/news/2016/07/data -police-racial-bias.

13. Martha C. White, "Locked-In Profits: The U.S. Prison Industry, by the Numbers," NBC News, November 2, 2015, https://www.nbcnews.com/business/ business-news/locked-profits-u-s-prison-industry-numbers-n455976.

14. Science Daily, "Cost of Incarceration in the U.S. More than $1 Trillion," September 7, 2016, https://www.sciencedaily.com/releases/2016/ 09/160907215543.htm.

15. The Pew Charitable Trusts, *Collateral Costs: Incarceration's Effect on Economic Mobility*, 2010, http://www.pewtrusts.org/~/media/legacy/uploadedfiles/ pcs_assets/2010/collateralcosts1pdf.pdf. United States Sentencing Commission, *Quick Facts: Minimum Penalties*, 2014, http://www.ussc.gov/sites/ default/files/pdf/research-and-publications/quick-facts/Quick_Facts _Mand_Mins_FY14.pdf.

16. The Sentencing Project, *Fact Sheet: Incarcerated Women and Girls*, November 2015, http://www.sentencingproject.org/wp-content/uploads/2016/02/Incarcerated-Women-and-Girls.pdf.

17. Federal Register, *Annual Determination of Average Cost of Incarceration*, July 19, 2016, https://www.federalregister.gov/documents/2016/07/19/2016-17040/annual-determination-of-average-cost-of-incarceration.

18. Associated Press, "At $75,560, Housing a Prisoner in California Now Costs More than a Year at Harvard," *Los Angeles Times*, June 4, 2017, http://www.latimes.com/local/lanow/la-me-prison-costs-20170604-htmlstory.html.

19. Science Daily, "Cost of Incarceration in the U.S. More than $1 Trillion," September 7, 2016, https://www.sciencedaily.com/releases/2016/09/160907215543.htm.

20. The Sentencing Project, *Fact Sheet: Incarcerated Women and Girls*, November 2015, http://www.sentencingproject.org/wp-content/uploads/2016/02/Incarcerated-Women-and-Girls.pdf. Prison Policy Initiative, *States of Incarceration: The Global Context*, accessed July 26, 2017, https://www.prisonpolicy.org/global.

21. "Got Your ACE Score?," ACES Too High, accessed July 26, 2017, https://acestoohigh.com/got-your-ace-score.

22. Jane Stevens, "The ABCs of ACEs #InsideOut," MomsRising.org, April 18, 2016, https://www.momsrising.org/blog/the-abcs-of-aces-insideout.

23. Centers for Disease Control and Prevention, *Adverse Childhood Experiences (ACEs)*, April 1, 2016, https://www.cdc.gov/violenceprevention/acestudy/index.html.

24. Jo Craven McGinty, "How Many Americans Have a Police Record? Probably More than You Think," *Wall Street Journal*, August 7, 2015, https://www.wsj.com/articles/how-many-americans-have-a-police-record-probably-more-than-you-think-1438939802. Andrea Caumont, "Chart of the Week: The Problem of Prison Overcrowding," Pew Research Center, August 2, 2013, http://www.pewresearch.org/fact-tank/2013/08/02/chart-of-the-week-the-problem-of-prison-overcrowding. National Resource Center on Children and Families of the Incarcerated, *Children and Families of the Incarcerated Fact Sheet*, http://nrccfi.camden.rutgers.edu/files/nrccfi-fact-sheet-2014.pdf.

25. Court Services and Offender Supervision Agency, *Statistics on Women Offenders 2016*, 2016, https://www.csosa.gov/newsmedia/factsheets/statistics-on-women-offenders-2016.pdf.

26. Washington State Institute for Public Policy, *Benefit Cost Results, Adult Criminal Justice*, May 2017, http://www.wsipp.wa.gov/BenefitCost?topicId=2.

27. The Pew Charitable Trusts, *Collateral Costs: Incarceration's Effect on Economic Mobility*, 2010, http://www.pewtrusts.org/~/media/legacy/uploadedfiles/pcs_assets/2010/collateralcosts1pdf.pdf.

28. BBC News, "World Prison Populations," accessed July 26, 2017, http://news.bbc.co.uk/2/shared/spl/hi/uk/06/prisons/html/nn2page1.stm.

29. Prison Policy Initiative, *States of Incarceration: The Global Context*, accessed July 26, 2017, https://www.prisonpolicy.org/global.

30. Amnesty International USA, *Women in Prison: A Fact Sheet*, accessed July 26, 2017, https://www.prisonpolicy.org/scans/women_prison.pdf.

31. Court Services and Offender Supervision Agency, *Statistics on Women Offenders 2016*, 2016, https://www.csosa.gov/newsmedia/factsheets/statistics-on-women-offenders-2016.pdf.

32. Malika Saada Saar, Rebecca Epstein, Lindsay Rosenthal, and Yasmin Vafa, "The Sexual Abuse to Prison Pipeline: The Girls' Story," Center on Poverty and Inequality, Georgetown University Law Center, 2015, http://rights4girls.org/wp-content/uploads/r4g/2015/02/2015_COP_sexual-abuse_report_final.pdf.

33. Allen J. Beck, Marcus Berzofsky, Rachel Caspar, and Christopher Krebs, "Sexual Victimization in Prisons and Jails Reported by Inmates," U.S. Department of Justice Bureau of Justice Statistics: May 6, 2013, https://www.bjs.gov/content/pub/pdf/svpjri1112.pdf.

34. Washington State Institute for Public Policy, *Benefit Cost Results, Adult Criminal Justice*, May 2017, http://www.wsipp.wa.gov/BenefitCost?topicId=2.

35. Lauren Evans, "Incarcerated Women Are Fighting on the Front Lines of California's Wildfires for $1 an Hour," *Jezebel*, October 11, 2017, https://jezebel.com/incarcerated-women-are-fighting-on-the-front-lines-of-c-1819376951.

36. United States Sentencing Commission, *Quick Facts: Minimum Penalties*, 2014, http://www.ussc.gov/sites/default/files/pdf/research-and-publications/quick-facts/Quick_Facts_Mand_Mins_FY14.pdf.

37. ACLU, *Facts about the Over-Incarceration of Women in the United States*, accessed July 26, 2017, https://www.aclu.org/other/facts-about-over-incarceration-women-united-states?redirect=facts-about-over-incarceration-women-united-states.

38. Rebecca Vallas, Melissa Boteach, Rachel West, and Jackie Odum, "Removing Barriers to Opportunity for Parents with Criminal Records and Their Children," Center for American Progress, December 10, 2015, https://www.americanprogress.org/issues/poverty/reports/2015/12/10/126902/removing-barriers-to-opportunity-for-parents-with-criminal-records-and-their-children.

39. Bryce Covert, "How the System Punishes Children If Their Parent Has a Criminal Record," Think Progress, December 10, 2015, https://thinkprogress.org/how-the-system-punishes-children-if-their-parent-has-a-criminal-record-ca9ccac0c762.

40. Jessica Jones, Katharina Obser, and Jennifer Podkul, *Betraying Family Values: How Immigration Policy at the United States Border is Separating*

Families, Women's Refugee Commission, Lutheran Immigration and Refugee Services, KIND, January 10, 2017, https://supportkind.org/wp-content/uploads/2017/03/BetrayingFamilyValues_Feb2017.pdf.

41. Suzanne Gamboa, "DHS Announces Arrests, Deportations as Groups Scramble to Warn Immigrants," NBC News, January 4, 2016, https://www.nbcnews.com/news/latino/dhs-announces-arrests-deportations-groups-scramble-warn-immigrants-n490011.

42. U.S. Citizenship and Immigration Services, *RAIO Directorate—Officer Training, International Human Rights Law Training Module*, September 12, 2012, https://www.uscis.gov/sites/default/files/USCIS/About%20Us/Directorates%20and%20Program%20Offices/RAIO/International%20Human%20Rights%20Law%20LP%20%28RAIO%29.pdf.

43. Jessica Jones, Katharina Obser, and Jennifer Podkul, *Betraying Family Values: How Immigration Policy at the United States Border is Separating Families*, Women's Refugee Commission, Lutheran Immigration and Refugee Services, KIND, January 10, 2017, https://supportkind.org/wp-content/uploads/2017/03/BetrayingFamilyValues_Feb2017.pdf.

44. Julia Edwards Ainsley, "Exclusive: Trump Administration Considering Separating Women, Children at Mexico Border," Reuters, March 3, 2017, http://www.reuters.com/article/us-usa-immigration-children/exclusive-trump-administration-considering-separating-women-children-at-mexico-border-idUSKBN16A2ES.

45. "Child Displacement," Wikipedia, updated August 4, 2017, 22:51, https://en.wikipedia.org/wiki/Child_displacement#cite_ref-Fitzgerald_19-0.

46. National Immigration Law Center, "Unconstitutional Conditions in Border Patrol Facilities," accessed July 26, 2017, https://www.nilc.org/issues/immigration-enforcement/hieleras.

47. The Pew Charitable Trusts, *Collateral Costs: Incarceration's Effect on Economic Mobility*, 2010, http://www.pewtrusts.org/~/media/legacy/uploadedfiles/pcs_assets/2010/collateralcosts1pdf.pdf.

48. Mark Berman, "Minn. Officer Acquitted in Shooting of Philando Castile during Traffic Stop, Dismissed From Police Force," *Washington Post*, June 17, 2017, https://www.washingtonpost.com/news/post-nation/wp/2017/06/16/minn-officer-acquitted-of-manslaughter-for-shooting-philando-castile-during-traffic-stop.

49. Mitch Smith, "Video of Police Killing Philando Castile Is Publicly Released," *New York Times*, June 20, 2017, https://www.nytimes.com/2017/06/20/us/police-shooting-castile-trial-video.html.

50. Thomas Frank, "Black People Are Three Times Likelier to Be Killed in Police Chases," *USA Today*, December 1, 2016, https://www.usatoday.com/pages/interactives/blacks-killed-police-chases-higher-rate.

51. Nicole Flatow, "Report: Black Male Teens Are 21 Times More Likely to Be Killed by Cops than White Ones," Think Progress, October 10, 2014, https://thinkprogress.org/report-black-male-teens-are-21-times-more-likely-to-be-killed-by-cops-than-white-ones-72fb08a1dbda.

52. Cristina Silva, "Black Lives Matter Wins Global Peace Prize for Championing Justice and Equality," *Newsweek*, May 31, 2017, http://www.newsweek.com/black-lives-matter-wins-global-peace-prize-championing-justice-and-equality-618217.

53. "Fatal Force," *Washington Post*, 2016, https://www.washingtonpost.com/graphics/national/police-shootings-2016.

54. Kali Nicole Gross, "We Must Make Police Brutality against Black Women an Issue in 2016," *The Root*, June 10, 2015, http://www.theroot.com/we-must-make-police-brutality-against-black-women-an-is-1790860110.

55. Kimbriell Kelly, Wesley Lowery, Steven Rich, Julie Tate, and Jennifer Jenkins, "Fatal Shootings by Police Remain Relatively Unchanged after Two Years," *Washington Post*, December 30, 2016, https://www.washingtonpost.com/investigations/fatal-shootings-by-police-remain-relatively-unchanged-after-two-years/2016/12/30/fc807596-c3ca-11e6-9578-0054287507db_story.html.

56. Alex Ronan, "It's Time to Talk about the Female Victims of Police Brutality," The Cut, April 29, 2015, https://www.thecut.com/2015/04/black-women-and-girls-face-police-brutality-too.html.

57. Jamilah King, "Michael Brown's Death Didn't Happen in a Vacuum," *Color Lines*, August 11, 2014, http://colorlines.com/archives/2014/08/michael_brown_st_louis.html.

58. Maia Szalavitz, "Study: Whites More Likely to Abuse Drugs than Blacks," *Time*, November 7, 2011, http://healthland.time.com/2011/11/07/study-whites-more-likely-to-abuse-drugs-than-blacks.

59. Glenn Blain, "Sean Bell's Mother Petitions Albany Lawmakers to Support Special Prosecutors in Cop-Related Shootings," *New York Daily News*, March 11, 2015, http://www.nydailynews.com/new-york/special-prosecutors-killings-vic-mom-article-1.2146348.

60. "Police Abuse Cases Need Special Prosecutors," *Washington Post*, December 6, 2014, https://www.washingtonpost.com/opinions/police-abuse-cases-need-special-prosecutors/2014/12/06/fcf57e28-7cd6-11e4-b821-503cc7efed9e_story.html.

61. Donovan X. Ramsey, "What Does It Take to Indict a Killer Cop?" Demos, December 3, 2014, http://www.demos.org/blog/12/3/14/what-does-it-take-indict-killer-cop.

62. Sarah Ryley, Nolan Hicks, Thomas Tracy, John Marzulli, and Dareh Gregorian, "Exclusive: In 179 Fatalities Involving On-Duty NYPD Cops in 15 Years, Only 3 Cases Led to Indictments—and Just 1 Conviction," *New York*

Daily News, December 8, 2014, http://www.nydailynews.com/new-york/
nyc-crime/179-nypd-involved-deaths-3-indicted-exclusive-article-1.2037357.

63. Sophia Kerby, "The Top 10 Most Startling Facts about People of Color
and Criminal Justice in the United States," Center for American Progress,
March 13, 2012, https://www.americanprogress.org/issues/race/news/2012/
03/13/11351/the-top-10-most-startling-facts-about-people-of-color-and-criminal
-justice-in-the-united-states.

64. Christopher Uggen, Ryan Larson, and Sarah Shannon, "6 Million Lost Voters: State-Level Estimates of Disenfranchisement 2016," Sentencing Project,
October 6, 2016, http://www.sentencingproject.org/publications/6-million
-lost-voters-state-level-estimates-felony-disenfranchisement-2016.

65. Adapted from "#KeepMarching: MomsRising Advocacy and Organizing
Tactics and Tips," https://s3.amazonaws.com/s3.momsrising.org/images/
Keep_Marching_Toolkit_2_1. pdf and https://www.momsrising.org/blog/
updated-keepmarching-meeting-guides-and-recordings. Beth Messersmith,
MomsRising senior campaign director, led the creation of this guide along
with the MomsRising team.

Conclusion

1. "2016 November General Election Turnout Rates," United States Election
Project, accessed July 23, 2017, http://www.electproject.org/2016g.

2. Erica Chenoweth and Jeremy Pressman, "This Is What We Learned by
Counting the Women's Marches," *Washington Post*, February 7, 2017,
https://www.washingtonpost.com/news/monkey-cage/wp/2017/02/07/
this-is-what-we-learned-by-counting-the-womens-marches.

Policy Recommendations

1. "Harassment," U.S. Equal Employment Opportunity Commission, https://
www.eeoc.gov/laws/types/harassment.cfm.

Index

MomsRising Together, https://www.momsrising.org, warrants that it is a 501(c)(4) nonprofit organization and represents that all amounts it receives from all sales of this book will be used to advocate for women, mothers, and families through MomsRisingTogether.